The Political and Social Theory of Max Weber

The Political and Social Theory of Max Weber

Collected Essays

Wolfgang J. Mommsen

The University of Chicago Press

The University of Chicago Press, Chicago 60637

Polity Press, Cambridge

© 1989 by Wolfgang J. Mommsen

All rights reserved. Published 1989

Printed in Great Britain

98 97 96 95 94 93 92 91 90 89   5 4 3 2 1

Library of Congress Cataloging-in-Publication Data

Mommsen, Wolfgang J., 1930–
    The political and social theory of Max Weber: collected essays /
Wolfgang J. Mommsen.
        p.   cm.
    Includes bibliographical references and index.
    ISBN 0-226-53398-0 (alk. paper)
        1. Weber, Max, 1864-1920—Contributions in political science.
    2. Weber, Max, 1864-1920—Contributions in sociology.   I. Title.
    JC263.W42M66   1989   88-36950
    306 ′.2—dc 19   CIP

Contents

Preface

In the spring of 1985 I was invited by Professor Anthony Giddens to give a lecture course on Max Weber in the Faculty of Social and Political Sciences at Cambridge University. Thus I was encouraged to present Max Weber's views on political and social theory in a series of lectures devoted to the main themes of his political and social thought. Weber's views on liberalism and constitutional democracy, on Marxism and Wilhelmine Social Democrats, on bureaucratization as a potential threat to liberal society but also as a tool of effective government, and lastly his theory of legitimate domination and charismatic leadership, are intrinsically linked with one another. Politics, social theory and history cannot be separated neatly in his thought; rather they must be seen as aspects of one and the same reality, and none of these aspects can be analysed in isolation. This was the message I wished to bring across to the students in my Cambridge lectures.

The material included in this book far exceeds the original series of lectures, amplifying the ideas I was able to develop there. It is based in part on essays which have already been published but which have been thoroughly revised and updated for this publication. The first part, 'Politics and Social Theory', is devoted to the intimate relationship between politics and social research in Weber's personal career. The first essay, on 'Politics and Scholarship', demonstrates that Weber's passionate political engagement and his scholarly activities cannot be simply divided into separate compartments. However much Weber himself strove for objectivity in his scholarly work, many of its fundamental features were derived from his political experience. Certainly he did not wish his academic work to be diluted by political partisanship; yet it was certainly influenced by the insights into the nature of political rule and the exercise of power which he acquired while being actively engaged in contemporary politics.

In his political views Max Weber never followed narrow party lines. Even though he considered himself a liberal and in 1919 even embarked upon active election campaigning for the German Democratic Party, in his political theory he accommodated altogether different political viewpoints. In doing so, however, Max Weber did not look for easy compromises or for pragmatic, commonsensical solutions. On the contrary, in a Nietzschean manner he attempted to follow alternative lines of inquiry at the same time, pursuing each political position to its ultimate conceivable conclusion so that he eventually arrived at what may be called antinomical positions of a mutually exclusive character. This is also reflected in his views on contemporary politics in his own time, in particular his ambivalent attitude towards liberal democracy. His theory of legitimate domination tries to steer clear of conventional views; with a sort of ice-cold reasoning he tends to describe legitimate domination primarily in terms of acceptance of effective leadership, rather than in any kind of value-oriented terms – a position which is certainly at variance with conventional notions of democracy.

The second part, 'Max Weber on Socialism and Political Radicalism', is devoted to Max Weber's attitude towards socialism and radical-democratic thought. The essay 'Capitalism and Socialism: Weber's dialogue with Marx' is concerned with the relationship between Weber and Marx on a theoretical level; while Weber objected strongly to Marx's political views, none the less there seem to be substantial parallels between himself and Marx in the analysis of the capitalist system. However, Weber considered Marx's account of how the alienation of the workers under capitalism might eventually be overcome to be not only wrong but positively dangerous for the survival of a liberal social order. Weber's views on the Social Democrats in Wilhelmine Germany, which are discussed in the essay 'Joining the Underdogs?', are, however, remarkably ambivalent. While in principle he took sides with the Social Democrats against their bourgeois adversaries, whose fear of the so-called 'Red Peril' he regarded as rather ridiculous, if not abhorrent, he blamed them for their mere verbal radicalism, accompanied by timidity and petty-bourgeois attitudes. He had considerable respect for radical politics, provided that its proponents were prepared to accept the consequences, but personally he considered a reformist strategy to be the only sound one under given conditions. On the other hand he was fascinated by anarchist and syndicalist positions, and it is for this reason that he was first drawn to Roberto Michels. In Roberto Michels he saw to some extent his *alter ego*, inasmuch as Michels seemed to follow the path of the ethics of conviction which Weber rejected, even though in his personal life-conduct he was driven by deep-rooted emotional commitments. Max Weber's personal relationship to Roberto Michels, which is the subject of the last essay of Part II, demonstrates perhaps best his personal views about the insoluble tension between an ethically oriented life-conduct and instrumental-rational social action.

The third part, 'The Development of Max Weber's Theoretical Ideas', deals with key aspects of Max Weber's sociological thought. In his sociological theory the political perspectives we encountered in Weber's political thought are turned into theoretical guidelines according to which he chose to analyse the fabric of society. This is particularly the case with Weber's theory of bureaucratization, the theme of the first essay in this part. Weber saw in bureaucracy both a potential danger to individual liberty and an effective instrument in the hands of great personal leaders who are thereby enabled to give new impulses to an existing social system. This essentially antinomical conception of the social functions of bureaucracy provides a key for understanding Weber's political and social thought alike. It certainly had a significant influence on his theories of legitimate domination and charismatic leadership. Similarly Weber's notion of rationality bears testimony to the antinomical structure of his reasoning. He was not just the prophet who heralded the modern age of modernity and instrumental rationalization; instead we observe a gradual change in his usage of the notion of rationality, which eventually comes to encompass completely different types of rational social conduct – those oriented by instrumental-rational considerations, and those oriented by substantive values of very different sorts. Alongside this goes a tendency towards a more formalized use of the ideal-typical method, as is demonstrated in detail in the essay on 'Ideal Type and Pure Type: two variants of Max Weber's ideal-typical method'.

In the later years of his life Max Weber turned his back on those varieties of social reasoning which were merely concerned with formal rationality and instrumental-rational social action. Pursuing the idea of 'disenchantment' through the progressive formal rationalization of all spheres of social interaction, he came close to rediscovering myth (although now within a thoroughly institutionalized world) as a source of individual lifestyles at variance with everyday life. He pointed to the eternal struggle between totally irreconcilable world-views that was now re-emerging in modern bureaucratic society, if on a different, far more elevated plane. In the essay on 'The Two Dimensions of Social Change in Max Weber's Sociological Theory', his theory of social change, which he never formulated conclusively, is reconstructed in a systematic manner. It can be demonstrated that neither idealistic nor neo-evolutionist interpretations are capable of correctly assessing Max Weber's conception of social change. His theory of social change seeks to do justice to the perennial interplay of individual and institutional forces in history. It is largely indebted to liberal individualism, and in some respects to Nietzschean ideas too; according to Weber, the individual, if oriented towards stringent 'otherworldly' ideas, may give new impulses to the course of historical events – a notion eventually conceptualized in the theory of charismatic authority – but he reconciled this radically individualistic conception with a sociological theory of social change which emphasizes the independent role of social and economic forces which operate according to their own inherent laws (*Eigengesetzlichkeiten*), a position strongly reminiscent of Karl Marx and the Anglo-Saxon empiricist tradition.

The final part, 'The Rediscovery of Max Weber', tells the variegated story of how Max Weber's ideas were gradually taken up by social and political thinkers in the West. Strangely enough, in the inter-war period his work was largely neglected, if not forgotten, perhaps with the exception of his famous thesis on *The Protestant Ethic and the Spirit of Capitalism*. During the 1930s his intellectual heritage found a temporary home in the United States, while in Germany under Hitler his sociology was rejected as a typical expression of late-bourgeois liberalism which National Socialism allegedly was about to overcome for good. It was only after the Second World War that Max Weber's work was rediscovered again, although sometimes (at any rate in the early years) for the wrong reasons. The astounding renaissance of his thought which we experience today throughout the whole world, including the countries of the communist bloc, tells us perhaps more about ourselves than about Max Weber. His social theory is embedded in a notion of universal history which is informed above all by one key question – namely, how the individualistic life-conduct of the personality, inherited from the age of liberalism, may be preserved in our own highly bureaucratized and thoroughly rationalized Western culture. This is certainly an issue which is still very much with us, however widely our answers may differ from Max Weber's own.

I wish to express my sincere thanks to Anthony Giddens for his encouragement and unswerving support without which this book would not have come about. I am also greatly indebted to Gary T. Miller, who undertook the arduous task of translating the essays on 'Politics and Scholarship' and 'Rationalization and Myth in Weber's Thought' from the German original, as well as editing the text throughout.

Wolfgang J. Mommsen
Düsseldorf, March 1988

Acknowledgements

Chapter 1 was originally presented as part of a series of lectures on Max Weber at the Istituto-Germano-Italico at Trent, and in a revised version at the Conference of the Deutsche Soziologische Geselleschaft at Kassel in 1986. This translation is by Gary T. Miller.

Chapter 2 was first published in *Historische Zeitschrift*, 233 (1981), pp. 35–64, with the title 'Die antinomische Struktur des politischen Denkens Max Webers'. It is republished here in the English version, translated by José Casanova, which originally appeared in Scott G. McNall (ed.), *Current Perspectives in Social Theory: A Research Annual*, vol. 4 (Greenwich, Conn., and London, 1983), pp. 253–88.

Chapter 3 was first presented as part of a series of broadcasts for the Open University in 1985.

Chapter 4 was first published as 'Max Weber als Kritiker des Marxismus' in *Zeitschrift für Soziologie*, 3 (1974), pp. 256–78, and was then included under the title 'Kapitalismus und Sozialismus: die Auseinandersetzung mit Karl Marx', in Wolfgang J. Mommsen, *Max Weber: Gesellschaft, Politik und Geschichte* (Frankfurt, 1974), pp. 144–81. It is here published with major modifications using the English version translated by David Herr with the co-operation of Gerd Schroeter and Robert Antonio, which appeared in Robert J. Antonio and Ronald M. Glassman (eds), *A Weber-Marx Dialogue* (Kansas University Press, 1985), pp. 234–61. An earlier English version was published under the title 'Max Weber as a Critic of Marxism' in *Canadian Journal of Sociology*, 2 (1977), pp. 373–98.

Chapter 5 was first presented as part of a series of lectures at Cambridge University in June 1985.

Chapter 6 was first published in Wolfgang J. Mommsen and Jürgen Osterhammel (eds), _Max Weber and his Contemporaries_ (London, 1987), pp. 121-38. It was translated by Erica Carter and Chris Turner. A German version appeared in Wolfgang J. Mommsen and Wolfgang Schwentker (eds), _Max Weber und seine Zeitgenossen_ (Göttingen, 1988).

Chapter 7 was first presented as part of a series of lectures at Cambridge University in June 1985.

Chapter 8 was first published under the title 'Idealtypus und reiner Typus: Zwei Varianten der idealtypischen Methode Max Webers', in Wolfgang Küttler (ed.), _Marxistische Typisierung und idealtypische Methode in der Geschichtswissenschaft, Studien zur Geschichte_, vol. 7, Akademie der Wissenschaften der DDR, Zentralinstitut für Geschichte (Berlin, 1986).

Chapter 9 was first published under the title 'Rationalisierung und Mythos bei Max Weber', in Karl Heinz Bohrer (ed.), _Mythos und Moderne: Begriff und Bild einer Rekonstruktion_ (Frankfurt, 1983), pp. 382-404. This translation is by Gary T. Miller.

Chapter 10 is in large part based on a presentation at the Congrès International des Sciences Historiques in Stuttgart in 1985. A German version was published in Jürgen Kocka (ed.), _Max Weber, der Historiker_ (Göttingen, 1986), pp. 51-72. However, it has been thoroughly revised and extended.

Earlier versions of essay 11 were presented at the Institut d'Histoire Contemporaine, Paris, in May 1985 and at Princeton University in April 1986.

Bibliographical Note and Abbreviations

References to quotations from Max Weber and to my *Max Weber und die deutsche Politik* are given, wherever possible, in both the German version and the published English translation. However, as a rule, my own translations are used in the text.

AfSSP   *Archiv für Sozialwissenschaft und Sozialpolitik*
EaS   Max Weber, *Economy and Society: An Outline of Interpretive Sociology*, ed. Günther Roth and Claus Wittich (Berkeley, Los Angeles and London, 1977)
Eldridge   *Max Weber: The Interpretation of Social Reality*, ed. J. E. T. Eldridge (London, 1971)
GARS   Max Weber, *Gesammelte Aufsätze zur Religionssoziologie*, vol. 1 (Tübingen, 1920), vol. 2 (Tübingen, 1921), vol. 3 (Tübingen, 1921)
GASS   Max Weber, *Gesammelte Aufsätze zur Soziologie und Sozialpolitik*, ed. Marianne Weber (Tübingen, 1924)
GPS   Max Weber, *Gesammelte Politische Schriften*, 3rd edn (Tübingen, 1971)
KZSS   *Kölner Zeitschrift für Soziologie und Sozialpsychologie*
Lebensbild   Marianne Weber, *Max Weber: Ein Lebensbild* (Tübingen, 1926)
MWG   *Max Weber-Gesamtausgabe*, ed. Horst Baier, M. Rainer Lepsius, Wolfgang J. Mommsen, Wolfgang Schluchter and Johannes Winckelmann (Tübingen, 1984), vol. I: *Schriften und Reden*:
                vol. I/2: *Die römische Agrargeschichte in ihrer Bedeutung für das Staats- und Privatrecht*, ed. Jürgen Deininger (Tübingen, 1986)

vol. I/3 (in two parts): *Die Lage der Landarbeiter im ostelbischen Deutschland*, ed. Martin Riesebrodt (Tübingen, 1984)

vol. I/10: *Zur Russischen Revolution von 1905: Schriften und Reden 1905-1909*, ed. Wolfgang J. Mommsen in collaboration with Dittmar Dahlmann (Tübingen, 1989) (forthcoming)

vol. I/15: *Zur Politik im Weltkrieg: Schriften und Reden 1914-1918*, ed. Wolfgang J. Mommsen in collaboration with Gangolf Hübinger (Tübingen, 1984)

vol. I/16: *Zur Neuordnung Deutschlands: Schriften und Reden 1918-1920*, ed. Wolfgang J. Mommsen in collaboration with Wolfgang Schwentker (Tübingen, 1988)

Mommsen, *Max Weber*	Wolfgang J. Mommsen, *Max Weber und die deutsche Politik 1890-1920*, 2nd edn (Tübingen, 1974)
Mommsen, *Max Weber*, English edn	Wolfgang J. Mommsen, *Max Weber and German Politics 1890-1920*, trans. M. Steinberg (Chicago, 1985)
NPL	*Neue Politische Literatur*
RS	Max Weber, *Rechtssoziologie, aus dem Manuskript herausgegeben und eingeleitet von Johannes Winckelmann*, 2nd edn (Neuwied, 1967)
WL	Max Weber, *Gesammelte Aufsätze zur Wissenschaftslehre*, 3rd edn (Tübingen, 1968)
WuG	Max Weber, *Wirtschaft und Gesellschaft: Grundriss der verstehenden Soziologie*, 5th edn, ed. Johannes Winckelmann (Tübingen, 1978)

PART I

Politics and Social Theory

I

Politics and Scholarship:
The Two Icons in Max Weber's Life

Max Weber was a deeply committed political personality throughout his life. From his early years right up to 1920 he was passionately involved in the politics of his day and he always reacted extremely forcefully to political events, even if this frequently never penetrated beyond his circle of closer acquaintances. Karl Jaspers found in hindsight that 'his thought represented the reality of someone who was political to the core, a will to act in the service of the historical moment.'[1]

The view has been put forward repeatedly, by Reinhard Bendix and Günther Roth, for example, that Max Weber's scholarship could be clearly separated from his politics.[2] Here the opposite view will be advanced – that contemporary politics exerted a great influence on Max Weber's academic work without thereby detracting from its scientific character. Even where he was not dealing expressly with political matters the political dimension of his analysis can be traced just beneath the surface. It can be shown, for example, in his work on 'the Protestant ethic and the spirit of capitalism' that this is concerned with an ethos specific to the bourgeoisie as an autonomous social class which has nothing in common with the feudalist fundamental ideals of traditional aristocracy. Hence the bourgeoisie must not accommodate itself to the insidious process of feudalization that could be observed in Imperial Germany.

With such deep-rooted political concerns it is little wonder that Max Weber repeatedly found himself confronted by the question of whether or not he should move over into practical politics. As early as 1894 the opportunity arose to take on a candidature in Mannheim for the Reichstag (the Imperial Diet). His rapid academic promotion then reduced his inclination to change over into active politics. Furthermore, in 1899 illness rendered serious work in any field impossible for some years, and especially so in active politics. However, from

1906–7 onwards Max Weber acted as political adviser to the Freisinnige Vereinigung (Liberal Union) (which later became the Fortschrittliche Volkspartei (Progressive Popular Party)) through the intercession of Friedrich Naumann (whose role in party politics has recently been clearly delineated for the first time by Peter Theiner[3]) and Ernst Mueller-Meiningen. His influence on the major decisions of the Liberals, particularly during the period of the so-called Bülow bloc from 1906 to 1909 which consisted of a somewhat unnatural coalition of the Liberal and Conservative parties, was undoubtedly restricted in scope but should not be underestimated. Weber's insistence on the adoption of a genuine parliamentary system and the curtailment of the so-called 'personal regime' of Wilhelm II did not indeed have any direct effect in the years leading up to the First World War, but on the other hand it helped gradually to bring round the Progressive Liberals to a firm political stance, especially on constitutional issues.[4]

After the outbreak of the First World War Max Weber did his utmost to find some opening for himself in politics so that he could at least perform some sort of service to the nation once armed service had been denied to him on health grounds. However, no suitable role could be found for him and especially not under the conditions of the 'domestic truce' which aimed to curb if not to suspend completely all internal political hostilities; under those circumstances a man with his volatile temper and his habit of speaking the plain truth was really not in demand. The opportunity to take up a post in Brussels as specialist adviser on the staff of Governor-General von Bissing, who was in charge of the German military administration of Belgium during the First World War, which suddenly presented itself in 1915 proved illusory in the end. It came to nothing because the imperial government did not show the slightest interest in having an independent 'brain trust' in Brussels working for the annexation of Belgium and therefore stifled von Bissing's plans right at the outset – fortunately enough, one might add in retrospect, for this saved Weber from a potentially damaging collaboration with the official 'war aims' policy.

From 1916 onwards Weber played a leading role in Friedrich Naumann's Arbeitsausschuss für Mitteleuropa (Working Party on Central Europe), a committee founded early in 1916 to promote the idea of a central European economic union. Weber joined the committee in the belief that it would be able to produce some solid groundwork for the policy of the Bethmann Hollweg government. It must be remembered that the programme to establish a central European economic bloc under German leadership was viewed in many quarters at the time as a reasonable and realistic alternative to a sweeping programme of overt annexations such as the extreme right propagated in its increasingly aggressive and excessive memoranda on what the war aims should be. Certainly the government of Bethmann Hollweg pursued a policy of annexationism; but it preferred indirect means of extending imperial Germany's hegemonic status to large-scale annexations. However, it dared not fight openly for this somewhat more moderate line; not only did it not support the Arbeitsausschuss für Mitteleuropa, but it looked upon it as an inconvenience by whose activities the government might be discredited, because it was afraid of being blamed as weak – and this despite the fact that decisions in this area had always fallen under the *de facto* if not the *de jure* competence of the joint chiefs of staff under Hindenburg and Ludendorff. In the end and in utter frustration Max Weber deliberately sought refuge in academic work far removed from the bustle of politics by devoting himself to his studies on Hinduism and Buddhism.

In October 1918, with the unexpected appointment of Prince Max von Baden as imperial chancellor, the initially vague prospect now presented itself of his attaining some public function in politics after all. Matthias Erzberger, who had become a key figure in the new government and who was soon to become chief negotiator in the armistice negotiations, tried to win Max Weber over in early November 1918 to join a group to launch a publicity campaign in support of Prince Max von Baden's government, and indeed, it appears, Max Weber was inclined to take up the offer. The Revolution then swept away the last imperial government under Prince Max and accordingly nothing was to come of this opportunity.

The Revolution, however, offered Max Weber surprising new chances for an active role in politics. In the second week in November the Council of People's Delegates (Rat der Volksbeauftragten) considered appointing Max Weber Secretary of State for the Interior and commissioning him to draft the first version of a parliamentary constitution for the whole Reich. Eventually, however, Hugo Preuss, one of the few liberal constitutional lawyers in Germany, was appointed Secretary of State instead, and for his part he initially intended to entrust Max Weber with responsibility for constitutional questions even if only as Deputy Secretary of State. Just as little came of this in the end as of the proposal by Conrad Haussmann and Ludo Moritz Hartmann that Max Weber should be appointed envoy of the German republic in Vienna, which would have been a politically significant appointment in view of the fact that the issue of an Austrian *Anschluss* with republican Germany was still open. None the less Weber was the only person at the time invited in an unofficial capacity to take part in the informal consultations on the drafting of a proposed imperial constitution for the Council of People's Delegates held in the imperial Department of the Interior between 9 and 12 December 1918.[5]

At the same time the opportunity arose for Max Weber to become politically

active in the Deutsche Demokratische Partei (German Democratic Party). He
was elected to the party executive. More important, he took on extensive
electoral work for the DDP in the campaign for the elections to the National
Assembly which began in early December 1918. The degree of Max Weber's
commitment to the DDP during those weeks was considerable and has not been
given sufficient attention up to now in the literature on the subject.[6] But late in
November Weber's candidature in the Reichstag constituency of Hessen/
Nassau failed among other reasons because the way in which he had spoken out
too openly in the initial stages of the electoral campaign in favour of co-
operation with the Social Democrats and for a partial nationalization of the
economy made him appear suspect to many of the delegates.

Compared to this, Weber's political involvement in the Heidelberger
Vereinigung für Politik des Rechts (Heidelberg Association for Legal Policy)
was much more detached. The Heidelberg Association planned to launch a
public campaign in defence of Germany, primarily directed abroad, against the
almost universal condemnation of Germany for her conduct in the war in the
Allied as well as the neutral countries. It aimed at improving the moral position
of the Reich government at the impending peace negotiations. The Heidelberg
Association objected especially to the 'war guilt' accusation, to Allied propaganda about German atrocities during the war and to misuse of the League of
Nations for the purposes of a policy of subjecting Germany to a harsh peace
settlement. In this respect it was indeed an advantage that Max Weber could
speak out on these issues from the independent standpoint of a scholar of international standing. Partly at Prince Max's suggestion Max Weber was eventually
invited by the German Foreign Minister Graf Brockdorff-Rantzau to take part
in the Versailles peace negotiations as an expert adviser. The purpose behind
this move, however, was to use Max Weber's great prestige to promote
Brockdorff-Rantzau's policy on the question of war guilt rather than to allow
him or the other specialist advisers a genuinely independent influence over the
handling either of the war guilt problem or, more especially, of the issue which
particularly preoccupied Max Weber: whether Germany should sign the Peace
Treaty at all or rather, as he thought fit, reject it, even at the risk of the possible
occupation of parts of the Reich by Allied troops. Indeed, Max Weber did take
an active role in the negotiations of the German delegation at the Versailles
conference in May 1919, in particular regarding the territorial issues in the east.

In the summer of 1919 Max Weber withdrew from politics, deeply dis-
appointed with the course of events. His appointment to a professorship in
Munich had played a decisive role in this, for he had considered right from the
start that accepting the appointment would be incompatible with any further
active political involvement. But then again it is doubtful whether the with-

drawal from politics which he undertook at that time, and which he rounded off afterwards by resigning from his executive seat in the DDP and even giving up his membership, would really ever have been final. There is much to suggest the opposite view, in line with his declaration on the occasion of disturbances at Munich University over the possible reprieve of Count Arco (who in May 1919 had received a death sentence for the assassination of Kurt Eisner), towards the end of which he said: 'The reason why I am no longer in politics, as you know, is because it is impossible to have politics in Germany so long as it is possible for madmen of the right and left to peddle their madness.'[7] In other words, even then he still considered his withdrawal from politics to be by no means permanent, but temporary only. Undoubtedly Max Weber would have been back in the political arena before long, had he been allowed to live longer. He once said to Mina Tobler that 'politics . . . had always been his secret love' and that 'these people . . . [i.e. the radicals on both the right and left] destroyed all that one held dear.'[8] Max Weber never succeeded in completely renouncing this 'secret love', no matter how hard he tried at times to distance himself from everyday politics, not the least in order to ensure his spiritual survival. We must therefore conclude that Max Weber stood on the threshold between politics and science all his life. He endeavoured to be of service to both at the same time, no matter how difficult this could be. Even if he really never crossed the threshold into active political life, this was not just because of political circumstances at the time or because he was misunderstood by the 'politicians without a vocation'[9] but also because of his personal attitude to politics: he wanted to give a lead to politics, not to become tangled up in the tactical machinations of the everyday political struggle, although according to his own understanding this formed part of the politician's job.

With the only real exception of the period between 1898 and 1905 Max Weber always followed up the political events of his day with journalism in powerfully worded articles in the *Frankfurter Zeitung*, *Hilfe* and the *Münchener Neuesten Nachrichten*, in various public statements and in works of an academic character but with a political orientation. Many of his writings on political subjects are derived from articles which were written in response to current political events or for a definite political purpose. This is the case, for example, with his essays of 1905–6 on Russia to which Weber himself ascribed a primarily journalistic function. In view of the general negligence of the daily press, he thought it his duty to inform the German public reliably and comprehensively about events in Russia, which he considered to be of world-historical importance. His 1917 article 'Parliament and government in the newly constituted Germany' ('Parlament und Regierung im neugeordneten Deutschland') also had chiefly political motives. Even in its later revised version published in book form, as he himself said, 'its character as political polemic should not be suppressed, for that is what it still is and that is what it should be.'[10] Yet crucial elements of his sociology of domination are to be found in this text. Exactly the same was claimed for the article written at the end of 1918 on 'Germany's future form of government' ('Deutschlands künftige Staatsform') – namely, that what we are dealing with here is 'occasional writing of a political character without any claim to "scientific" validity'.[11] Finally, even his great speech 'Politics as a vocation', which arose from a particular historical situation and which is unmistakably directed against the pacifist tendencies of the time, contains fundamental statements about the nature of politics that are still valid to this day, even though Weber himself only found the text 'very mediocre' when he revised it for publication.

Contrary to customary opinion, Weber in no way thought it inappropriate for science to find its inspiration in passionate involvement in political events and vice versa. What he could not tolerate was the uncritical admixture of both spheres, especially in the form of using the lecture to propagate political value-judgements. Two conditions were absolutely necessary: first, to declare one's own standpoint as openly as possible; and, second, to distinguish consistently between scientific analysis and political premises and deductions. Values and scientific deductions were to be examined for their validity on a separate basis, the former on the basis of personal preferences, the latter on the grounds of rational criteria. Yet in no way did he thereby want to support a purely positivistically understood conception of science as 'value-free' or even in the radical sense as 'value-judgement-free', that is, far removed from politics or values.

The principles of this position are already clearly formulated in the Freiburg inaugural address of 1895. Already here Weber sharply rebuked those historical positions which presented their own quite subjective value-orientations as if constituted by the objective process of history itself. Instead he forcefully emphasized that in political economy there are no scientific standards of value of an objective nature which are consequent on its subject matter – for instance, such possible standards as the goal of achieving maximum productivity or the principle of social justice or the idea that there should be a permanent social redistribution between the classes so as to avoid a widening of class distinctions. He held it to be much more proper and more objective to declare unambiguously the value-positions governing one's approach, and indeed not only on scientific but just as much on political grounds. He did this then with remarkable consistency: 'The national economic policy of a German state and standards of value of a German national economist cannot be anything else but German.'[12] In principle Max Weber held to this notion for the rest of his life. He never shied away from openly declaring to his audience his own value-preferences. One only has to think of his severe critique of the 'passion for bureaucratization', which led him to despair, his bitter polemic against the 'pseudo-constitutionalism' of Imperial Germany and the 'personal regime' of Wilhelm II in the debates of the Verein für Sozialpolitik (Social Policy Association).[13]

Certainly Weber later defined his position on this point more precisely in the sense of logically differentiating between 'value-judgement' and 'value-relation'. In scientific analysis value-judgements have to give way to value-related judgements, which elevate certain values to the point of reference for analyses in political and social science, without asserting anything about their validity as such. Values as such, according to Weber, are not capable of scientific validation; but on the other hand there is also in principle no possibility of restricting the theoretically endless spectrum of value-positions or eliminating certain extreme value-orientations in favour of a realistic orientation by scientific means, such as in the way Jürgen Kocka spoke of a range of empirically acceptable theoretical positions. The decision to consider certain values as personally binding on oneself and to arrange one's life-conduct strictly accordingly belongs to the autonomous sphere of personality, according to Weber. Thus political value-decisions are in principle inaccessible to scientific verification or disproof no matter how understood. On the other hand science is indeed quite capable of elucidating the possible or probable consequences of certain decisions in concrete situations in the light of the respective ideal values governing an individual's actions or even of competing ideal values and so of rationalizing value-decisions to the extent that the achievement of the highest ideal values of the individual is given optimal chances.

In the so-called 'value-judgement controversy' conducted in the Verein für Sozialpolitik from 1908 onwards Weber never succeeded in gaining acceptance of his views. Originally he had taken on this fight above all with a view to countering the prevailing influence of the 'old-conservative' tendency as represented by Gustav von Schmoller, the Grand Old Man of the German historicist school of national economics after a frontal assault had failed to repel it. Schmoller in Weber's view represented a prototypical case of the dovetailing of value-judgements with scientific judgements in the name of a historicist conception of scholarship. Even Max Weber's colleagues in the Verein für Sozialpolitik misconstrued his line of argument in a thoroughly objectivist way, to go on to conclude that absolute value-neutrality was unattainable in any case, so that they thought Weber's ideas could be discarded as impracticable. Yet recent research has followed them in part whenever it maintains that Weber's theory of value-neutrality results in a strict separation of scholarship and politics.

Weber was concerned on the contrary to bring both spheres into relation with each other in such a way that on the one hand their transparency was consistently maintained and on the other the ground was taken from under the feet of all lectern demagoguery once and for all. This should not mean, however, that the political viewpoints which form the impulse of scientific research and flow into the formulation of the questions which guide scientific research should not be declared openly. This meaning can be discerned throughout Max Weber's work. Essential elements of his sociology of domination and especially his theory of democratic rule are owed directly or indirectly to insights he had gained in the contemporary political struggles of his day. And the sociology of domination in its turn is oriented around the central issue of how freedom, however understood, may be possible under different social conditions, and in particular in the conditions of highly bureaucratized capitalist societies.

Max Weber was extremely irritated by the political arrangements in Imperial Germany. He diagnosed as the chief characteristic of the existing political system that it had left the political leadership to a civil service that was well-meaning but incapable of political leadership and far-sighted political judgement. From the point of view of constitutional policy, in Weber's opinion it was a case of a pseudo-constitutional system that possessed all the disadvantages but none of the advantages of parliamentary forms of government.[14] Imperial Germany was led by good civil servants, even outstandingly good civil servants, but it lacked politicians – not just great politicians but politicians in the ordinary sense of the word. Accordingly he ascribed structural leaderlessness to the political system. This condition was additionally made worse by the 'personal regime' of Wilhelm II, that is the irresponsible governmental interventionism of the monarch in all political decision-making, especially foreign policy. In Weber's view this was rooted in social conditions and in the mental disposition of the leading classes of the nation. The existing bureaucratic regime was above all concerned to preserve the traditional political and social pre-eminence of the big landowning aristocracy, although this class had lapsed in the meantime into the role of receiver of state subsidies and accordingly no longer possessed the most important qualification that enables a class to provide political leadership, namely, an economically secure existence. In fact the higher civil service was pursuing a policy which sought to protect the *Junker* from their own narrowmindedness.

These conditions were reflected in the political immaturity of the middle classes. In purely economic terms they would have been called upon to take over control in state and society; instead they sought protection against the rising lower classes from the conventional hierarchical-authoritarian state. This was, as Weber perceived it, partly a result of Bismarck's imperious rule which had represented the exact 'opposite of the political education of the nation'.[15]

Weber judged the working class scarcely less favourably. It was pushing to get into power, without having any concrete ideas of how it could achieve this, not to mention to what use it should be put. Weber charged the German Social Democrats with an apolitical attitude, lack of a sense of power and a petty-bourgeois mentality. Instead of pursuing a sensible policy of reform in co-operation with the progressive elements of the bourgeoisie, it confined itself to a 'revolutionizing of minds'. Its appearance in the political arena had the effect of a 'shot in the arm for the existing order'. Max Weber used the British example here as a counterfactual model, although idealizing it in many respects. In Britain there was a parliamentary monarchy which assigned to the monarch a great degree of *de facto* political influence although constitutionally the monarch was confined to representative functions. In Britain it was a matter of a 'kingdom of influence', not, as in the case of the Wilhelmine empire, of 'mere pretence'. In Britain there was a powerful parliament which, precisely because it was not just relegated to purely negative politics, had always brought forward great political leaders. And these politicians had known how to pursue a thoroughly successful imperial policy and to achieve the mostly voluntary subordination of the colonial peoples to British domination. Moreover, the world power status of Britain had had positive effects on the attitude of British labour: unlike their German counterparts the British workers possessed a well-developed sense for issues involving political power. Quite apart from that, they pursued a realistic strategy as regards the promotion of their concrete class interests, instead of adhering to a strategy of mere verbal radicalism.

This highly critical diagnosis of the structural defects of the German political system, developed with British conditions in mind, became intensified during the First World War. In Weber's opinion not only was the outbreak of the war under circumstances that were extremely unfavourable to Imperial Germany a consequence of these failings, but furthermore they increasingly reduced Germany's chances of surviving the war relatively unscathed. The superiority of the parliamentary systems of the West over the German 'semi-constitutional-ism' was in his view incalculable. In Weber's opinion the 'ideas of 1914' – which symbolized a specially German variety of political culture whereby imperial authority and bureaucratic order were seen as guarantors of a type of civil society striking the right balance between the principles of freedom and authority – were pure 'literary verbiage'. He thus considered the achievement of domestic political reforms to be the first condition for a successful conduct of the war.

Weber wholeheartedly supported a powerful imperialistic foreign policy in the interests of increasing the power status of the nation, but that policy had to be carried out with a sense of reality and proportion. This was precisely what appeared to be less and less assured. The decision in favour of unrestricted submarine warfare in the summer of 1916 he considered to be the first extreme of absolute arrogance, which was then to be followed with a second in the conclusion of the imposed peace of Brest-Litovsk. In view of these hopeless conditions, which he attributed to the lack of a genuinely responsible political leadership, he could see only one effective solution: the parliamentarization of Imperial Germany. A policy of effective domestic reforms, associated with the introduction of a genuinely parliamentary system of government, was above all to achieve the following:

1 strengthening the political consensus of the nation and its readiness if necessary to do its utmost to survive the war successfully;
2 securing an effective political leadership, which, precisely because it would be based on democratically formed majorities, would be in a position to pursue a realistic, well-judged policy, with the goal of safeguarding the power position of Imperial Germany in the world in the long term, well beyond the foreseeable end of the war;
3 connected with this, putting an end to the irresponsible agitation for extreme and increasingly utopian war aims;
4 the effective elimination of the persistent interventionism of the military hierarchy in political decisions.

Against this current political background Max Weber gradually developed his theory of democratic rule of the parliamentary type. Essentially here he started from the classical model of representative democracy as it had developed in western Europe, namely a parliamentary system on the basis of the liberal model of individual self-determination protected from state despotism by basic rights in the context of a constitutional order. However, Weber saw himself compelled under the influence of contemporary events to place special emphasis on the need for political leadership. In accordance with contemporary ideas, he thus described the production of great political leaders as the most important function of parliamentary democracy and in a way the most important source of its legitimacy. Weber's model of democratic rule, in view of its conscious emphasis on the dominant role of political leaders within the parliamentary process of policy formation, thus tended to run into conflict with the liberal postulate of the self-determination of the active citizen, although, as will be shown below, he fundamentally adhered to the principle that democratic rule, even if it may be completely based on personality, at the same time still required the consensus of the citizens.

The political circumstances in Wilhelmine Germany induced Max Weber to develop his theory of democratic rule not from the premises of individual self-determination and popular sovereignty – although indeed hints of this can be found in his work – but rather from the superior performance of parliamentary democracies. In concrete situations, however, this meant relying particularly on their ability to produce a truly effective leadership. Weber in principle adhered to the basic precepts of a liberal conception of democratic rule: personal liberties, the idea of representation and the requirement that all democratically responsible action necessitates the political consensus of actively involved citizens. But increasingly he emphasized by contrast the opposite principle: that great politicians must create their political following on the strength of their personal charismatic qualifications; in other words, that the formation of political opinion flows essentially from the top downwards and not from the base upwards to the elected leader, whether by the principle of delegation or by the conferring of a political mandate. Deeply convinced of the need for great political leadership under the contemporary political circumstances in Germany, which were threatening to endanger the very existence of the Reich, Max Weber had no reservations about pushing the idea of the political leader's personal responsibility to its utmost conceptual limits, although thereby he brought himself into diametrical opposition with the classical precepts of liberal democracy.[16] In this context at least the legal and constitutional political norms of democratic rule are treated merely as formal preconditions for the rise of great leader figures who have gained their positions of power exclusively on the strength of their personal charisma – that is, on the strength of the belief of the masses in their capacity for leadership.

At the same time the gradual unfolding of this position, which was to receive its most radical expression in the theory of 'plebiscitarian leader democracy', must be seen against the background of Weber's universal-historical theory of Western rationalization as an essentially irreversible process of increasing formal rationalization of every aspect of life and of the progressive bureaucratization of all institutional forms. From this point of view, plebiscitarian leader democracy appeared to be a suitable means of preserving intact a dynamic order of politics and thus at the same time political freedom, in whatever sense of the world, in modern bureaucratic societies.

It is well known that according to Max Weber one of the most significant achievements of the West was the creation of a bureaucratically organized institutional state, with a clearly delimited territory, a rational legal order and its own staff of bureaucrats serving only the reasons of state and operating within the framework of clearly defined competences, but above all in possession of the monopoly of physical violence; the latter distinguishes the state from all other institutional forms of domination in society. From the point of view of the efficiency, stability and reliability of its apparatus of rule, this type of bureaucratic domination was far superior to all other known forms of domination in history. There seemed to be no turning back from this organizational form of domination at least in the historical situation in which Weber found himself. The triumph of bureaucratic forms of the exercise of domination seemed to be merely a question of time. Even in the USA, which for a long time had known only the 'spoils system' and a purely amateur administration, since the Americans looked upon a bureaucratic organization of state administration with the deepest suspicion, it was only a matter of time before administration by bureaucrats according to the European model would establish itself. In Weber's estimation, however, bureaucratic machines belonged to those social institutions that were the most difficult of all to destroy.

All the same, bureaucratization seemed to be on the advance across the globe, not only in state and local administrations but also in the economic sphere and in social life and not least in the field of party organization. Relying on studies by James Bryce and Maurice Ostrogorski, and with reference to American and British examples, especially Chamberlain's 'caucus' as first practised in Birmingham, and the party machines of the major American cities, Max Weber predicted the replacement of the type of honorific party (*Honoratorienpartei*) characteristic in particular of traditional liberalism by tightly organized bureaucratic mass-membership parties. Social democracy was the most obvious example of this new type on his own doorstep. Unlike Roberto Michels, Weber did not consider the rise of mass bureaucratic parties and the associated oligarchization of internal party structures to be a disaster, or the beginning of the end of genuine party democracy and thus of democracy in general, but saw this development as inevitable under the circumstances of the advanced industrial state of the capitalistic type.[17] Indeed, he even saw positive aspects in this, for bureaucratic party machines could help to increase the social dynamism of the capitalist system, which had taken a regressive trend after the formation of monopolistic structures. The party apparatuses functioned so to speak as a reinforcement for the initiatives of the leadership and enabled the latter to implement their political objectives more effectively. In this way the great personalities who, because of the relative underdevelopment of political systems in the early nineteenth century, could still have claimed the political leadership for themselves came into their own, as it were, on a higher plane. At the top of well-organized, strictly obedient party machines there opened up for them the prospect of creative politics. The combination of charismatically legitimated leadership and the bureaucratic underpinning of their rule, even in the conditions of egalitarian industrial society, held the promise of a far-sighted policy capable of innovation and thus of an indirect increase in social dynamism. This was of the greatest importance. In the course of the development of the institutional-bureaucratic state in large parts of Europe, there arose an increasing lack of political leadership, especially in the pseudo-constitutional system of Imperial Germany which preserved the undiluted autocracy of a bureaucratic power elite. In Weber's view the main thing was to oppose this trend, initially in the interests of national power politics, but in general also in the interests of the preservation of the liberal order itself.

Considerations of this sort led Max Weber to highlight most emphatically the contrast between politician and bureaucrat in his sociology of domination, not only from the point of view of practical politics but also in purely theoretical terms. Bureaucrats must act strictly in accordance with instructions, within the bounds of rigidly defined competences, without personal considerations but above all without revealing their personal convictions and ideals. That is why bureaucratic apparatuses are capable of achieving maximum efficiency and, almost more importantly, why they can serve as reliable and predictable instruments in the hands of whoever controls them. Precisely because their code of behaviour is prescribed and decisively influences their life-conduct, which is oriented to the dispassionate and impartial fulfilment of the instructions given to them, bureaucrats are unsuited to political leadership. However, for the politicians at the head of these bureaucratic machines who are responsible for giving them objectives and direction, other laws apply. By contrast with bureaucrats, political leaders must possess exactly the opposite qualities, in particular the capacity to pursue their own objectives, systematically and stubbornly, at whatever cost to themselves and with relentless personal engagement. Their duty is not to adapt to pre-existing conditions but to fight for something they personally hold to be an important value. But leading politicians must create a following for themselves as well by making use of their demagogic skills. In this, however, they must not simply appear as the representatives of the interests of their followers or electors, but rather the reverse: they must supply them with their political objectives. Ultimately these objectives will be derived from their innermost personal value-orientations and not somehow from the tacit or expressed will of their political supporters or electors.

The extremes to which Weber goes in determining the role of political leaders as acting exclusively on their own responsibility while on the other hand emphasizing how rigidly constrained bureaucrats are in carrying out their instructions, bound up as they are within a bureaucratic administrative apparatus, correlate with the sharp contrast he makes between political action as a type and bureaucratic-administrative action. With this characterization of the functions of political leadership, particularly as it applies in modern democracy, which then took on its general form in the theoretical requirement of charismatic leadership qualifications even for the democratic politician, Weber's theory of democratic domination necessarily came into conflict with generally accepted conceptions of democracy, which view the political leader primarily as the representative if not just the mandatory of the electorate. Max Weber indeed does not especially dispute this. For him it was self-evident that small groups of politicians always determine political action. However, he distanced himself from democratic elite theories of the sort propounded by Gaetano Mosca or Wilfrido Pareto essentially through his individualistic model of political action. Weber's sociology of domination does not involve leading elites or *classes dirigeantes*, but always some outstanding personalities who of course are in constant competition with one another for the voters' favour and who thereby have to assure themselves of the political consent of the citizens. The latters' political maturity functions as a negative condition for the securing of genuine charismatic leadership; and in this respect the democratic selection of leaders can be realized only in democratic political systems which put into practice the principle of the equality of every citizen in the state and of equal rights of participation.

From this point of view it follows that Max Weber found it necessary to restate the classical theory of democracy. In his view, the natural-law justification of democratic domination – even if he did not expressly reject it, but rather emphasized its significance in the creation of modern democratic systems – had lost all its concrete relevance for the present day. Democratization had, as he once said, if 'any precise meaning at all, then only that of the "minimalization" of the domination by "professional civil servants" in favour of the most direct possible dominion of the people, which in practice means of its respective party leaders'.[18] One can view this as an inappropriate abridgement of the concept of democratic rule. Yet Max Weber considered the principle of free leadership selection to be the essence of democratic rule under whatever circumstances. In so far as the unqualified adoption of this principle succeeded, that was 'not so insignificant' an achievement. For fundamentalist justifications of democracy, on the other hand, he reserved only contempt. From this point of departure Max Weber gradually developed a functionalist model of parliamentary democracy at the centre of which stood the great leader figure, in the last instance responsible only to himself and bound only by his self-chosen 'ultimate values'. The omnipotence of bureaucratic routine, embodied in the ever rapidly expanding bureaucratic institutions of modern society, served as an ideal-typical opposite of this model and supplied it with its legitimation.

Max Weber developed his model of the parliamentary system following the example of contemporary British constitutional conditions, but not without embellishing it with elements from German political tradition. In comparison with other contemporary types of democratic rule, such as the American presidential system in particular, but also the Swiss system of direct democracy and an extremely weak executive, the parliamentary system for him seemed to be the best suited to securing a maximum of political dynamism and optimal political leadership under conditions of increasing bureaucratization in all spheres of social interaction. Not least because of the unrestricted right of inquiry assigned to it by constitutional law, parliament was still best able to keep in check the bureaucratic governmental apparatus, which had at its disposal an increasing amount of expertise in the exercise of power (*Herrschafts-wissen*). In addition, parliament's primary function is to select political leaders. Yet it can fulfil this only if it carries political responsibility and if it has unrestricted participation in the political decision-making processes – in other words, in so far as it is a working parliament and not just an arena for ideological debate. Max Weber exemplified this with the case of the British parliament, which again and again had brought forth outstanding political leadership figures of a high quality, while the same could not be said of the German Reichstag precisely because it was condemned to pursue a merely negative form of parliamentary politics. As argued by Weber, parliament functions chiefly as a proving ground for politicians with a vocation for political leadership but at the same time as an organ of control which brings about the retirement of states-men and politicians from positions of responsibility whenever they have forfeited their leadership qualities. With the rise of plebiscitarian democracy, political initiative had transferred to the respective party leaders or statesmen who with the support of their following in parliament directed their political appeal primarily at the broad mass of the electorate in order to elicit from it the necessary consensus for their policies.

Democratic leader-rule thus cannot do without a powerful parliament. Only in the antagonistic interplay between the two institutions of government and parliament can first-rate political leadership develop. In spite of its deliberately antinomically arranged structure, this model of democratic rule does not evade the danger of a functionalistic abridgement of parliament's role in the democratic-constitutional state and of parliament's being viewed chiefly as an organ for the maintenance and supervision of strong political leadership. This tendency comes fully to the fore between 1919 and 1920. As regards this period of his political thought, one can speak of a 'turning against pure parlia-mentarianism';[19] Weber distinguished now between 'leader democracy' and 'leaderless democracy', that is to say the 'rule of professional politicians without a vocation', without the internal charismatic skills which are exactly what makes a leader.[20] This can be interpreted partly as a reaction to his own not very encouraging experiences with the DDP (German Democratic Party) party organization in Hessen/Nassau, but was basically derived from his conception of political leadership which in turn originated in his philosophical view, here influenced by Nietzsche, that in practice only outstanding individuals have any chance of putting forward objectives for and giving new directions to society by virtue of their personal charisma.

Max Weber's theory of democratic domination emphasizes onesidedly the process of policy formation from the top downwards and the significance of the leading politician, while the great majority of citizens as such tend to recede into the background. This is at least in part a result of the climate in which Max Weber developed his sociology of domination. At the time the enemies of freedom almost uniformly seemed to be on the side of the bureaucratic machines. The precept of individual self-determination remained for Max Weber the ideally suited measure of democratic systems; yet it had lost its direct relevance in the conditions of developed bureaucratic societies. Only with the help of charismatic skills and only by using special techniques for winning over followers and for exercising domination by way of bureaucratic organization did the individual still have any chance, in Weber's opinion, of really bringing his or her influence to bear in the political sphere.

The apparent top-heaviness of the structure of political leader-rule in parliamentary democracy as it appears here should certainly not be mistaken as authoritarian. For the taking to extremes of the principle of the political leader's personal responsibility is matched by the requirement that great political leadership can only emerge within a genuinely democratic system and that it is bound by the necessity of continual self-legitimation within the framework of the democratic process of policy formation. Thus a democratic constitutional framework and, even more importantly, a democratically constituted society in which the precept of individual self-determination is recognized as a basic structural principle at every level of the state order represent indispensable preconditions for the functioning of 'charismatic leader democracy'. For Weber this goes without saying; because of the aforementioned reasons arising from the contemporary political climate and conditioned by the historical situation, he stressed this aspect much less forcefully.

As is demonstrated in more detail in a later essay, what we have here is an antinomical model, both sides of which are simultaneously and separately pushed in extremely radical fashion to their conceptual extremes. In Max Weber's work the principle of forming a gathering of followers in parliamentary democracy on the strength of a charismatic gift for leadership and the principle of individual self-determination are in essence equally valid and equally important. Charismatic leadership of the democratic type requires not only a democratic constitution but also a politically self-conscious citizenship. On the other hand, the achievement of liberty in whatever sense of the word – and thus also the realization of the principle of individual self-determination in constitutional practice – can only be secured under conditions of charismatic political leadership, because this alone can prevent a gradual petrification of modern bureaucratic societies in sheer routine and still preserve a sphere of liberty for the individual. A reconciliation of the principle of individual self-determination and the principle of charismatic leader-rule is theoretically unattainable; rather, they possess the quality of antinomies. Only in practical life-conduct does the possibility arise of giving preference to one or the other in a particular context of action. Not the least because of this is the model of parliamentary democracy, as we find it in Weber's work, presented in a bipolar structure. According to whether the problems of democratic rule are formulated from the point of view of individual self-determination and self-realization or from the point of view of political leadership, differing conclusions result. They are reconciled if at all only in the prescriptive idea that everything must be done in the conditions of the bureaucratic state so as to ensure a maximum of liberty and opportunity for creative political action.

The bipolarity of this model of democratic government is reflected in the field of political ethics. Max Weber, as is well known, distinguished two forms of political ethics, the *ethics of conviction* and the *ethics of responsibility*. Ethics based on conviction make the pursuit of certain values or ideals an imperative duty for an individual, no matter how great the chances for the achievement of these ideals in the current social situation may be and no matter what direct or indirect, intentional or unintentional, forms may be adopted by the political action that is committed to these ultimate values. In the final analysis, for the actor it is chiefly a matter of confirming the validity of or 'preserving' those values he or she holds to be absolute; the actor feels duty-bound to comply with them even in the most adverse circumstances and even if necessary by sacrificing his or her own life, as in the case of the syndicalist or the anarchist. Ethics deriving from a sense of responsibility, on the other hand, require the constant weighing-up of the possible consequences of one's actions, with a view to the optimal possible realization of whatever ideal values one has, and if necessary employing the rational knowledge available to the actor about their possible consequences or their unintentional side-effects.

In Weber's view the ethics of responsibility represented the ethic specific to the politician, and more particularly to the democratic politician. But he could not see any chance of somehow denying those who acted out of ethical conviction the justification for their own actions – and certainly not by means of rational science. Furthermore, indeed, great political leadership always contains an element of conviction ethics, by imposing certain objectives on its respective supporters which are to be absolutely binding. Weber thus in principle viewed both ethics as equally valid. Wolfgang Schluchter tried to demonstrate that only the ethics of responsibility corresponds to Max Weber's personality ideal, which requires a rational life-conduct in keeping with ultimate values which constitute the stuff of personality in the first place, and that it must therefore be seen as an essentially superior ethic.[21] Without doubt the concept of responsibility ethics contains elements of a material ethic of values. Yet for fundamental reasons Weber did not permit himself to follow such a course; for this would have resulted in a dilution of the respective ultimate value-decisions, whether on the basis of pragmatic or scientific criteria. But this is precisely what Weber considered neither practically desirable nor theoretically feasible.

Moreover, it is true of both variants of political ethic that they maintain an insolubly tense relationship with the precepts of all religiously founded ethics, for the simple reason that force and the exercise of force represent their specific mode of action. In his emphasis on force as an autonomous irreducible category of politics Max Weber follows in the tradition of Niccolò Machiavelli. According to Weber, 'legitimate violence', or the exercise of domination by means of force by a regime accepted or recognized as legitimate by those who are ruled, also stands in an antinomical relationship of insoluble tension to the principles of all religious ethics but especially to Christian ethics. Here as well the mutually competing or even opposing positions involved are pushed to their respective conceptual limits in a Nietzschean style of reasoning which tries to express the antinomies immanent in politics in the purest possible form instead of opting for a middle course and justifying it pragmatically or morally.

The essential incompatibility of politics and ethics as we find it in Weber's sociology of domination is reflected in the theory of the three pure types of legitimate domination. The antinomical structure of the political as an autonomous sphere of values is again much in evidence here. The way in which Weber tried to determine the legitimacy of political systems excludes from the start any recourse to normative criteria of a moral or ethical kind. In this respect he broke with a long tradition in Western political theory which traced the legitimacy or illegitimacy of domination (as the case may be) back to a system of moral norms, whether it be Hobbes's argument for the moral desirability of ending the anarchic condition of 'war of all against all' by the establishment of unrestricted domination, if necessary with the help of unrestrained violence; or Machiavelli's idea of the circulation of 'virtù', that is, the creative vitality of individuals or peoples capable of rulership; or the natural-law dogma of the likes of John Locke, which tried to impose fundamental limits on the exercise of state power. Max Weber's sociological theory of legitimacy instead started from the factual observation of how much consent to legitimacy is given by the 'ruled', that is in the empirically discernible willingness to subject themselves to a particular system of domination and to accept its norms as personally binding. Seen from this perspective, for Max Weber 'illegitimate domination' could not exist at all as a type, but there could only ever be a greater or lesser degree of empirically extant consent to legitimacy.

As is well known, Max Weber distinguished three different pure types of legitimate domination: *legal domination*, in which the belief in the legality of law which is posited in the correct form and according to the usual procedural rules is the basis of legitimacy, quite irrespective of the question as to which substantive legal principles are respectively at issue thereby; *traditional domination*, in which custom or precedent – in other words, 'prescriptive law' – is the foundation of legitimacy; and finally *charismatic domination*, which possesses or may make legal claim to legitimacy on the strength of the belief in the charismatic qualification of the leader in question and thus also in the lawfulness, indeed the absolutely binding force, of the values, norms and goals laid down by him. Thus it is not normative criteria of a moral or ethical nature that decide the legitimacy of a system of domination but the subjective disposition of its subjects in practice to accept the authority in question. This comprehensive typology claims to take into consideration all forms of legitimate domination at one fell swoop and to be applicable in theory to every system of domination known to us in history. Furthermore, this model also displays an antinomical structure. Inasmuch as legitimacy ought to be more than just the acceptance of the immutability of a system of rule on the basis of the existence in practice of domination, it always ultimately originates in one single form, namely the charismatic foundation of political authority. Legal domination, on the other hand, survives chiefly on the strength of what in practice exists. Legal domination, as Weber emphasizes, owes its legitimacy for the most part to the routineness of the rules that take effect through it. Compared with this the conceptually feasible model of a value-oriented legal order fades into insignificance. On the other hand Weber presumes that legal domination cannot be stable in the long term without elements of charismatically legitimated leadership. Patriarchal legitimacy derives its power essentially from charismatic authority which has taken on an institutionalized form and which so acquires a sort of permanence. Taking these ideas into consideration, it becomes clear why Max Weber did not categorize parliamentary democracy, at least in its only variant that was dynamic and could survive in the long term – as 'leader democracy' – in the model of the three types of legitimate domination as a subtype of legal rule based on rational values, which, certainly, he might well have originally intended,[22] but categorized it as a variant of charismatic legitimacy, and in fact as a version of charismatic rule supposedly 'free of domination'. In *Economy and Society* this is expressed with admirable clarity: '"Plebiscitarian democracy" – the most important type of "leader democracy" – is in its genuine sense a type of charismatic rule which is concealed behind a type of legitimacy that is *formally* derived from and persists as a result of the will of the ruled.'[23] These comparatively late passages from part 1 of *Economy and Society* must be read in association with the formulations in 'Politics as a vocation', which were written at roughly the same time, about the necessity of a 'leader democracy with a machine', that is, the necessity of a combination of charismatically based leadership authority and bureaucratic techniques of domination.[24] Even if Weber did not develop this new conception any more systematically, it does represent his final answer to the question of how democratic authority is still possible in an age of increasing bureaucratization and how maximum social dynamism and individual freedom, however understood, can be achieved.

In a way these remarks lead us back to where we started. Max Weber's theoretical ideas on 'plebiscitarian democracy' reflect his political opinions during the foundational phase of the Weimar Republic. In the debates about the new imperial constitution in 1919–20 he supported systematically and with powerful rhetorical contributions constitutional solutions which pointed in just this direction, in particular by his insistence on a popularly elected president; by virtue of his direct links with the will of the masses the *Reichspräsident* was to be an opening for the rise of political leaders over and above party machines and parliaments. In this way Weber hoped to assist a 'leader democracy' to come to the fore in Germany, in which charismatically qualified politicians with a sense of foresight but also with a sense of proportion are at the helm, instead of a 'leaderless democracy of professional politicians without a vocation'.

Political science has viewed these suggestions of Max Weber with a certain scepticism, or has taken them up in diluted form which leaves the problematic elements of his theory mostly untouched. In the 1950s and 1960s especially there were only a few political scientists who were really willing to give their unconditional acceptance to Weber's conception of exceptional political leadership oriented around the idea of charisma. This is true even of those political scientists who were closely associated with Max Weber, such as Karl Löwenstein or Ernst Fraenkel. Their reception of his sociology of domination (and, incidentally, this is just as much true of the sociologists) occurred in a rather selective fashion. They accepted Weber's model of parliamentary democracy in so far as it had been developed in the context of a devastating critique of the pseudo-constitutional system of the German Wilhelmine empire, but tended to reduce the 'time-bound' elements of his theory, above all the elitist bias of his conception of political leadership, to a pragmatically acceptable level, to say nothing about his underlying nationalistic inclinations. Only rarely did anyone completely follow Max Weber's theory, with its explicit antinomies and its extreme radicality of thought, which had so little in common with the empiricist modes of thought prevailing at the time. Nowadays this has changed. Max Weber is again attracting great interest as a thinker who strove to base political theory and political action on fundamental value-attitudes which related to a definite image of humanity. Individuals, who must find their own way in a world increasingly dominated by anonymous forces, are thrown back upon themselves and their personal value-attitudes; given the lack of imperative objective norms they are confronted with more and more new decisions for which no easy way out can be found in political reality.

With some justification, Wilhelm Hennis recently pointed out that Max Weber has nothing in common with that version of liberalism which attempted to replace the domination of individuals over other individuals with the administration of things and thus assumed that it could suppress strife and violence once and for all. 'To force the individual into political arrangements, to make him participate in the responsibilities and the risks of these arrangements, and if necessary even deliberately to submit these arrangements to external and internal risks, in other words not to exclude strife by institutional provision, but rather in fact to provoke it' – that is, according to Hennis, at the centre of political theory from Machiavelli and Rousseau right up as far as Max Weber.[25] This is particularly true of Max Weber's theory of democratic domination. This was constructed of antinomies precisely because he did not want to see the idea of strife eliminated; he wanted, on the contrary, to see it properly accentuated. The special advantage of parliamentary democracy lay not in the fact that the struggle between political tendencies and philosophies could be mediated through it but much rather that the way of conducting this struggle could be perfected within the parliamentary constitutional system.

However, it does not follow from this that Weber was no liberal at all, as Hennis would have it. On the contrary, there can be no doubt about Max Weber's political stance. He was a liberal who was no longer satisfied with the simple repetition of the traditional liberal dogmas, because deep down inside he could feel how profoundly liberal thought and liberal ways of life were under threat in this modern world of ours. He sought radical solutions that made it possible to further dynamic, far-sighted policies even in conditions of increasing bureaucratization. His role in the German politics of his day and his academic pursuit of a contemporary theory of democratic government are two aspects of one and the same basic attitude.

2

The Antinomical Structure of
Max Weber's Political Thought

Once in the midst of his discussion with Heidegger, Karl Jaspers spoke of Max Weber's 'questions of great world-historical import which, though answerable in part through concrete critical research, become, as questions, ever greater and more unanswerable'.[1]

Referring to Weber's philosophical and sociological work, Jaspers is saying that in the concrete process of research it leads to the very limits of knowledge and that the partial empirical solution to the questions posed only raises new, far more complex questions. The same can be said particularly of Max Weber's political thought. His probing questions led again and again to the very limits of the political positions which he held to be valid, laying bare the insoluble conflict between alternative ideal values in ultimate situations. This chapter will examine this phenomenon more closely in a particular area of Weber's political thought, namely, his basic attitude towards liberal democracy.

Politically, Max Weber belonged to the tradition of German National-Liberalism of the post-Bismarck era. Very early on, however, he began to commit himself to the left wing of liberalism. He belonged to the group of German thinkers who, already before the turn of the century, consistently demanded the parliamentarization of Imperial Germany. Yet his support for the liberalization of German society was tied to an impassioned nationalism which, already in the 1890s, meant a commitment to German world politics on a large scale.[2] Within the context of the German politics of his time, Max Weber can best be characterized as a prominent representative of the kind of cultural imperialism that became fashionable in the late 1890s in German intellectual circles, especially among university professors. The question whether his liberal convictions were self-sustaining or rather just a means of enhancing the internal cohesiveness of the national power state is not easy to answer. Yet there can be no doubt that, for Weber, a strengthening of German liberalism was thinkable only in conjunction with vigorous national power politics. Authors such as Jürgen Kocka, David Beetham and Anthony Giddens[3] have objected to this interpretation, arguing that even though Max Weber may have made some important concessions on this point to the spirit of the age he was none the less fundamentally a true liberal, and thus his nationalist views are to be rated only as secondary.[4]

It would seem that there was an inherent contradiction manifest in Weber's thought which has to be dealt with as such and which is in need of being further investigated. This points to one of the parameters of his thinking in which the contradictions between alternative value-positions stand out sharply.

It is true that Max Weber did not always present his nationalistic goals as emphatically as in the 1890s, but in principle the ideal of a strong nation-state remained a dominent leitmotiv in his political thought throughout his life. Weber pointed out explicitly and repeatedly that in his personal hierarchy of values the national idea took precedence over questions of a liberal constitutional order: 'The arguments advanced here will not influence those who do not hold, in principle, the historical tasks of the German nation as having precedence over all other questions concerning the form of government nor will they influence those who view these tasks in a fundamentally different light.'[5] Elsewhere Weber formulated this issue even more sharply: 'For me, "democracy" has never been an end in itself. My only interest has been and remains the possibility of implementing a realistic national policy of a strong, externally oriented Germany.'[6] Such a position does not lend itself to facile compromise. Rather one has to take as one's point of departure the fact that Weber was a nationalist as well as a liberal, even though both positions are not readily compatible with one another. We are confronted here with an antinomy in Weber's political thought which will not simply disappear by way of compromise; it can be resolved only within the framework of a systematic interpretation.

The conflict which emerges here between two different ideal values appears to be symptomatic of an important feature of Weber's thinking. Weber always advanced the rationalization of a given position in the light of certain ultimate ideals to the outermost limits, in this case, the ideal of a strong German nation-state on the one hand, and the ideal of a liberal social order on the other. Recently, Rehberg has aptly pointed out that 'Weber incorporated models of action which were class-bound and time-conditioned, but in having intensified them he forced them through unsolvable conflict situations to their consequent realization.'[7]

In this way, the fundamental value-conflicts and antinomies which are customarily concealed by the pragmatic compromises of everyday life now become evident.[8] Such a position brings Max Weber together with Friedrich Nietzsche. Nietzsche had already maintained the basic principle that out of intellectual honesty one always had to follow any issue to the most consistent position thinkable, which should then become the yardstick for one's thinking, regardless of the consequences for oneself, even when this could ultimately lead to self-destruction. In this absolute unconditionality of the will to knowledge Weber had much in common with Nietzsche. One can also find certain analogies in their lives. Max Weber's attitude towards life has often been aptly described as that of 'heroic pessimism', an attitude characterized by an inherent conflict between antagonistic value-positions in contradistinction to the abandonment of self to comfortable everyday resolutions. Max Weber used the expression 'I want to see how much I can endure.' This statement is to be understood fully in the Nietzschean sense. Yet in the case of Weber this fundamental attitude of 'heroic pessimism' also take on a rationalistic form. Like the Puritan who conducted his life with iron discipline, orienting it towards certain normative values whose origins were outside everyday life and rationalizing it to the utmost, Weber saw it as the duty of every individual to face the problems and conflicts with which one was confronted in complete sobriety and without any illusions and to reduce the given options to the underlying fundamental problems of values, without paying heed to the dominant opinions of the day.

Hence there are great similarities between Weber's and Nietzsche's basic structure of thinking. Both men always traced the concrete problem back to the level on which the value-questions which were normally hidden emerged to full view. It is true that one rarely finds Nietzsche being explicitly quoted in Weber's sociological work, even though he is quoted, and not by chance, precisely in those places where Weber addresses fundamental ideological problems or world-historical perspectives, as is the case at the end of *The Protestant Ethic* or in 'Science as a vocation'. In any case, there can be no doubt that Weber was profoundly influenced by Nietzsche, although it may be going too far to interpret Weber's work as the result of a permanent dialogue between Nietzsche and Marx, as has been suggested by Baumgarten.[9] Weber shared with Nietzsche the conviction that only the individual, as a rule only the outstanding individual, was capable of setting new goals and of imparting a new drive to society, out of personal value-orientations whose origins were to be found beyond the routine everyday life. The innerworldly asceticism of the Puritans which led to the revolutionary transformation of the modern world can be ascribed to otherworldly value-convictions. Modern natural-rights theory and the modern industrial capitalist system of production also issued from the latter. The role of the charismatically gifted politician is to be seen in an analogous light. He alone, on the basis of personal convictions which are not simply a reflection of given conditions, but are rather rooted in fundamental value-orientations, is in a position to give society the force needed to go beyond the routine of everyday life. Weber explicitly rejected, however, the extreme consequence of an aristocracy of the spirit which Nietzsche derived from this fact, namely, the notion that only the outstanding individual had the calling and the capacity to establish new values. Weber did not share Nietzsche's dislike for the masses (*die Vielzuvielen*). Nietzsche's view that 'the meaning of world history resides exclusively in its highest exemplars' was even less acceptable to him. On the contrary, only those individuals who are able to induce the masses to follow them voluntarily are truly great and capable of creative and formative politics. In contrast to Nietzsche's ethic of the master which culminated in the outright rejection of all democratic politics, Weber adhered to the fundamental principles of liberalism which hold sacrosanct the dignity of the individual and aspire to see society organized in such a way that all individuals may preserve a maximum of free initiative.

At the same time, however, Weber approached with a Nietzschean radicalism of thinking the question how far the classical liberal theory still maintained its inner consistency and stringency under modern conditions. In certain areas and with a limited purpose Weber brought about a reformulation of the content of liberal theory in a way which could definitively be compared with Nietzsche's postulate of 'the transvaluation of all values'. Progressively, as part of his endeavour to formulate a definitive conception of parliamentary-democratic domination which would correspond to the times, he felt the need to discard or rather reformulate in the process generally accepted liberal conceptions. Once again, positions which had originally coexisted in an unclear relationship started progressively to diverge until, finally, they took on an antinomical structure. The unconditionality of Weber's thinking, which the latter owed to Nietzsche, and the clear appreciation of the power character of all social relations, which he learned from Marx, led him finally to abandon the framework of classical liberal theory and to search for new, more solid foundations for liberal postulates. This extreme radicalization of alternative positions, so typical of Weber's political thinking, reveals as it were the flaws and contradictions within the liberal system of values which appear when the latter is confronted with the conditions of advanced industrial societies. Thus the antinomies and contradictions which Weber's theory of the constitutional state ran into are a reflection of the crisis of liberalism in the age of transformation from a civil-bourgeois to a mass society.[10] In the following pages I will try to show, by focusing on a series of specific issues, the tensions and inherent conflicts which become manifest in Max Weber's political philosophy of values the moment the ideal values which come into play are pushed to the limits of their validity.

Let us first examine the question how it was possible for Weber to be at the same time a resolute liberal and a rugged nationalist, one for whom it was imperative that Imperial Germany conduct vigorous world politics, even to the point of not excluding the option of war, if necessary. From our present-day perspective it becomes clear that both these ideals stand in contradiction to one another. Indeed, the principle of 'individual self-determination' is hardly compatible with a 'world politics' which had as its objective the establishment of a hegemonic supremacy of Imperial Germany over the European continent *vis-à-vis* the smaller nations. There are some valid grounds for assuming that Max Weber advocated a vigorous German imperialism primarily for tactical reasons; that is to say, that he saw the inauguration of German imperialism primarily as a means to achieve a fundamental liberalization of German society. As it were, Weber propagated the imperial idea in order to fight the conservatives with their own weapons. A consistent imperialist policy implied an option for the industrial state; the latter, however, was at the same time directed, at least indirectly, against the traditionally pre-eminent position of the agrarian conservatives in state and society. A rational imperialist policy called for the modernization of German society; on the one hand, to provide the necessary material resources and, on the other hand, to make possible the kind of internal national unity needed for such a policy. In this sense, the imperialist idea could serve precisely as a kind of ideology of emancipation directed against the hegemony of the Prussian aristocracy in German society, thereby leading to a liberalization of the political system. Weber thought that in this way liberalism would take up again a new positive task and receive new momentum as the carrier of a grand programme oriented towards the future.

However, irrespective of these primarily tactical points of view which permitted him as a liberal simultaneously to propagate imperialist policies, Weber was an imperialist out of conviction. He thought that in an age of imperial power conflicts it was simply the duty of the German Reich to assert itself as a world power if only in order to assure a place on earth for German culture in the centuries to come. Apparently, even in 1911, when Weber was for a time actively supporting a policy of international understanding, he did not really shrink back from the idea of a major European war, should it prove inevitable in the course of pursuing a vigorous imperialist German policy. It is true that he felt great apprehension over the concrete circumstances under which the First World War finally broke out. Yet he did not desist from using passionate rhetoric to justify the German war effort from a universal-historical perspective: 'We had to be a power state and we had to risk this war in order to have a say in the decision-making process regarding the future of the world.'[11] In the light of the available data one cannot but conclude that for Max Weber an active German imperialistic policy was more than just a clever strategy to give new life to German liberalism. He passionately supported internal reforms at home, moreover, as a necessary counter-measure to the policy of pursuing a vigorous course in politics abroad. In any case it was also more than just a tactical means of enhancing the power of the German nation-state, even though it was frequently expressed in such a manner as to suggest such a conclusion. Indeed, the question which of the two hierarchies of values, the nationalist or the liberal, had pre-eminence for Weber cannot be answered unequivocally. Rather one has to proceed from the assumption that one is dealing with an antinomy of a fundamental nature in Weber's thinking. In fact, one could say that for the most part Weber scorned facile compromise or middle positions. Even though he recognized in principle the need for pragmatic solutions in politics, he did not admit of such solutions when dealing with conflicts of fundamental values. He repeatedly pointed out that it was the fate of modern man to have to deal simultaneously with different ideas and value-orientations which were in conflict with one another in his own heart. This appears to be particularly the case as regards his political attitude, which was at once that of a convinced liberal and that of a relatively moderate German nationalist.

None the less, it is possible to trace these two apparently incompatible positions back to a common fundamental premise. Max Weber's point of departure was the conviction that society was threatened in its basic elements by the universal processes of bureaucratization and rationalization of all spheres of life. It was therefore necessary to preserve at all levels of social life a maximum of dynamic forces or to promote them with all the means available. In a certain sense, Weber wanted to maintain as unrestricted as possible, even under the conditions of mass industrial society, the classic principle of competition, that is, the struggle between the various individuals and groups in society for their ideal or material interests. Thus he called for a liberalization of the constitutional system at home which would at once set free the spontaneous activities of groups and organizations within the social system. Weber viewed the existence of a highly pluralistic social structure as an essential element of a liberal order, one which would permit a maximum of free space where political parties, groups and interest organizations could freely contest their particular ideal or material interests. This same conception also found its counterpart in the sphere of international relations. Weber welcomed, in principle, an international system in which a number of strong nation-states confronted each other in permanent rivalry. He viewed the military arms race among the superpowers as an unfortunate but inevitable side-effect of a welcome state of affairs.

Once it became clear to him after the outbreak of the First World War that the heyday of the autonomous nation-state had passed and that a few hegemonic power structures would come in time to replace the many sovereign nation-states of varying rank, Max Weber wanted to secure a hegemonic position for Germany within Europe. This hegemonic position, which he, for one, wished to be restricted to informal methods of domination, was necessary in order to guarantee the nation-states of central Europe above all a proper and secure place within the system of world powers that was in the process of being formed. A plurality of national power states and a system of powers in which the individual political and social systems would confront one another in permanent contest seemed to him to be a precondition for the preservation of a high degree of freedom and dynamism within the society of European and even world powers.

In this respect there is a link between Weber's advocacy of a comparatively moderate German imperialism and his liberal ideas, a link which is able partially to bridge the above-mentioned contradiction between both positions. The competitive struggle of the superpowers within the international system and the tensions between the different social structures and social orders were not merely a threat to peace. They also had a positive function, even though Weber himself lamented the fact that the European states were forced to invest a far from insignificant part of their gross national product in the relatively unproductive arms race.

In Weber's theoretical statements on the nature of democracy and the liberal order, one can also find the same tendency to balance out positions which are diametrically opposed. Weber was convinced that, given the social conditions which emerged in the advanced industrial societies of the West, classical liberal ideas had largely lost their concrete power of expression or, at least, their unequivocal meaning. For him liberal constitutional rights had become either truisms or empty formulas which as such could not offer any orientation although, like daily bread, one could not do without them.[12] Weber recognized the major historical relevance of the theory of natural rights as it was first developed by the Levellers, but he believed that under modern conditions the theory had progressively lost its significance and was being replaced by positivistic, formal-legal norms. Thus Weber believed that a revival of liberal-ism could not simply fall back upon the classical theory of human rights. It was necessary to interpret them anew in relation to the concrete social relations of late capitalist industrial societies. Many elements of the orthodox liberal doctrine, such as the postulate of the self-determination of the individual, seemed to him to have become largely meaningless under the conditions of advanced industrial societies.

Weber soon realized that, following the emergence of late capitalism, far-reaching transformations had also appeared in the character of the decision-making processes and the types of policy formation within liberal societies. The rise of plebiscitary democracy, together with the emergence of modern, bureaucratic party organizations, had radically transformed the conditions under which the individual could still have an influence upon political events, thereby fundamentally transforming the premises of democratic politics. Max Weber's conception of parliamentary democracy had little in common with the fundamentalist justifications of democratic authority which had customarily been part of the ideological tradition of the West since Rousseau.

One has to admit that it is not easy to reconstruct precisely Max Weber's 'late liberal' position. He was in agreement with the liberal tradition in assuming that a free society had in principle to grant all its citizens a maximum of self-determination and, therefore, of participation in all political decisions. Yet for him this was a stipulation which, given modern conditions, had lost practically all its meaning. He thought it was naïve to believe that under modern conditions the people as a whole were in a position to determine their own political destiny through free elections. The only trait distinguishing constitutional democracies from other forms of domination was the fact that the former had a system of 'formally free' elections of their leaders; in other words, the people themselves selected their own 'rulers', while in other systems the selection of the political leadership was always made from a more or less closed ruling class. Once Max Weber expressed this position most emphatically when addressing Roberto Michels: 'How much more resignation will you still have to endure? Concepts such as "popular will", and genuine will of the people do not exist for me any more. They are fictions.'[13] Diverging from the classical foundation of democracy in natural law, constitutional democracies are distinguishable from other forms of domination primarily by the fact that the people are in a postion to choose in a formally free way those leaders who appear more suited than others to represent their interests and their goals. Yet, according to Weber,[14] and from the perspective of the individuals making up the masses, this fact did not measurably change, if at all, the structure of domination inherent in the democratic system. For Weber, 'any notion of abolishing the domination of man over man by whatever sort of socialist system by however attenuated forms of "democracy" is utopian.'

Thus one can find in Weber's theory of parliamentary democracy two positions which stand in insoluable tension with one another and which he advances with intellectual rigour to the very limits of the thinkable. There is, on the one hand, the principle of individual self-determination, which derives ultimately from the primary value of the dignity of all human beings who, as persons, should act out of their own free initiative and should never be subjected to external determination. There is, on the other hand, the insight that all social relations are ultimately relations of domination and that even the different types of democracy do not basically overcome domination, that is, the external determination of individuals by other individuals. At best democracy can create the optimum conditions in which the individual's own initiative is subjected to the least possible restrictions. Max Weber's reflections on the best possible form of democratic domination moved within the area of tension between these two fundamental principles, that is, between the principle of individual self-determination as the formal condition for the possibility of freedom in general, and the principle of domination as the material precondition for a social order in which a maximum of freedom is possible in the first place.

The postulate that democratic domination should always be based on the consent of the subjects was for Weber as obvious as it was trivial. Under modern conditions this was materially inevitable. According to Weber, if democratization was to have a precise meaning at all, it could only be that of 'a minimalization of the power of the civil servants in favour of the most "direct" rule of the "demos" that was possible, and in practice that means the rule of its party leaders.'[15] Thus Weber wanted to reformulate the classical liberal demand for the self-determination of the people to mean the right of the people to choose their own leaders in a formally free way, together with institutional arrangements which guaranteed the resignation or the replacement of their leaders whenever they had lost the trust of the masses. From a realistic perspective, according to Weber, democracy can at best mean domination by freely elected leaders, who are then in a position to proceed essentially at their own discretion. It can never mean the superseding of domination by a system of policy formation from the bottom up.

If measured according to the classic criteria of democratic authority, 'the right to free election of leaders' is insufficient as such. Yet Weber was convinced that this was 'not so insignificant', rather that it was actually the very substance of democratic domination.[16] In contrast to the formal basis of democratic domination in the consensus of the people who elect their legislators for the running of the state apparatus, Weber introduces the idea of competition among those who are capable of leadership and have the inner 'calling' to set objectives for the masses. In this process, the plebiscitarian techniques of demagogy and the emotional binding of the masses to the leaders constitute legitimate methods. In opposition, therefore, to the principle of legitimation of domination through a process of policy formation from the bottom up, an alternative principle will assert itself to some extent, namely the legitimation of domination by virtue of personal authority based on the special charismatic qualities of those who have the calling to lead and to rule. Through the use of their personal charisma and their - in the positive sense of the word - demagogic capabilities, the leaders procure for themselves a following from among the people whom they need in order to achieve their own personal ends. Throughout this process the people play merely a passive role. For Weber, at least in the modern mass states, this personal plebiscitarian form of establishing political authority and, with it, individually accountable domination was simply inevitable. Only under the conditions of small geographical areas like the Swiss cantons did Weber conceive of direct forms of political policy formation from the bottom up as a practical possibility.

We are faced here with yet another antinomical position in Weber's conception of democracy. On the one hand, the principle of individual self-determination was to be guaranteed by the principle of the formally free, that is, substantially unrestricted choice of the respective leaders, as well as by the additional support of elections through parliamentary institutions. On the other hand, democratic leadership is in principle a variant of charismatically based authority which, as such, derives from and is legitimized by the will of the ruled only in form but not in substance. According to Weber, the leaders rule exclusively by virtue of their own personal responsibility. In any case, they are not to be viewed substantially or materially as executors of the will of the electorate. Moreover, their ruling authority is based largely, if not exclusively, on the emotional belief of the voters and of their supporters in their formal qualification for leadership. The substantive issues, meanwhile, recede into the background and have a direct influence upon the relations between the leaders and their followers only in extreme cases. According to Weber, only in this way, thanks to the extraordinary ideals of committed individuals, could leadership be ensured. Weber advanced this position with the utmost rigour to its utmost conceptual limits precisely because under the influence of the developments taking place in Germany after 1918 he was convinced that an effective democratic order and, in a broader sense, a free society were simply not possible without great leaders who would act out of their own sense of personal responsibility. Thus he was being thoroughly consistent when, in the context of his theory of the three pure types of legitimate domination, he defined parliamentary democracy as being in all respects an 'anti-authoritarian' variant of charismatic domination: '"Plebiscitary democracy" - the most important type of "leader democracy" - is in its genuine sense a type of charismatic rule which is concealed behind a type of legitimacy that is *formally* derived from and persists as a result of the will of the ruled. In fact, the leader (demagogue) rules by virtue of the devotion of his political followers and their faith in him as a person.'[17]

It is here that the antinomian structure of Weber's theory of democracy emerges most clearly. The demand for the strongest possible personal plebiscitary rulership and the postulate of the self-determination of the citizens as guaranteed through a parliamentarian system of representation are in what at first appears to be an insoluble antinomical relationship. Yet, at the same time, they are complementary elements of an efficient parliamentary democracy. In Weber's conception, the logical consequence of the second principle, namely, the unrestrained enforcement of the will of the masses *vis-à-vis* the state rulers, together with the demand for the greatest possible 'minimalization of the domination of man over man', would lead to the emergence of a 'leaderless democracy' (*führerlos*), one characterized by the rule of politicians who did not have those internal charismatic qualities which make the leader.[18] In such a system, politics becomes mere routine with no room for creative political acts. From a universal-historical perspective Weber saw in this form of democratic domination a serious danger for the continued existence of independent and free stuctures in the Western world. By contrast, he regarded as comparatively negligible the danger that the democratic rule of the *Führer*, legitimated through personal plebiscite, could turn into a dictatorial (or even fascist) regime, even though he himself had pointed out that in general 'leader democracies' were 'characterized' by a highly emotional type of devotion to and trust in the leader and that this accounted for a tendency 'to follow as a leader the type of individual who is most unusual, who promises the most or who employs the most effective propaganda measures'.[19]

This antinomical model of democracy finds its full formulation for the first time in Weber's later writings. In any case, the situation is complicated by the fact that after 1918, particularly for reasons of a universal-historical nature, Weber's antinomical model of democracy underwent a shift of emphasis in favour of the role of the leader. Weber's position derived from the realization that in the historical context of emergent mass industrial society the issue was no longer how to ensure that the government in a democratic system was effectively controlled by the people or, especially, that the government's decisions were closely bound to the will of the people. Weber was convinced that the rise of industrial capitalism, which he sometimes called the most revolutionary power in world history, was closely tied to the irresistible progress of bureaucratization and rationalization. In the wake of the development of capitalism, bureaucratized and rationalized forms of social organization and of social conduct had been growing rapidly. The latter, in turn, tended to undermine traditional liberal ideals and values and ultimately could even in some ways undermine the freedom of the individual. Weber thought that the free societies of the West were undergoing a process of routinization and rationalization of all aspects of social life which would slowly but steadily lead to a paralysis of all individual initiative. At the end of this process one would no longer be able to speak of any sort of freedom at all. Weber thought there was a possibility that the free societies of the West could sink gradually into a new version of late antiquity. Thus the most decisive question for him was 'how, in view of the prevailing tendency to bureaucratization, would it *still be possible* to salvage *some kind* of vestigial freedom of movement for the individual'.[20] Weber was convinced that this demand was especially relevant for the political regimes of his time. He saw as an immediate possibility the danger that the modern welfare state and mass democracy would degenerate into a static society and that political and social mobility would increasingly decline. This would imply, however, that the room for freedom (in what ever sense one would choose to define the word), which for the time being still existed in industrial societies, would progressively be reduced.

Weber evidently had good reason to be inclined to the view that under the conditions of modern industrial society not only authoritarian state systems such as that of Imperial Germany but even parliamentarian democracies had a tendency to become 'leaderless'. The appeal of the charisma of the great politician appeared to him to be the only means of ensuring a maximum of effective political leadership in modern societies. He hoped that the combination of these two alternative types of domination would restore the conditions under which 'freedom' could henceforth be more than a mere formula – even in late capitalist mass society with its numerous bureaucratic organizations. The two types were: democratic domination, which derived from the consensus of a sovereign people, a type which tended towards the loss of authority; and a specific variant of charismatic domination based on the personal authority of the great charismatic politician.

Under modern conditions, however, even a charismatically based plebiscitarian 'leader democracy' could not manage without the elements essential to a bureaucratic administrative apparatus or without a bureaucratic party organization, both acting as the 'obedient servants' of their respective leaders. Their role is to ensure that the decisions of the leaders, which originated in the leader's own personal responsibility, be accepted and, at the same time, efficiently enacted in the state as well as in society. Here, again, we are confronted with an antinomical model. The personal plebiscitarian authority of the great democratic politician has to make use of the techniques of bureaucratic domination, even though this may entail the risk of exposing the leaders to the danger that their charisma will be gradually undermined by routine.

Max Weber studied thoroughly the various types of modern democratic systems which attempted to operate with a non-professional administrative machine or with an elected officialdom like the old American system.[21] Weber concluded that under modern conditions they were no longer viable. Only the combination of charismatic leadership with strict bureaucratic discipline appeared to him to hold any promise. Weber expressed this position most clearly in 1919: 'there is only the choice between "leader democracy" with a "machine" or "leaderless democracy", i.e. the rule of "professional politicians without a calling", that is, without the inner charismatic qualities which go to make up a true leader.'[22] One could say that for Max Weber the best chance for securing an open society with a maximum degree of freedom and an optimum degree of individual self-determination for all was to be found not so much in the mixture of alternative political principles of organization as in their dialectical combination.

Weber came to similar conclusions in his analysis of the economic subsystem. Very early on he became concerned with the question of the origins of capitalism, and especially with its long-term socio-historical consequences. It was his view that modern industrial capitalism, which was essentially a creation of the Protestant bourgeoisie and which had triumphed in its early capitalist phases of development over the older, traditional feudal and corporatist societies, created historically unique preconditions for the emergence of liberal ideas in state and society. But he doubted that the same conditions were still valid for a capitalism which had developed into its mature form.

In his analysis of the 1905 Russian Revolution, which Western liberals had viewed for the most part as a secular breakthrough of liberal principles which would lead as well to the triumph of a liberal order in Russia, Weber wrote: 'One can only laugh at the tendency to ascribe to present-day late capitalism – this "inevitability" of our economic development – of the kind being imported into Russia and already existing in America elective affinities with "democracy" or even with "freedom" in any sense of the term. The question to be posed is: how can all these things (individual liberties, the rights of man and so forth) be possible at all in the long run?'[23] Weber was convinced that economic development itself was leading to an ever-increasing restriction of freedom and that, therefore, one had to struggle to enforce liberal principles in late capitalism 'against the tide of material circumstances'.[24]

Weber was deeply concerned that the rapidly developing monopolistic-capital structures were making the classical liberal model of society obsolete and that the trend towards the formation of ever more powerful bureaucratic machines would accelerate immensely. In 1905, on the occasion of the trade-union debates in the Verein für Sozialpolitik, he took the stand that it was no longer possible to proceed from the assumption that, given the emergence of 'giant concerns', the trade unions would still be powerful enough in the future to assert themselves against the big concerns and enterprises without the necessity of additional protective measures from the state or that they could still be effective in securing appropriate wages for the working classes. Yet he rejected most emphatically a mediation of trade union power through direct state intervention or through state-regulated arbitration. He wanted, namely, to avoid a curtailment of the competitive struggle between the working classes and the employers' associations. He deemed it was necessary, instead, to look for ways of improving indirectly, through appropriate methods, the starting conditions of the working classes in potential labour struggles.[25] In 1912 he tried to bring new life into the stagnating social politics of Germany by founding an association of people active in social policy. The objective of such an association was to ease the relations between employers and employees and to pave new ways for the emancipation of the working classes within the existing system.[26]

In his essays on *The Protestant Ethic and the Spirit of Capitalism*[27] one can find the most powerful formulation of Weber's fear that if left to run its course undisturbed 'late capitalism' would bring 'a new age of serfdom' not unlike the one of late antiquity. Modern capitalist industrial society, organized according to the principle of purely formal rationality, could lead into a dehumanization of the world of work and further the displacement of the individual personality from social life. Weber failed, however, to find a real solution. The alternative proposed by Marx, that is, the socialization of the means of production as a panacea to free the working classes from oppression, was for Weber only a surrogate and not a solution, since the socialization of the means of production would only strengthen even more the already existing universal trend to bureaucratization. Apart from this, the modern industrial system could simply not do without the initiative of energetic, individualistic entrepreneurs.[28]

Already in *The Protestant Ethic and the Spirit of Capitalism*, Weber had clearly pointed out that capitalism, which was entering its mature stage, no longer needed the specific individualistic driving force to which it owed its origins. Rather it enforced, whether those affected by it liked it or not, a type of life-conduct in accordance with its technocratic needs: 'The Puritan *wanted* to work in a vocation; we are *forced* to do so.'[29] According to Weber, the advanced capitalist system was exhibiting increasingly mechanical, ultimately 'inescapable powers over man such as have never before been seen in history', enforcing in the process forms of life-conduct which were no longer in accordance with the classic ideals of individual freedom. At best, it was only in the private sphere that one could still preserve the value-creating spontaneity of the individual.

Weber's gloomy, at times even apocalyptic, predictions were based on a precise analysis of the basic model of capitalist economic and social organizations. In this he followed to a large extent Karl Marx's classical analysis. For

Max Weber, highly productive modern capitalism in all its manifestations was based on the principle of 'formal rationality', that is, on the uniform rational calculation of all its operations for the purpose of ensuring a maximum degree of performance and efficiency. The decision whether to submit to the iron rule of formal rationality or not was simply no longer in the hands of the individuals and groups to which it was applicable, in the hands neither of the entrepreneurs nor of the labour force. It was simply enforced by market competition. 'Formal rationality', at least as a regulative idea, was the basic principle of the capitalist order. A capitalism structured for the purpose of maximizing its own fundamental law requires, first of all, 'the constant struggle of autonomous groups in the market place'; second, 'the possibility of a rational calculation of prices under conditions of unrestricted competition in the market'; third, 'formally free labour', in other words, labour based on free wage contracts, which made possible a direct correlation between actual production and the wage; and, finally, something which was specifically stressed, 'the expropriation of the means of production from the workers'. This meant that in its pure form the capitalist system not only imposed conditions over which the individual no longer had any influence but actually, in order to maintain itself, required the use of instruments of domination and oppression. It is well known that Weber again and again explicitly characterized the formally free labour relations which workers under capitalism had to enter into *vis-à-vis* their employers as yet another form of domination. At times he even stressed that a maximum of 'formal rationality' in the capitalist system was inevitably bought at the price of 'substantive irrationalities', such as 'the subjugation of the workers under the domination of the employers'.[30] One can also note here that Weber greatly emphasized the innate tendency of capitalism to shackle man in a system of unbroken dependence,[31] thus even accentuating Marx's thesis.[32] Weber's intention was to show that in developed industrial societies the capitalist principle of social organization, that is, the principle of 'formal rationality', was almost inevitably in contradiction with the principle of 'substantive rationality'. The classical liberal ideas, especially the principle of individual self-determination, can be considered as substantive rational principles. This means that in the course of its development the capitalist system almost inevitably had to come into conflict with the classical liberal system of values. Ultimately, according to Weber, capitalism is 'an iron cage' which tends to leave less and less room for spontaneous individual behaviour.

This sobering observation notwithstanding, Weber was fully convinced that there was no real way out of this situation. He saw no possibility whatsoever of eliminating, through some kind of revolutionary transformation of the social order, the fundamental conflicts which had revealed themselves. He viewed the strategy proposed by Marx – namely, that of a socialist revolution through which the masses would liberate themselves from their 'alienation' – as inapplicable in every respect. On the contrary, a socialist revolution which entailed the expropriation of the means of production and its control by a class of state functionaries – this being the only form of socialist economy which to Weber's mind presented any chance for survival – would only exacerbate the existing problems, since it would advance even further the universal tendency of the bureaucratization of all social relations, including those of the economic sphere. Besides, the expropriation of the means of production would not of itself eliminate the class struggle, nor would it improve the conditions of the workers in any significant way. On the contrary, the chances for the latter to represent their specific interests successfully *vis-à-vis* the class which owned the means of production would be far worse than under the conditions of the private capitalist system, where there was still room to play off the class which owned the means of production and the political rulers against each other. According to Weber, a dynamic market-oriented economic system still offered the best preconditions for guaranteeing a maximum of dynamism and thus, indirectly, a maximum of freedom in modern society. Accordingly, Weber was in principle in favour of the retention, whenever possible, of the free market, since he wanted to preserve at all costs the dynamic effects it had upon society as a whole. That is why in 1919, at the height of the German Revolution, he rejected all forms of the so-called 'mixed economy' and called for a return to pure competitive capitalism of the classic type. If German society ever wanted to regain its former position in the world market, it simply could not do without the dynamic force of entrepreneurs like Thyssen or Stinnes.

There is a paradox here. On the one hand, Weber argued that the immanent tendencies of capitalism were working for stagnation and for the ossification of social relations. Yet, on the other hand, he viewed the principle of capitalist market competition as an instrument which above all would guarantee a maximum of dynamism in the economic as well as in the political system. This paradox found a partial resolution in the political sphere. Weber assumed that the state could play a relatively autonomous role within the total social system, notwithstanding the fact that, as a rule, it was simply the instrument of the hegemonic group in society at any given moment. As an institution equipped with specific prerogatives different from other institutions of society, the state had the task not only of determining the legal framework conditioning the economic sub-system, but also of intervening whenever necessary in economic and social processes when those led to destabilizing effects. Here again one finds a combination of principles in opposition to one another. On the one hand, the economy, and to some extent also society, is to be organized according to market–economic, i.e. competitively oriented, criteria, and should therefore be free of direct state control. On the other hand, the state has to operate at times as an 'interventionist state' – if one may use a concept which was not yet in use in Weber's time. Certainly for Weber the most important task of the liberal state was to guarantee those pluralistic structures which would allow for the free competition of conflicting interests within a legally defined framework.

This becomes especially clear in Weber's attitude towards labour legislation and towards the principle of 'the welfare state', which began to evolve in his lifetime. Weber's attitude, which at first seems ambivalent, points once again, when viewed more closely, to an antinomical position. Weber was a dedicated champion of a progressive social policy whose objective was to compensate for the existing inequality of opportunities which affected different social groups. Weber supported such a policy even when it was secured at the expense of a less rational organization of capitalist production. Yet, at the same time, he repeatedly argued that social policy should not simply allocate certain fixed material advantages to the various groups. Its function rather was to create the contextual framework in which the parties could contend for their ideal and material interests within the existing legal order. For Weber feared nothing as much as a form of social organization in which certain social groups could, so to speak, automatically come up with fixed claims upon specific shares of the social product, and thus bring a kind of deadly artificial peace to social relations. Because of this, he occasionally expressed serious reservations concerning the modern welfare state. For Weber the welfare state presented great dangers for a free society inasmuch as it would grant social security to the masses under conditions which would undermine their readiness to struggle constantly for the safeguarding or amelioration of their own economic and social position and thus would contribute to the formation of an attitude of passive adaptation and complacency in the same way it had created a rentier mentality in sections of the German bourgeoisie. In 1905 Weber wrote:[33] 'In America's "benevolent feudalism", in the German so-called "welfare institutions", in the Russian "factory system", everywhere the system of serfdom is already at hand; we just have to wait until the diminishing speed of technological and economic progress ... eventually pushes the masses into accepting the situation and entering into it.'[34]

Weber was highly suspicious of any form of social policy which furthered the development of a social system which would deprive individuals of the responsibility to provide for their own life and which would uncouple the securing or betterment of life-chances from the sphere of individual personal effort. For Weber the primary task of the economic and social policies of the state should be that of safeguarding in every case the social balance between the particular social groups in society, without, however, mediating their competitive struggle with one another. In *Economy and Society*, following Marx rather closely, Weber essentially proceeded to reconstruct the classical liberal model of a pure market-oriented capitalism. This was to serve as the standard when ascertaining in each case the social costs resulting from policy measures which deviated from the ideal course of the formal rationality of a free, competitively oriented social order.

A policy of state intervention in the social and economic sub-systems for the purpose of maintaining the existing pluralistic structures, and thus guaranteeing a maximum of dynamics within the social system, demanded a strong and at the same time independent state power. In contrast to the liberal tradition, Weber openly advocated a strong state as the very condition making freedom possible, however it is understood. Once again, one finds here a classic postulate of liberalism – namely, the independence of society from the state – combined with its antinomical counter-principle, that of a powerful interventionist state. Weber scoffed at the old liberal ideology demanding the greatest possible restraint of the state in the economic and social spheres, for 'the roots of democracy cannot grow in the sky'.[35] To the traditional ideal of 'the minimalization of the domination of man over man' in favour of 'the administration of things', Weber consistently opposed the ideal of a strong state (although, of course, with parliamentary controls) whose leader was capable of purposeful action and was in a position to lay down the objectives for economic and social groups.[36]

The dialectical opposition between 'leader' and 'followers' which one finds in Weber's theory of democratic domination has to be seen in the same light. It is well known that Weber rejected outright the so-called mandate principle which formally bound the ruling politicians to the will of their electors. Likewise, he understood that the obligation of democratic politicians to take into account the consensus of the voters was for the most part a mere formality, at least to the extent that the great political leader always had to act solely in accordance with his personal convictions, and therefore whenever necessary had to obtain the consent of his followers through demagogic means (in the most favourable sense of the word). Only a plebiscitarian democracy, one led by great charismatically qualified politicians and which, in contrast to 'the outmoded negative democracy which only demanded freedom from the state', would strive for effective rule and for the greatest use of the means of power at its disposal in internal as well as in external relations – only such a democracy, according to Weber, would be capable of implementing a dynamic policy in a society which was increasingly defined by bureaucratic structures.[37]

The antinomical structure of Max Weber's political thought is most evident in the contrast between 'leader democracy' and 'leaderless democracy', as well as in the dialectical opposition between, on the one hand, the political leader who acts exclusively out of his own sense of responsibility, drawing inspiration from his own ideals, and, on the other, the masses who are inevitably condemned to passivity. As a rule 'plebiscitary democracy' still makes use of conventional instruments, such as parliament and a constitutional system, which ensure that political conflicts are kept within limits. At the same time, however, he emphasizes the charisma of the great plebiscitarian politician who, when in power, is in a position to go beyond parliament and the administrative apparatus in order to appeal directly to the masses. The model of the constitutional state in its parliamentarian variant, which as a type belongs to that of legal domination, is here combined with the charismatic principle of domination by virtue of personal authority which derives formally, but not substantively, from (and is legitimated by) the consensus of 'the ruled'. Apparently Weber saw no reason to mitigate in any way, much less to abandon, the antinomical character of his theory of democratic domination. For his part, Weber believed that this problem could never be resolved, be it on the level of constitutional procedures or on the level of theoretical reflection. Ultimately, it was up to the responsible political leader to deal with these contradictions in his own person.

In the light of the subsequent experience with fascism, one cannot but find objectionable a theory of democratic domination which accentuates rather too emphatically the pre-eminence of the political leader in contrast to the mass of citizens. Such a theory has not always been able to prove itself immune to a reinterpretation in an authoritarian, even fascist, direction, as demonstrated after all by the case of Roberto Michels, who justified his support for Mussolini and Italian fascism by explicitly referring to Weber's theory of the charismatic politician.[38] Yet, at the same time, one should not overlook the fact that such a meaning was certainly not intended by Weber. The strong emphasis he placed upon the principle of democratic leadership in his writings and lectures of 1918–19 to the relative neglect of the opposite principle of legitimation of personal authority through the plebiscitarian formation of consensus was brought about for the most part by specific historical circumstances. Presumably, under different circumstances, Weber would have emphasized other aspects.

This particular problem notwithstanding, the force of Weber's political thought manifests itself precisely in the fact that he was able to advance with extreme intellectual rigour to their very conceptual limits political positions, theories and tentative conclusions in order to test their potential development.

In the process, and in accordance with the intellectual rigour so peculiar to him, Weber was constantly confronted with antinomical structures for which he claimed it would be scientifically dishonest to find a resolution either through compromise or with the help of a materialist theory of society which was ideological in nature. He was inclined instead to accept as the only viable solution the dialectical combination of antinomical positions within an open system where each responsibly acting individual would have to deal with the given conflicting values. Within the parameters he laid down, which derived from liberal as well as Nietzschean positions, one could not go any further at the theoretical level. Science found itself reverting to a condition in which it was not in the position to formulate definitive truths, but only a number of alternative models of thinking or alternative models of conduct which ultimately cancelled each other out. Thus everything would again come down to the autonomy of the individual person who, though having a moral obligation to rationality, was basically free to choose.

This circumstance also explains the ambivalence of many of the concrete political positions and strategies maintained by Weber. With a clarity unrivalled anywhere else, his work reflects the fact that liberalism was no longer viable as a self-contained political philosophy with clear-cut solutions available for every social and political problem.[39] Determined to advance liberal and democratic postulates to their ultimate limits, while at the same time confronting them with the social reality of advanced industrial society, Weber was led to develop systematically the antinomical potential inherent in these postulates. Weber elaborates on the dichotomous contrasts by cutting through the at first seemingly harmonious surface and revealing its antinomical structure. Here Weber saw the only chance for a maximum degree of real freedom. The same is also valid for his specific views in everyday politics. Irrespective of the time-conditioned nature of many of the solutions he proposed, his postion was marked above all by a principled openness in relation to alternative solutions taking account of new political or social developments. Weber believed, from the perspective of a position which was decidedly liberal and nationalist, that it would be necessary to sustain highly differing models of action and different political strategies in order to counter the secular trend towards the petrification of free society in routine, mediocrity and general misery. It was the task of the politician to secure the conditions under which creative social action could still remain possible. It was the task of science to provide the knowledge which would make it possible to choose responsibly from among the greatest possible number of alternative options, instead of submitting more or less unhesitatingly to supposedly factual constraints or pursuing 'professional politics without a calling', without long-term social objectives.

3

Max Weber's Theory of
Legitimacy Today

By the early 1960s many social scientists assumed that the traditional political ideologies of the nineteenth century had lost their momentum in the advanced industrial societies of the West. Ernst Topitsch argued that a new era in the history of mankind was about to begin in which politics would no longer be determined by holistic philosophies and meta-scientific ideologies. Karl Popper's famous book *The Open Society and its Enemies* appeared to have decided the case against the fundamentalist ideologies of the nineteenth century, in particular the varieties of Marxism, once and for all. Daniel Bell heralded the 'end of ideology'. It appeared that in the democratic societies of the West a general consensus had been reached about the principles of political rule; in future political and social problems ought to be open for solution by the rational techniques of the empirical social sciences. 'Piecemeal engineering', not wholesale reconstruction according to grand schemes or ideological blueprints, seemed to be the order of the day. In the light of such assumptions the traditional problem of the legitimacy of the political order had receded into the background while practical issues had moved to the forefront.

However, a number of scholars strongly objected to this trend of opinion, in particular Jürgen Habermas. Habermas argued that the 'scientification' of the political process, as it were, would lead to a crisis of legitimacy of the political systems in the advanced industrial societies of the West. It goes without saying that the twin forces of bureaucracy and science had indeed altered the character of political decision-making. The increasing trend of ascertaining political issues in pragmatic rather than in ideological terms on the assumption that in principle at least they could be resolved satisfactorily with scientifically designed social technology was seen by Habermas as necessarily leading to a weakening of the democratic consensus. The decline of meaningful ideological orientations, which, as he admitted, was a corollary of the decline of traditional political philosophies, would backfire in the end. In advanced Western societies the state had ceased to be a meaningful entity, other than as a guarantor of increasing prosperity and social security for all. The advance of bureaucratic modes of decision-making, and the increasing reliance of parties and governments alike on scientific expertise of diverse sorts, amounted to a pseudo-depoliticization of politics. The process of political decision-making gradually evolved into a mere technical affair which the individual citizen had no chance of effectively influencing one way or the other. Habermas predicted that when the period of steady economic growth came to an end, faced with increasing economic difficulties, a crisis of belief in the legitimacy of late capitalist society and its governmental system was likely. The gradual weakening of the traditional political consensus would become a serious problem. To put it another way, advanced industrial societies were progressively losing their legitimacy.

Today it can be seen that none of these predictions, neither those of empirical social science nor those of the Frankfurt School, turned out to be true. There has been no 'end of ideology'; rather we have experienced a new upsurge of ideological politics, not just outside Europe, most noticeably in the Third World, but also in Europe itself. The 'student revolt' of the late 1960s, which was very much an ideological phenomenon, blew over rather quickly, but with it the idea of politics as some sort of sublime form of social technology also went by the board. The worldwide recession, caused or perhaps only accentuated by the first oil crisis in the 1970s (which might also be described as a crisis caused by a loss of unrestricted control on the part of powerful Western multinationals), left governments unprepared and helpless. The economic policies of Keynesianism (or what was thought to be Keynesianism) failed dismally and exposed the limits of governmental power in the economic sphere in a rather spectacular way. This became all the more obvious in the last decade when some Western societies experienced not only zero but even negative growth (something unheard of for many years) and unemployment rose to unprecedented levels. On the other hand, ideological politics surfaced again even in the most advanced industrial societies in the West, as, for instance, in Great Britain and West Germany. Often nationalist emotions were mobilized in order to strengthen the political fabric; on the other hand, doctrinaire socialism, which had been confined to marginal groups only, was revived and gained considerable influence over the policies of the socialist parties. However, the belief that this turn of events could seriously endanger the existing political consensus proved unfounded. To put it in another way, the economic recession did not engender a crisis of legitimacy in the political systems of the West. There is as yet no crisis of 'late capitalism'. The political systems proved to be remarkably stable, even with a high rate of unemployment which only a few years ago had been considered altogether unacceptable politically. On the other hand there is undoubtedly a widespread disillusionment with politics among the public. We can observe an increasing disaffection with the institutions which dominate the political arena today and which in a way have appropriated the state for themselves.

These phenomena can be described rather well by Max Weber's sociological model of legitimate rule. He was the first to point out that bureaucratization was both a necessary tool and a curse. Under modern conditions political success is possible only if the political leader makes full use of bureaucratic techniques of government. On the other hand the widespread use of bureaucratic methods in order to create or retain political support is bound to create new hierarchical structures in politics; only a few groups have any chance of effectively influencing the process of political decision-making while the great majority is reduced to playing a more passive role.

The advantage of formal-rational techniques of government was described by Max Weber as indispensable; however, a price had to be paid for this in the form of 'substantive irrationalities', for instance the loss of genuine participation by all citizens in the political process or the widening of the gap between private and public life orientations. The advantage of having overcome the holistic ideologies of the past was accompanied by a serious disadvantage. Instrumental-rational forms of social conduct were making headway everywhere, while the spontaneity of the individual was subjected to severe restraints. The new technocratic procedures of politics left little room for individual creativity, unless the individual was able to establish personal influence through bureaucratic techniques of mass control and by turning to plebiscitary or even charismatic modes of leadership.

Weber's appeal for great political leaders who are supposed to invigorate stagnant political systems by virtue of their strong personal charisma has been criticized from many quarters. Indeed, it remains to be seen whether the personal legitimacy of the political leader can be a permanent substitute for the belief in the legitimacy of the political system as such, as Weber seems to have assumed at times. His sociological model of parliamentary democracy which he defined as 'an anti-authoritarian variant of charismatic rule' has not been well received in modern political theory.

Even so, Weber's typology of 'three pure types of legitimate domination' provides important insights into the problems of legitimacy in advanced industrial societies. As is well known, Weber distinguished between three 'pure types of legitimate rule' – namely 'legal rule', 'traditional rule' and 'charismatic rule'. Taken together, these three types of legitimate rule are supposed to cover all historically possible forms of legitimate government. This is to say that all empirical cases of legitimate rule are combinations of these three essential sources of legitimacy (or rather belief in the legitimacy of government, to use Weber's own rather pedantic phrase). None of these 'pure types' is to be found in empirical reality; they are theoretical constructs which were designed in this way so as to represent three substantially different sources of legitimacy as clearly as possible. Charismatic legitimacy, to begin with, depends entirely on the readiness of the charismatic leader's followers to accept the ideals which that leader represents and the orders derived from them as absolutely binding. To put it another way, charismatic legitimacy as such originates in the personality of the leader. However, once a charismatic authority is established it is transferred to the leader's followers. Traditional legitimacy can be described as the routinization of charismatic authority; it rests upon the belief that what has always been is legitimate. That is to say, 'prescription' decides the issue of whether a particular political authority is considered legitimate, not substantive principles of some kind, such as the 'rights of man'. Legal legitimacy (which is the most common of all) depends on the belief that everything that has been enacted in accordance with established procedures may be considered legitimate. There may be cases in which value-rational beliefs provide support for certain forms of political rule. However, according to Weber, this was not specific to legal rule. On the contrary, the purely formal procedures according to which rules are enacted and political decisions reached are, in his view, the very foundations on which the legitimacy of a political system rests. As long as political rule is conducted according to procedures and regulations considered legitimate by the public, no decision arrived at in such a manner will be considered unlawful, however outrageous it may be in terms of a substantive moral standard. This may seem to be fairly far-fetched, but it illustrates a very important aspect of legitimacy through 'legality' under modern conditions of government by means of bureaucratic techniques. The Holocaust might never have occurred if those involved in it had not believed that the individual measures which made its implementation possible were formally correct. Accordingly, there were no objections to the policy of depriving the Jewish population of their civil rights as a first step towards deporting them to what were allegedly 'labour camps'; it was only under such conditions that the gigantic clandestine operation of genocide could ever have succeeded.

Perhaps this is an extreme example. Yet the strictly impersonal nature of governmental authority in the modern state does contain a dangerous potential for gross abuse, even in parliamentary democracies of the Western type. Modern government exercises power through a multiplicity of bureaucratic institutions rather than in a personalized way and therefore it is often difficult effectively to evaluate its actions according to political or moral standards. This is the gist of Weber's argument that under modern conditions governmental legitimacy as a rule depends solely on 'the belief in the formal legitimacy of enacted rules and the right of those elevated to governmental offices to exercise power according to these rules'. 'These rules may be established by agreement or imposition, on grounds of expediency or value-rationality or both' – that is, specific value-attitudes may provide a justification for these rules. Yet this is by no means necessarily the case. On the contrary Weber emphasized that the former usually prevails, namely the enactment of law according to mere expediency or, as he has put it, according to the principles of instrumental rationality – that is, without regard to value-rational principles of whatever sort. This is not exclusively but nevertheless predominantly the case. This type of legal government is typical of all modern industrial societies. Indeed, most people are prepared to assign legitimacy to established authority so long as it conforms to the letter of the law and keeps itself within the established procedures. The highly bureaucratized nature of modern government makes it difficult for the citizens to judge for themselves whether governmental actions are legitimate or not as measured against value-rational standards. The more bureaucratic government is and the more removed the experience of ordinary people is from any actual exercise of power, the more likely it is that the system will be considered formally legitimate unless it embarks upon policies which deviate from normal expectations to a very great extent. However, what works in favour of the established order is not only the belief that formal legality always legitimizes governmental actions, but also tradition. In fact, as Weber points out, the belief in the legitimacy of an established order is strengthened in most cases by the fact that people have grown accustomed to it, and thereby assign legitimacy to it on traditional grounds as well. This is not to say that only rule based on 'prescription' is legitimate; on the contrary, any system of formally correct imposed or enacted laws may possess rational-legal legitimacy, but this is strengthened if the respective legal system is considered to be a customary one, or, as Weber put it in an untranslatable German term, if it is *'eingelebt'*.

One may well ask whether Weber's theory of formal legal legitimacy does not in fact have a conservative bias. Indeed, according to this conceptualization, established authority enjoys a distinct advantage, and the more so, the more bureaucratized or institutionalized it is. To put it another way, the 'law of gravity' at work here always operates in favour of the established formal-legal system of government regardless of whether it is supported on substantive grounds, say, because the citizens agree with particular political objectives or because the established order conforms with constitutional principles commonly held to be valid; for instance, it is usually argued in terms of natural law that democratic government depends upon certain inalienable 'rights of man'.

Perhaps Weber went too far when he argued that bureaucratic domination, once it has been firmly established, is almost indestructible; on these grounds, in his view, revolutions are extremely unlikely to succeed. But his observations about formal-legal legitimacy remain valid all the same. Legitimate domination does allow for social change so long as government keeps within the confines of what is customary, for otherwise its legitimacy may be negatively affected. However, there is always a danger that established political systems will become 'leaderless' and stagnant. Under such circumstances charismatic revolutions may occur to break the deadlock, although under modern conditions this has become rather less likely than in earlier periods of history.

The modern bureaucratic state, provided it is governed in accordance with formally established legal rules, is likely to enjoy a substantial degree of legitimacy whatever its constitutional structure. This is true, to some degree at least, for non-democratic and authoritarian forms of government as well, including Marxist-Leninist governmental systems, although they may be judged according to substantive principles, notably the principle of individual liberty. This explains the remarkable stability of most governments in the present world in face of the disaffection of large sections of the population with the existing order and growing discontent over its inability to deliver the 'economic goods' which they have become accustomed to, namely prosperity and full employment. Yet one should not overestimate the degree of political stability derived from this state of affairs. Formal-legal legitimacy may not be strong enough to contain the forces of discontent which exist on the fringes of modern industrial society. Sooner or later they will demand a thoroughgoing reconstruction of the social system on value-rational grounds, even though 'charismatic breakthroughs' are unlikely to occur in the foreseeable future.

PART II

Max Weber on Socialism and Political Radicalism

4

Capitalism and Socialism: Weber's Dialogue with Marx

The advance of modern industrial capitalism and consequent social developments are the dominant themes of Max Weber's sociological work. As early as 1893, Weber predicted that, within a few generations, capitalism would destroy all tradition-bound social structures, and that this process was irreversible. He described modern capitalism as an essentially revolutionary force and believed that it was not possible to arrest, by any means, its triumphal march. Much of his scholarly work was concerned with investigating the societal and cultural effects of industrial capitalism from the standpoint of their meaning for the future of Western liberal societies. Consequently, it was inevitable that Max Weber would confront Karl Marx's analysis of modern capitalism and his ideas about a future socialist society. Weber's sociology can be viewed as an attempt to formulate an alternative position standing in harmony with his own bourgeois-liberal ideals, but one that does not simply dismiss the socialist critique of bourgeois society as being without foundation.

Weber belonged to a generation that stood midway between the generation of Marx and our own. His socio-political views were formed under the influence of the extraordinarily rapid growth of modern industrial capitalism in the last decades before 1914. The development of large industrial combinations, trusts and monopolies, all typical of a maturing capitalist system, took place before his eyes, and he could not but note how this new reality conflicted with classical political economy's ideal image of capitalism. Although Weber did not ignore these developments, he remained throughout his life a passionate champion of a liberal brand of dynamic capitalism. Weber was perhaps Marx's greatest theoretical opponent; given the range of his sociological work he has been rightly called a 'bourgeois Marx'.[1]

Weber occasionally referred to himself as 'a member of the bourgeois class' who was 'educated in their views and ideals'.[2] In 1907, in an argument about the German Social Democrats, he requested expressly that Roberto Michels simply regard him as a 'class-conscious bourgeois'.[3] Nevertheless, one hesitates, in the light of Weber's constant striving for critical self-examination, to call him a bourgeois in the ordinary sense of the word. Rather, to use his own terminology, he is better located in the intelligentsia, a social group that cannot be assigned to any of the economic classes. Weber was less a 'bourgeois' than a liberal intellectual for whom the autonomy of the individual was an indispensable principle, and it was from this perspective that he approached the nature of capitalism and Marxism. As a result, Weber's attitude towards capitalism as a total societal configuration proved to be thoroughly ambivalent; this will be shown in greater detail. Although he vigorously defended the capitalist system against its critics on the left (whether they were from the workers' movement or from those intellectuals whom he described as having succumbed to 'the romanticism of the general strike' or to 'revolutionary hope'), he did not hesitate to criticize the system's inhuman consequences.

The starting-point of Weber's analysis of modern capitalism was not as far removed from Marx as Weber himself assumed. His concern for the preservation of human dignity under the social conditions created by and typical of mature capitalism (particularly, the severe discipline of work and exclusion of all principles of personal ethical responsibility from industrial labour) is entirely consistent with Marx's effort to find a way of overcoming the social alienation of the proletariat under industrial capitalism.[4] But Weber's sociological analyses of industrial societies led him to conclusions that were, in many respects, opposed to those of Marx.

It is hardly necessary to point out that Weber always took Marx's theoretical work seriously. Weber labelled the *Communist Manifesto* 'a pathetic prophecy', but at the same time, despite his decidedly different views, he considered it 'a scholarly work of the highest order'.[5] Eduard Baumgarten reported that, in the last years of his life, Weber told one of his students:

One can measure the integrity of a modern scholar, and especially of a modern philosopher, by how he sees his own relationship to Nietzsche and Marx. Whoever does not admit that he could not accomplish very important aspects of his own work without the work that these two have performed deceives both himself and others. The world in which we ourselves exist intellectually is largely a world stamped by Marx and Nietzsche.[6]

Weber achieved his own intellectual position through constant grappling with these two completely opposite thinkers. Weber's pronounced aristocratic individualism can be traced largely to Nietzsche. This was held in check, of course, not only by Weber's liberal convictions, but also by the insight that the fate of the individual is determined extensively by material and economic factors and to a very great degree is dependent upon anonymous socio-economic processes – an insight which is ultimately traceable to Marx.[7]

Nevertheless, it seems that in his early writings Weber paid little attention to the original writings of Marx and Engels.[8] We find, however, an extensive treatment of Marx and Marxism in his early lectures on national economics in Freiburg in the 1890s, but they seem not to have had a direct impact on his published work. Up to 1906 he referred primarily to vulgar Marxist interpretations; direct references to Marx were almost totally absent. During these years he confronted Marx and Marxism primarily in his methodological writings. There, Weber distanced himself sharply and repeatedly from what was then called 'historical materialism'. In principle, Weber rejected all material philosophies of history. He considered these and other approaches that claimed to discover objective historical laws or even an inner meaning to history 'charlatanism'.[9] From his own standpoint, perhaps best characterized as a neo-Kantianism combined with Nietzschean principles, there could be no objective ordering of the historical process. In Weber's opinion the Marxist theory of history, which described historical change as a determinate sequence of social formations with each characterized by its respective mode of economic production and propelled by class conflict, lacked any scientific basis. For Weber, there were no objective laws of social reality. At best, it might be possible, with the aid of ideal types, to construct law-like theories of societal processes. These can serve as criteria for determining the degree to which certain segments of social reality depart from such nomological models.

Weber's radical position followed inevitably from the fundamental premise that history is meaningless in itself and that, at least from the standpoint of a random observer, it appears as more or less chaotic. Only when specific concepts and categories, formulated from the perspective of ultimate cultural values, are applied to a limited segment of reality (which in itself is limitless), does it become meaningful. Accordingly, Weber considered Marx's theory about the succession of different modes of production to be no more than a sociological hypothesis that provides essential insights into the nature and development of modern industrial societies, but on no account does Weber consider it as objectively valid scientific knowledge. In the former sense, namely as an ideal-typical construction, he regarded Marx's theory as extremely significant.[10] On the other hand, he was not prepared to accept it as ontological truth. He expressed this in 'Objectivity in social science and social policy':

Liberated as we are from the antiquated belief that all cultural phenomena can be *deduced* as a product or function of the constellation of 'material' interests, we believe nevertheless that the analysis of social and cultural phenomena with special reference to their economic conditioning and ramifications is a scientific principle of creative fruit-fulness, and, if applied carefully and free from dogmatic restrictions, will remain so for a long time to come. However, the so-called 'materialistic conception of history' must be rejected most emphatically in so far as it is meant as a *Weltanschauung* or a formula for the causal explanation of historical reality.[11]

In these remarks Weber did not differentiate between Marx and Marxist theory in his own time.[12] Marx's conception of a necessary and irreversible process, leading from feudalism to capitalism and eventually to socialism, was not a purely ontological statement; it was also a theory for practical orientation, requiring human action to become reality. Capitalist society comes into being only through the actions of the bourgeoisie, and without a socialist revolution carried out by the proletariat there can be no socialist society. This activist element in Marx's theory was obscured by the later interpretations by Engels and, finally, Kautsky.[13] It was they who turned it into that rigid, mechanistic theory commonly called historical materialism.

When he wrote the above-quoted passages, Weber was apparently not fully aware of the substantial differences between Marx's theory and orthodox Marxist interpretations in his own time, even though it would appear that he discussed some of Marx's texts in his early academic lectures in the 1890s. A careful comparison of their methodological procedures[14] shows that the two thinkers were actually not as antithetical as Weber himself claimed. Both Weber and Marx were concerned with extrapolating certain sequences of causal chains of events from the historical process. To be sure, unlike Marx, Weber emphasized that one could grasp only segments of social reality, never its totality. Weber thought it impossible, indeed dishonest, to go beyond the construction of ideal types: models that are used for describing particular historical sequences and for analysing their social effects and human con-sequences. In other words, from Weber's methodological perspective, claims about the objectivity of the historical process were fictitious. It is no coinci-dence that he repeatedly took offence at precisely this element of Marx's teach-ings. Weber considered this view of history to be false not only on epistemological grounds but also in principle, or, if one prefers, for ethical reasons highly questionable. In his view it fatally weakened the responsibility of the autonomous individual, who is called upon constantly to decide between different ultimate values. The belief that history is determined by objective pro-cesses seduces individuals all too easily into adapting to the presumed objective course of things, rather than remaining faithful to their own ultimate con-victions and value-positions.

We also encounter this viewpoint in Weber's comments on the German Social Democrats.[15] He repeatedly expressed utmost contempt towards them precisely because they asserted persistently that world history was on their side and that, therefore, the victory of socialism over the bourgeois world was merely a question of time.[16] Not only the liberal in Weber, but also the follower of Nietzsche, protested against such an orthodox variety of Marxism and vehemently rejected socialism dressed in pseudo-scientific garb which seemed to guarantee scientific certainty of final victory. On the other hand, he had the greatest respect for socialists who, regardless of the chances of success, fought for their ideals.

For Weber, Marxism was acceptable in only two forms: (1) as a political theory which, instead of invoking objective scientific truths, proclaims revolutionary struggle against the purportedly unjust social order on the basis of ethical convictions and without regard for the possible consequences for the individual, or (2) as a system of brilliant ideal-typical hypotheses, which in themselves deserve closest attention from all sociologists and which are capable of substantially advancing knowledge of modern societies.

A more detailed analysis of Weber's views of Marxism shows that Weber took exception, above all else, to the Marxist theory of 'superstructure'. Weber never accepted the thesis that all social phenomena could be explained sufficiently by relating them to economic causes: 'the common materialist view of history, that the "economic" is in some sense an "ultimate" in the chain of causation, is in my estimation totally worthless as a scientific statement.'[17] Weber ignored the fact that Marx and Engels's position on this matter was much more sophisticated.

Weber held that social phenomena could not, even in the final analysis, be explained by economic causes. However, he did not express an idealist counter-position. Weber's famous essays on *The Protestant Ethic and the Spirit of Capitalism* are commonly viewed as an attempt to prove that idealist, and especially religious, factors play an independent role in the historical process. In 1918 Weber presented the results of this study in a series of lectures at the University of Vienna under the title, 'A positive critique of the materialist view of history'. However, he did this with thoroughly ambivalent feelings.[18] He never claimed that his 'Protestant ethic' thesis completely answered the question of how and why industrial capitalism arose. He pointed out repeatedly that he uncovered only one group of factors among others that had contributed to the rise of capitalism.[19] Incidentally, Weber drew considerably closer to Marx when he indicated that mature capitalism no longer needed the Protestant ethic. In almost Marxian language, he described modern capitalism as a social power that forces people to subject themselves to the social conditions it has created, regardless of whether or not they are willing. They have no choice; they must be professionals (*Berufsmenschen*) because modern industrial capitalism does not permit otherwise.[20] In almost apocalyptic terms he argued that capitalism is forging the conditions for a new 'iron cage of serfdom', which humanity will have to occupy as soon as the current phase of dynamic economic growth has reached its natural limits.[21] In describing the capitalist system's almost mechanical domination of man, which in the long run threatens to become a modern form of slavery, Weber came close to Marx's conviction that capitalism is an inhuman social order that contains the propensity for self-destruction.

On the other hand, Weber refused to identify this immanent trend in the capitalist system (which he endeavoured to define precisely using sociological methods) with an objective developmental law. The universal-historical perspective of an approaching age of bureaucracy recurs repeatedly in Weber's scholarly writings; however, it is never hypostatized into an ontological statement of a philosophy of history. Here, the decisive difference between Weber's and Marx's conceptions of history becomes obvious. While Marx, in Hegelian fashion, framed his analysis in an almost apodictically conceived theory of history (although partly with political intentions), for Weber every holistic view of the historical process had only a hypothetical quality, serving orientation but not understood by itself as true and immutable. Accordingly, Weber was only being consistent when he gave particular attention to those forces and tendencies which were counteracting this process and sought to discover the conditions under which these can display their optimal effectiveness.

Weber's reaction to individual elements of Marxist theory also conforms to this fundamental attitude. He accepted the thesis that the material conditions of existence pervasively determine human action only as a nomological model for the definition of concrete social conduct, but not as conceptualized truth; and it was precisely the significant deviations from this model that he sought to establish. With respect to the role of material and particularly economic interests, Weber was fundamentally pluralistic. Weber found that, even under industrial capitalism, development is not determined exclusively by 'material interests'. Alongside their dynamics stand the dynamics of 'ideal interests';[22] every analysis must take both sets of factors into account. In his essays on the Protestant ethic and later studies of world religions, Weber was above all intent upon demonstrating that ideal interests can initiate social change of considerable magnitude; indeed, under certain circumstances they can have revolutionary effects although – or, better, precisely *because* – they have nothing in common with economic motivations.

On this point Weber perhaps stood furthest from Marx. In contrast to Marx, he was firmly convinced that individuals who are consciously guided by ultimate values of whatever sort – and the more these values stand in opposition to everyday reality, the more far-reaching their effects – can be an irreducible force that reshapes a given social reality so as to conform with their ultimate values. Naturally, the actual results of such individual actions are conditioned by the specific social situation. But the original motivation of action cannot be explained perfunctorily by referring to the social conditions, which significantly shape the eventual results.

This concept of social change, which is directed primarily towards value-oriented actions of individuals or groups, corresponds to Weber's strictly individualistic thinking, and is, in principle, irreconcilable with Marxist theory. Nevertheless, there is common ground between Weber and Marx (at least with the *Philosophical Manuscripts* of 1844). In a brilliant essay, which still ranks among the best ever written on Weber, Karl Löwith has shown that both thinkers were concerned with the same central problem: how a dignified human existence can be secured under the conditions of industrial society. However, the realization that Marx was concerned equally with the liberation of 'alienated man' was obscured, in Weber's earlier work, by vulgar Marxist interpretations.[23]

As a few scattered comments indicate, Weber doubted Marx's prognosis that, because of its inherent contradictions, the collapse of the capitalist system was inevitable. He believed that the pauperization theory, crisis theory and concentration theory were all unsound, and in this respect he agreed fully with contemporary critiques of Marxism. After a long and uninterrupted rise in real wages, the pauperization theory, even in modified form, was no longer tenable. Weber regarded the assumption that the transition to socialism would occur after a series of constantly intensifying economic crises with a mixture of disdain and irony, as can be gathered from his occasional polemical remarks about the 'so-called anarchy of production', which nevertheless produces tremendous material achievements.[24] Weber's lecture on 'Socialism' delivered to Austrian army officers in 1918[25] used arguments of then contemporary political economists (also those of Eduard Bernstein) in pointing out the likelihood of increased capitalist self-regulation through the formation of cartels, syndicates, and the like, which would reduce the intensity of recurrent economic crises.[26] Specifically, Weber contradicted Marx's view that further capitalist development would cause an inevitable polarization between the bourgeoisie and the overwhelming majority of the proletariat, absorbing all remaining social strata. Weber referred expressly to the rapid increase in '"white-collar workers" and, hence, of bureaucracy in the private sector', a development which, he believed, indicated increasing differentiation within the workers' ranks as well as within the middle classes.[27] Consequently, Weber regarded the German bourgeoisie's fear of revolution as pitiable and the Social Democrats' slogans of revolutionary agitation as a symptom of both political immaturity and the backwardness of the German political and social system, which denied workers political equality just as it denied them recognition as social partners of the entrepreneurs. Thus Weber repeatedly castigated the patriarchalism of German entrepreneurs, who could not free themselves from the authoritarian attitude towards their employees; he also considered them partially responsible for the radicalization of the workers.[28] Even so, Weber assumed that a socialist revolution was extremely improbable in his time. In his view, the Russian 'October Revolution' was a military revolt veiled in socialist drapery.[29]

Quite apart from the question of the prospects for socalism, Weber rigorously disputed that the abolition of private appropriation of the means of production and the transition to a demand-oriented economy (*Bedarfsdeckungswirtschaft*), of whatever type, would substantially improve the lot of workers. Weber believed that the separation of workers from the means of production, which Marx emphasized so strongly, was by no means limited to a social order based on private property. Rather, he considered it to be an essential precondition of all modern, highly developed societies, capitalist or otherwise. 'It is', he argued, 'a serious error to think that this separation of the worker from the tools of his trade is something peculiar to industry, especially to *private* industry. The basic state of affairs is unaltered when the person at the head of the machine is changed – when, for example, a state president or prime minister controls it instead of a private industrialist.'[30] On the contrary, the separation of workers from the means of production exists in state-directed socialism just as much as in capitalism. In both, an increasing divergence of formal ownership and managerial control becomes manifest, a split which Weber saw as a mark of advanced industrial systems and which, as we will see below, he took as the starting-point for an ideal-typical theory of social stratification that differs significantly from Marxist theory.

From the foregoing, it can be concluded that Weber was convinced that neither private appropriation nor the uneven distribution of property can be regarded as the essential causes of the alienation and deprivation of the working classes. The elimination of private control over the means of production leaves the fundamental problem untouched, namely, the superiority of those in dominant economic positions who exercise control over the masses of workers. It is the problem of control, not the formal disposition of property, which is crucial. Therefore, Weber saw the roots of alienation, not in property relations, but in omnipotent structures of bureaucratic domination, which modern industrial capitalism produced in ever-increasing numbers. Accordingly, he considered the demand for abolition of private control of production to be a fetish, which ignored the true state of affairs and glossed over the fact that individual workers had nothing to gain by such measures. 'This would also be true particularly of any *rationally* organized socialist economy, which would retain the expropriation of all workers and merely bring it to completion by expropriating the private owners.'[31] However, this would mean a further strengthening and bureaucratization of the economy and, indirectly, of the social system. Socialization would not liberate workers; it would make them more dependent upon those who control the means of production.

For workers it makes little difference whether the masters of the means of production are capitalist entrepreneurs or managers or government officials with entrepreneurial duties. In contrast to Marx's expectation that socialism would eliminate the profit motive, Weber soberly predicted that individual workers would continue to be concerned only with their constellation of personal interests, whatever the structure of the society. Weber aimed at demonstrating that nationalization of production would lead only to a shift of interest positions, and it would certainly not eliminate 'the domination of man over man'. Workers would be confronted with a new, still more powerful bureaucracy, and one far harder to control, whose members one might well call, with Djilas, 'the new class'. Consequently, any possibility of improving their concrete working and living conditions within the system would be further restricted. According to Weber, it made no basic difference whether the transition to a socialist, planned, demand-oriented economy was achieved by a revolutionary or evolutionary path. Such a transition would considerably curtail the chances of attaining a maximum of freedom, however understood.

In 1917 there was much discussion in Germany about whether the forms of the wartime economy, with their high level of government control, should be maintained after the war and gradually turned into a socialist system. Weber protested passionately against such suggestions.

A progressive elimination of private capitalism is theoretically conceivable, although it is surely not so easy as imagined in the dreams of some literati who do not know what it is all about; its elimination will certainly not be a consequence of this war. But let us assume that some time in the future it will be done away with. What would be the practical result? The destruction of the iron cage of modern industrial labour? No! The abolition of private capitalism would simply mean that the *top management* of the nationalized or socialized enterprises would become bureaucratic as well.

This would endanger a free society's chances of survival in an age of bureaucratization; for it is bureaucracy that poses the real threat to a humane society.

Together with the inanimate machine it [i.e. bureaucracy] is busy fabricating the cage of serfdom which men will perhaps be forced to inhabit some day, as powerless as the fellahs of ancient Egypt. This might happen *if* a technically good, i.e. a rational bureaucratic, administration and provision of social services *were to be the ultimate and sole value* in the ordering of their affairs.[32]

From a universal-historical perspective, Weber regarded the abolition of private ownership with great scepticism. In his view, nationalization of the means of production is incapable of contributing to a solution of the most pressing problem of our time. This is the question how, in the face of 'omnipotent tendencies towards bureaucratization . . . some remnants of "individualistic" freedom of movement' can still be rescued?[33] Nationalization would make the situation still worse and only lead to an increase in the power of functionaries, not of workers. 'It is the dictatorship of the official, not that of the worker, which, for the present at any rate, is on the advance.'[34]

Yet Weber distinguished himself radically from Marx not only in his estimation of the chances for eliminating the structural deficiencies of industrial capitalism but also in his analysis of the nature of capitalist society. According to Weber, even mature capitalist societies are not as monolithically structured as the Marxist class model postulates. In principle he accepted the concepts 'class' and 'class struggle', unlike many of his bourgeois contemporaries, but he refused to assign them the dominant role that they play in Marx's theory.

Weber believed that class interest in the Marxist sense could be decisive in certain situations, but that this is not necessarily so. Only in extraordinary historical situations, according to Weber, are there collective class actions that conform unambiguously to this behavioural pattern, and even in such cases the population achieves nothing without the leadership of persons (normally intellectuals) from other classes. Weber tersely rejected the so-called 'false class consciousness' solution of Georg Lukács, who held that segments of a class can be mistaken concerning their actual class interests and that these interests are established objectively. Weber considered this to be a pseudo-scientific strategy that obscured the key issues.

The fact that people in the same class situation regularly react in mass actions to such tangible situations as economic ones in the direction of those actions which are most adequate to their average interest is an important and simple fact after all for the understanding of historical events. However, this fact must not lead to that kind of pseudo-scientific operation with the concepts of 'class' and 'class interests' which is so common nowadays and which has found its most classic expression in the statement of a talented author, that the individual may be in error concerning his own interests, but that the 'class' is 'infallible' about its interests.[35]

Weber also rejected Lukács's thesis because he was convinced that the social action of particular groups is never determined solely by economic interests. People do not always act in accordance with their objective class situation; they are influenced by a multitude of other factors as well, including religious beliefs, traditional modes of behaviour and particular values. This means that, instead of class, much more differentiated explanatory models of social action are necessary to deal with the complexity of social relations in industrial societies. Although Weber feared that, in the long run, capitalism would become a rigidly monolithic and bureaucratic system of gigantic proportions, he was convinced, contrary to Marx, that capitalist societies are, in principle, pluralistically structured. Class conflicts play an essential role, but actual social developments depend on many other social factors, such as strong, dynamic leadership.

Especially within complex industrial societies, distinctions between the individual's class situation and class interests are generally not clear. This is reflected in the ideal-typical schema of class stratification developed by Weber in *Economy and Society*, which differs most significantly from Marx's approach.[36] Instead of a single model of class stratification, Weber developed three different models, each based on a different criterion: the disposition of property; 'the chance of utilizing goods and services in the market-place'; and the social status of the respective social groups or strata. From these criteria, Weber distinguished between property classes, economic classes and social classes. He did so to make clear that a class situation, defined as a set of shared interests of groups of individuals, is many-layered and totally unequivocal only in the exceptional case.

Weber also distinguished between property classes and commercial classes because, in his view, their social interests are quite different. A society based predominantly on class stratification according to property tends to stagnate, because the 'positively privileged classes' are composed primarily of *rentiers*, who draw fixed revenues from private property. As a result, their central interest is maintaining the status quo; they are threatened by rapid economic growth and strong economic competition. The 'negatively privileged classes' are, for the most part, either not free or directly dependent upon their masters. Because the *rentiers* are not interested in social change and the lower classes are unable to alter their lot, class stratification based on property is non-dynamic. However, this model is not ideally suited for describing class relations in industrial societies. A more adequate approach emphasizes the chances of a specific class being able to exercise control of the means of production and the chances of its being able to obtain goods in the market-place. Formal possession of property is not decisive in determining the economic and social position of the various social groups in a capitalist system; rather, the degree of their effective participation in the functions of economic leadership is the decisive factor. Admittedly, these functions are frequently closely associated with the possession of property, but this is not necessarily so, particularly where highly specialized knowledge and managerial skills are of increased importance. Here also Weber distinguished between positively and negatively privileged classes, while groups such as craftsmen and independent farmers stand between them. The positively privileged classes consist of entrepreneurs, managers and members of the various professions 'with sought-after expertise or privileged education' (e.g. lawyers, scientists, physicians and artists), as well as, in rare cases, highly skilled workers who are not easily replaceable. The bulk of workers comprise the negatively privileged classes.

This bipolar model of class stratification, based on possession of property on the one hand and professional status on the other, is consistent with recent developments in industrial societies; science and technology are daily gaining in importance. Consequently the social status of those groups which supply the necessary specialized knowledge rises in importance, while the role of the formal proprietors of the means of production declines. What is the significance of this ideal-typical schema? First, under advanced capitalism, formal possession of property is less important than what Weber calls 'the monopolization of entrepreneurial management for the sake of the business interests' of one's own class.[37] Second, the two models show that even within the ruling classes of industrial societies there exists a great diversity of economic and political interests. *Rentiers* usually favour a stable economic system and, accordingly, are more likely to be politically conservative. On the other hand, managers, filling important entrepreneurial positions, are supportive of dynamism and rapid growth, and therefore they are often more liberal in their political attitudes and more flexible in their social behaviour.

Something similar can be said of workers. Weber concerned himself intensively with the progressive differentiation of status groups within the working class, and he pointed out that Marx, in his last years, also paid special attention to this issue.[38] Weber indicated that increasing differentiation would lead to corresponding differences in respect of economic interests and political views. Accordingly, he thought that the Marxist concept of class (i.e. that all social conflict is ultimately attributable to conflicts between capitalists and their various bourgeois accomplices on the one side and workers on the other) was not sufficiently differentiated to do justice to the extraordinarily complicated network of competing material interests within capitalist societies. Weber did not deny that there is class struggle and class interest within capitalist societies, but he disputed the contention that these factors alone determine how things develop. The status of particular groups or individuals within the production process, even more than the disposition of property, influences their interest positions within societal structure. The ideal-typical model of social-class stratification that Weber developed, using social status as a standard, is designed to take account of this fact. Weber distinguished between four classes: (1) the working class; (2) the petty bourgeoisie; (3) the propertyless intelligentsia, highly qualified specialists and white-collar workers; and (4) 'the classes privileged through property and education'.[39] This classification is admittedly rather imprecise, but it indicates, none the less, that Weber made a clear distinction between class affiliation and social status and that he regarded them, to a certain degree, as independent variables.

At this point, our observations on Max Weber not only as a critic but also as a student of Karl Marx may be summarized as follows. Weber's objections to the Marxist solution to the problems of industrial capitalist society have been confirmed, in many respects, by the development of socialist systems. Today it is evident that eliminating private appropriation of the means of production does not solve the problems involved; it merely results in a displacement of the fundamental conflict of interests, determined by the technological constraints of industrial production, on to a different plane. Nationalization may lead to a replacement of the social strata in control of the means of production, but not, however, to the elimination or even the alleviation of the domination exercised by those groups over the working class. The problem of establishing effective social control from the point of view and in the interests of the bulk of the population proves much harder to solve in Marxist-Leninist societies than in the capitalist West. Accordingly, one must agree with Weber that, instead of the particular form of ownership, the omnipotence of bureaucratic structures (unavoidable as they are under modern industrial conditions) represents the real cause of alienation in the world of industrial work and jeopardizes personal freedom. Dispassionately Weber identified the crucial problem, namely that in socialism merely a new stratum of bureaucratic masters had gained control. His scepticism about the claim that socialist society would gradually engender a new type of man has also been justified. The insight expressed in his theory of the various types of class stratification – it is not property ownership but rather the degree of control of the entrepreneurial function that is of decisive importance – has turned out to be valid. The key issue, namely how a humane existence can be assured for the working classes in industrial societies, is just as pressing as ever in existing socialist systems.

However, Weber's criticism of socialist theories does not mean that he was satisfied with capitalist social conditions. To be sure, he did not regard the workers' situation in Marx's despairing terms, and he considered Marx's proposals for helping workers as highly problematic. Nationalization could not end class struggle because it would only modify the composition of the 'positively privileged classes', without significantly improving the lot of workers. Worse still, workers henceforth would be subjected to the omnipotent control of anonymous government bureaucracies. These would be far more powerful than a multitude of private entrepreneurs, who, among other things, always have to reckon with government intervention in the case of serious class conflicts. 'While at present the political and private industrial administrations (of cartels, banks and giant concerns) stand side by side as separate bodies, and therefore industrial power can still be curbed by political power, the two administrations would then be one body with common interests and could no longer be checked.'[40]

Weber faced this problem on an even more fundamental level. He doubted whether the humane ideals of socialism could ever be realized. In a highly developed industrial society, full emancipation of workers from the yoke of the owners of the means of production was, in his opinion, unattainable.[41] This, of course, does not mean that he considered the social consequences of industrial capitalism, particularly with regard to the working class, to be in any way satisfactory. Accordingly, he had great sympathy with political movements that directed all their energies towards winning a maximum of social and political freedom for workers within a liberal, market-oriented capitalist economy.

Again the question arises of how the sphere of individual personality could be affirmed under capitalism and its great ally, modern bureaucracy, or, in other words, how the long-term dehumanizing tendencies of modern industrialism might be counteracted. At first glance, Weber's answer seems paradoxical. Starting from the conviction that there was no simple solution to this problem and that nationalization would only worsen the situation, he inclined towards making the best of the capitalist system rather than abolishing it.[42] Weber defended liberal capitalism because it guaranteed a maximum of free competition on both the economic and social levels. His ideal was an expanding capitalist system with a high degree of social mobility and dynamism; he thought this would permit the greatest possible emancipation of the working classes. He considered two things vital: first, strengthening the dynamic factors within the capitalist economy, rather than encouraging bureaucratization through socialist measures; and, second, creating a truly democratic political system, in which all social groups would be given the opportunity to pursue vigorously their social and economic interests within the limits of legal order. Weber conceded readily to Michels that this solution left much to be desired, but he added that its attainment would be 'no small achievement'.[43]

Weber's position contains problems, if not downright contradictions. On the one hand, Weber counted upon the dynamic effects of free competition in the economic as well as in the general societal realm, while, on the other, he viewed apprehensively the constant growth of cartels, trusts and other monopolistic structures as typical forerunners of a bureaucratized economy. Weber never systematically discussed this contradiction. By 1906, at the latest, Weber questioned whether his model – in which conflicts of interest between the working classes and entrepreneurs were freely fought out in trade-union struggles – was not outdated in the face of the development of giant corporations and powerful employer organizations. He emphatically advocated suitable legislative measures to restore the equality of opportunity between the working classes and their unions and the entrepreneurs in their continual struggle over wages and working conditions. Of course, the free, spontaneous action of the working classes should be encumbered with the fewest fetters possible. Therefore, Weber would hear nothing of governmentally established consolidated unions or of arbitration bodies on which government officials would be represented. Likewise, Weber strongly supported progressive social legislation; this was not to serve ethical or moral ends, but rather during a period of growing entrepreneurial power it was supposed to improve the position of the working classes in their battle with entrepreneurs.[44]

These observations could be generalized: the state should be, in some measure, a corrective to bureaucratization and petrification of the social fabric. This was one of the reasons why Weber emphasized so strongly the need for dynamic, future-oriented leadership and an effective system for the selection of qualified political leaders. It is open to question whether, under advanced capitalism, Weber would have favoured a liberal or interventionist economic policy, or, to put it bluntly: would he have given preference to Keynes or Friedman? We can find support for both views. In principle, Weber favoured the liberal model of freely contested conflicts within the confines of the rule of law. Yet, where the preconditions for this were imperilled, he did not hesitate to assign the state the task of intervening with appropriate corrective measures. Moreover, in Weber's view, as the political organization of society the state can be a source of dynamic economic growth and consequently of increased social mobility, though only by indirect means. Resolute and far-sighted politicians in top government positions are able, owing to their charismatic qualities, to set new goals for society and thereby counter routinization and petrification. This is also important because the underprivileged strata, especially the working classes, are particularly disadvantaged by economic stagnation and social petrification and their opportunities for emancipation are the first to suffer.

Such a solution presupposes that the government possesses a degree of independence from the economically powerful strata, or, in Marx's terms, that the state is more than just a tool of the ruling classes. Here, difficulties appear which are not resolved sufficiently in Weber's political sociology, and make his conceptual alternative to Marxism appear vulnerable. Certainly, Weber was quite clear that one could not simply grant the state the function of a neutral agency in the conflicts of social interests within industrial society. His battle against Schmoller's policies in the Verein für Sozialpolitik was directed primarily towards destroying the illusion that the state could ever stand above the social classes. Occasionally Weber made this explicit.[45] In his view, it was important to organize the governmental system in such a way that all social strata and groups, aided by plebiscitary leaders who have the people's confidence, could achieve a due share in political decisions. Weber did not doubt that, through their leaders, the working classes were capable of exerting a definitive influence upon the control of the governmental apparatus, thereby improving their social situation by political means.

Aside from this, there is the question whether the state possesses a position of independent leadership as regards economic forces. In this respect Weber never clearly articulated his opinion. In principle he did not distinguish between the state and the various social or economic institutions of society. To them essentially the same sociological terms applied. Yet he believed the state to be superior to these other institutions because of its special legal privileges, in particular the right to employ physical violence; and it was, moreover, organized basically as an 'autocephalous' institution. The state ought to exercise its independent authority, particularly with respect to the economic sphere; instead of being constantly influenced by economic interests, it was, on the contrary, supposed to influence economic activities and dictate their political parameters.

Starting from these premises, Weber looked primarily to the political realm, rather than to profound changes of the capitalist economy, for a solution to the structural problems first addressed by Marx. In this connection Weber's advocacy of plebiscitary 'leader democracy', with a charismatic element, deserves special notice (something to which Herbert Marcuse has already drawn attention, although, in my estimation, accompanied with an unacceptable interpretation).[46] A formally democratic political system, led by far-sighted, energetic and skilled politicians with demagogic qualities, favoured a high degree of social mobility. Consequently, this system had indirect emancipatory effects upon the lower classes without ever breaking the rule that the actual exercise of power rests in the hands of small groups. Beyond this, it allowed the underprivileged, at least formally, the possibility of overcoming the disadvantages of their social condition by political means. Weber considered as utopian the socialist option (i.e. smashing the power of the state), formulated by Lenin and then put into practice. In the long term history has shown Weber, rather than Lenin, to be right.[47]

Weber understood that there are possible socialist systems that would minimize the domination of workers by those controlling the means of production, for example, through extreme decentralization of economic organization and worker participation in management. Yet he believed that this could be achieved only under conditions that would have to do without both the regulatory mechanism of economic competition in the market-place and the money economy. Thus the cost of realizing certain socialist ideals would be a considerable reduction of formal rationality. Although Weber considered a variety of possible types of socialist societies, he assumed – and, so far, existing socialist systems have proved him right – that a socialist economy could survive only as a centralized, state-operated system.

State socialist economic organization, with its powerful bureaucratic machinery to control production, distribution and management, had, in Weber's view, obvious disadvantages when compared to the capitalist market economy (*Verkehrswirtschaft*). In *Economy and Society* Weber treated this problem in an ideal-typical schema. In a sense it was his last word on the relation between capitalism and socialism.[48] Weber contrasted the market economy with the planned economy. Although he explained clearly that it could not be determined on scientific grounds which of the two systems ought to be given preference, it is obvious that Weber believed market economies to be more effective. Socialist economic systems would have to cope with a considerable reduction in the formal accountability (*Rechenhaftigkeit*) of the production and distribution system, especially if they broke with the capitalist practice of market-oriented pricing. Although Weber expressed himself very carefully, his argument nevertheless returned again and again to the thesis that capitalism was infinitely superior to all known economic systems because it alone was capable of rationalizing all economic operations on a purely formal basis. If one chooses the standard of highest achievement as the criterion for judging the market economy against the planned economy, the former is far superior.

In contrast to some recent neo-Marxist interpretations, Weber was in no way inclined to glorify capitalism, and certainly not a capitalist system with a maximum of formal rationality in all its social dimensions. Closer analysis reveals that the pure type of market economy, as Weber developed it in *Economy and Society*, is anything but attractive and is not at all identical with that form of capitalism which Weber favoured. This model postulates that a maximum of formal rationality is attainable only if the following conditions are met:

1 'Constant struggle between autonomous groups in the market-place';
2 the rational calculation of prices under conditions of unrestricted competition in the market-place;

3 'formally free labour' (i.e. work performed on the basis of freely contracted
   wage agreements, as distinct from fixed salaries or the like);
4 'expropriation from workers of the means of production';
5 private ownership of the means of production.[49]

The majority of these conditions were no longer sufficiently met under the
advanced capitalism of Weber's time (assuming, for the moment, that they had
been present in early capitalism, which apparently served as Weber's model).
Was he then describing a ghost that already belonged to the past? Such a
question fails to grasp the core of the issue. Weber intended to describe the
specifics of capitalism in its pure form (a procedure which had methodological
similarities to Marx). Thus Weber's process of concept formation must not be
dismissed as a throwback to Manchester liberalism. As already mentioned, he
conceded, indeed emphatically advocated, that under certain conditions
deviations from the pure form of capitalist market economy would be necessary
– deviations effected through appropriate state interventions and in some cases
through a change in the legal and political parameters of economic activity. In a
way, Weber anticipated the neo-liberalism of the 1950s. In fact, he influenced
its leading exponents (e.g. Friedrich Hayek, Hannah Arendt and Alfred Müller-
Armack) to a considerable extent.

By stressing formal rationality as its basic characteristic, Weber never
intended to immunize modern industrial capitalism against criticism, as
Herbert Marcuse and Wolfgang Lefèvre attempted to demonstrate.[50] Weber
did not intend to elevate capitalism ontologically and thereby justify it ideo-
logically, as Marcuse claimed. Marcuse's argument that Weber's emphasis on
the formal rationality of all capitalist operations obscured capitalism's substantive irrationality is quite misleading. Weber discussed this very point repeatedly
in *Economy and Society*, although not always without ambiguity.[51] Weber distinguished explicitly between formal and substantive rationality, though
perhaps not as consistently as the issue demanded. He was fully aware of the fact
that a maximum of formal rationality was inseparably linked with substantive
irrationalities, for example, 'the submission of workers to the domination of
entrepreneurs'.[52] Likewise he never obscured the true nature of 'formally free
labour contracts', which are fundamental to capitalism; he described them
neutrally as a special form of domination. Weber proceeded from the premise
that under the conditions of mature capitalism formal rationality and substantive rationality are always in conflict with each other, just as in other
economic systems; it depended on the concrete situation what compromises
had to be made in order to find a balance between these antagonistic principles.

In developing such a conceptualization Weber cleared the path for a critique of capitalism, a critique which rated substantive value-positions, regardless of their sort, more highly than the formal rationality of the system. He pleaded for practical measures of social reform rather than for radical remedies which would lead to the destruction of the capitalist market economy. He warned, however, that the implementation of substantive principles would bring an inevitable reduction in the efficiency and productivity of the economic system, or, to put it otherwise, they could be had only at a price. Proceeding from concrete substantive value-positions, he indicated that a large number of critical alternatives to the capitalist system were conceivable but in each case some reduction of the formal efficiency of the economic system must be accepted as part of the bargain – an argument he used occasionally against Roberto Michels.[53] The manifestly dogmatic point in Weber's position was his nearly boundless confidence in both the formally rationalizing effect of the economic struggle between competing groups in the market and, in a broader sense, the competition of political groups within society.

The typological dichotomy of the market economy on the one hand and different forms of socialist planned economies on the other was by no means an apology for industrial capitalism. Weber did not aim to refute the socialists and Marxists with this extremely formal typology. Rather, his goal was to provide a value-free clarification of the respective social costs and consequences that the two opposing systems unavoidably generate. Thus he stated: 'The *purpose* of the discussion has been to determine the optimal preconditions for the *formal* rationality of economic activity and its relation to the various types of *substantive* "demands" of whatever sort.'[54] Weber wished to make perfectly clear that deviations from the pure type of market-oriented competition in capitalist economy entail a necessary reduction in the formal rationality of the entire system or, in other words, a diminution of its economic efficiency.

Weber was certain that none of the conceivable theoretical models of ideal economic systems could be translated into social reality without compromising at least some of the aims and values which they were intended to serve. According to his position, it was, in principle, impossible to determine the best economic system. Moreover, 'substantive and formal (in the sense of exactly *calculated*) rationality', as he put it, were 'inevitably largely separate. This fundamental, and in the last analysis, inherent element of irrationality in economic systems is one of the important sources of all "social" problems and, above all, of the problems of socialism.'[55] As early as his Freiburg inaugural address, Weber had made it clear that happiness and peace could not be had on this earth,[56] and he stuck to this conviction for the rest of his life with a 'heroic pessimism' reminiscent of Nietzsche. Weber believed that a definitive answer to the question of the nature of a just economic order could never be found. For the foreseeable future constant compromises between the principle of formal rationality and substantive value-principles seemed to be the only humane solution.

It should be evident why Weber never idealized capitalism, although he decided unequivocally in its favour. One the one hand, he was an enthusiastic partisan of capitalism as an economic system sustained by bourgeois values and as a source of rational social conduct largely experienced as binding; further-more, he supported it as a system with a maximum of economic dynamism and social mobility. On the other hand, he was deeply concerned about the ultimate socio-political consequences of capitalism, which, in the long run, would inevitably undermine dignified human life founded on the principle of the free, autonomous personality. The cool and matter-of-fact analysis of modern industrial capitalism in *Economy and Society* corresponds to this perspective. Indeed, Weber did not hide the defects of capitalism, yet in his view there was no workable alternative. Despite the high regard he had for the motives of sincere socialists, he did not believe the Marxist prescription could solve the real problems of modern Western society. Despite all of capitalism's shortcomings, he preferred it to every conceivable form of socialist economy. He was con-vinced that socialists, in so far as they wished to be serious about realizing their moral principles, would either have to accept a considerable regression in both technology and civilization or else be compelled to create gigantic bureau-cracies in the face of which the people, including the workers, would be unable to accomplish anything. Compared to any form of socialism, capitalism appeared to offer far better conditions for the survival of free societies in the age of bureaucracy.

Following this basic conviction, Weber spoke out consistently for the pre-servation of the capitalist system in the last years of the First World War and especially during the Revolution of 1918–19 in Germany. As early as 1916 he vigorously defended entrepreneurs against the mounting criticism of capital-ism. The war could never have been waged so successfully without their services, and even in the post-war years it was necessary to retain the motto: no curtailment of entrepreneurial activity but 'more capital, more capitalist activity and dynamism'. In this way the economic losses incurred by the war might be made good again, and Germany's position in the world markets recap-tured even in the face of superior competition from the United States.[57]

However, during the German Revolution of 1918 he made significant tactical advances towards socialism in order to make a coalition with the pro-gressive sections of the middle classes attractive to the Majority Social Demo-crats.[58] He admitted occasionally that some socialization was necessary under the prevailing circumstances. But, in principle, he always stuck to his convictions that only a free dynamic entrepreneurial class could restore Germany's economy. Yet neither on the political nor on the theoretical level did he consider the dialogue with socialism to be definitely closed. He felt that the final word on this issue had not yet been spoken. Earlier, in 1911, he had planned to write an essay on Marxism for the Russian journal *Logos* which did not come about after all.[59] Now he intended to take up the topic again on a systematic level. For the summer term in 1920 at the University of Munich he had planned to deliver a lecture course on 'Socialism' and had already started on this when he died of pneumonia in June 1920.[60] Had Weber been granted a longer life, he surely would not have further postponed that systematic treatment of Marxism, which we look for in vain in his work; he would have set it forth, whether in the ambitious *Political Sociology* on which he was then working or as a separate inquiry. However, even in its present form, his sociological work can be regarded as an alternative to Marx's theory, one which is on a par with the latter in both breadth of vision and the rigour of its argument.

Clearly, any evaluation of Weber's critique of the Marxist idea should bear in mind that he only lived through the first years of the Bolshevik regime and, therefore, he lacked concrete experience of socialist systems. Regardless of this, his essential points are still worthy of consideration. His thesis – that the distribution of property is not as important as the groups who control entrepreneurial positions – deserves special attention, as today's stagnating communist systems demonstrate. The abolition of private appropriation of the means of production, under certain circumstances, may be the way of resolving the pressing problems of our time, but it could also make things worse. A modern theory of socialism must, above all, be able to handle the problem of how economic decision-making can be effectively controlled by the people at large instead of falling into the hands of indecisive bureaucrats or new authoritarian elites. In this respect, Weber's analyses deserve attention even from those who do not share his convictions.

Weber presented no simple recipes for restructuring capitalist societies in order to end working-class alienation and exploitation, but at least he emphasized the crucial problems. Thus we are thoroughly justified in calling him a liberal sociologist who matched his great intellectual opposite, Marx, in probing deeply into the problems of industrial capitalism.

5

Joining the Underdogs?
Weber's Critique of the Social
Democrats in Wilhelmine Germany

Max Weber's views about the character and role of the German Social Democratic Party in Wilhelmine Germany are of considerable interest in many respects. He considered the Social Democratic Party to be one of the most advanced examples of a bureaucratic mass party of the type which in his opinion was about to become dominant in modern parliamentary government. More importantly, he was interested in the Social Democrats as a political party which had tied its political fortunes to a considerable degree to the Marxist theory of historical materialism. But paramount in his views about the Social Democrats were considerations regarding the concrete role they played within Wilhelmine politics. Above all he concentrated on one issue, namely whether the policies of the Social Democrats were likely to promote or retard a democratization of the political system. In his opinion the middle classes and the working classes ought to operate jointly in the political arena in order to put an end to the rule of the aristocracy and its fellow travellers within the governmental bureaucracy. Weber considered this to be necessary not only because he believed in the superior qualities of democracy but also for nationalist reasons; only an Imperial Germany whose policies enjoyed the full support of all sections of society including the working classes would be able to play a major role in future world politics. It is this viewpoint which was paramount in Weber's assessment of the German Social Democrats.

It should be noted to begin with that Weber never hesitated to declare that his own views were conditioned not least by his own personal class status; he repeatedly stated that he was a member of the bourgeoisie, even in the literal sense of this term, since his wife Marianne drew on income from her co-

ownership of a small family owned textile mill in Westphalia.[1] None the less his
views on Marx and Marxism were perhaps never quite as biased as he himself
was ready to admit, as was shown above in some detail: though a radical critic of
Marxism, his own sociology was in no small degree developed in a perpetual
intellectual debate with Karl Marx and his theories.[2]

Indeed, I have already demonstrated that Weber integrated important
elements of Marx's theories into his own 'interpretative sociology'. The ideal-
typical assessment of the capitalist system in its pure form which we find in
Economy and Society in many ways parallels Marx's own analysis half a century
earlier. The 'formal rationality' of fully developed capitalism is not all that far
removed from Marx's notion of the 'alienation' of the workers as a result of
their disappropriation of the means of production. Weber described just as
Marx did, and in a similar language, the subjection of workers to a strict
discipline of work in the factory. Work contracts entered into on the basis of the
principle of 'formally free labour' are, according to Weber, tantamount to subjection to the domination of entrepreneurs. The modern industrial system is
based just as much as older socio-political systems – and possibly even to a
larger degree – on the 'domination of man over man', and the fact that it is
formally based upon free decisions in the market-place rather than on any kind
of forced labour does not make it less so.

These few remarks may indicate that a large area of consensus is to be found
in the theoretical thought of Marx and Weber, as far as their assessment of the
nature of the modern industrial system is concerned. However, while there are
striking similarities in their *diagnosis* of the evils of capitalism, Weber did not in
the least consider Marx's suggestions for how to cure these evils to be valid. In
his opinion, they were neither theoretically sound nor a suitable programme for
practical political activity in advanced industrial societies. On the other hand,
Weber was prepared to pay tribute to Marxism in its original form as propagated by Marx from 1847 onwards as a heroic, albeit utopian creed which in
the first place had helped the working class to establish itself as an independent
political force in a society which utterly rejected workers' claims to a fair share
of the social product and to a decent living. Weber considered the *Communist
Manifesto* as well as the so-called *Katastrophentheorie*, which predicted an inevitable and indeed early end to capitalism, as prophecies of considerable suggestive
power. In his view they provided the backbone of the early fervent, semi-
religious socialist creeds; they believed that theirs was a fight for a just new
society and that victory was not far off.

By contrast, however, Weber found that in his own day this socialist creed
had deteriorated into a sort of self-perpetuating mechanistic ideology which
assumed that history was on the side of the working classes and that they would

be swept to victory by the automatic operation of the laws of economic development. In his view socialist ideology had become a mere ritual of abuse directed at all the social institutions within capitalist society, which were summarily dismissed as bourgeois without any serious attempt to assess their true nature. In other words, what in the early days had been a heroic creed had become merely radical rhetoric devoid of any rational assessment of social reality. This refers of course in particular to the Social Democrats in imperial Germany. To put it in a nutshell: the Social Democrats had failed to get rid of the ideological modes of thought typical of a political sect but entirely unsuitable for a political party. Hence they were incapable of facing up to present-day reality. Accordingly they were unable and unwilling to work for the improvement of the workers' lot on the basis of a realistic assessment of existing conditions. The opportunities for moving forward in specific areas by means of political alliances with the progressive sections of the bourgeoisie were therefore ignored.

Already in his inaugural lecture of 1895 Weber had argued, though characteristically as an aside, that the German working class was in no way ready for political leadership, however advanced it had become in economic terms: 'Politically the German working class is infinitely less mature than is maintained by a clique of journalists who aspire to monopolize its leadership.'[3] It was above all the lack of any sense of power which he considered the most critical deficiency of the German working class, in marked contrast, as he pointed out, to the British and French working classes; in this respect he referred to the support given to British imperialism by important sections of the British working class who allegedly fully understood the need for empirical and power politics, whereas their German counterparts excelled in a doctrinaire anti-colonialism. For the leaders of the Social Democratic Party – 'those declassed bourgeois' – he felt little more than contempt: 'They are pathetic experts in political triviality: they lack the deep instinct for power that a class which is called upon to take over the political leadership in a society ought to possess.'[4]

Since the turn of the century Weber's imperialist convictions were no longer as powerful a determining factor in his opinion of the Social Democrats. But, in principle, his views had changed little. In his opinion the Social Democratic Party had in no way substantially matured. It continued to pursue an orthodox Marxist strategy devoid of any real revolutionary spirit, a strategy which totally relied upon the mechanistic process of history to eventually bring victory. As a matter of fact, the revolutionary propaganda of the Social Democrats was not followed up by revolutionary deeds; instead they were content to denounce the existing social order in vitriolic language. It was seen as totally unjust, wretched and bound to collapse in due course, for the gradual unfolding of the capitalist process of production and its immanent contradictions would dig capitalism's own grave. In his view this mental attitude was merely a variety of petty-bourgeois thinking that was guided above all by the idea to be on the winning side, come what may. To put it bluntly, Social Democratic agitation amounted to merely a verbal radicalism which stood in sharp contrast to what may be termed the 'propaganda by deed' of anarchism.

Between 1906 and 1909 Weber discussed these issues at considerable length with Roberto Michels, who had attracted his interest as a young scholar of remarkable gifts notably because he was a devoted left-wing socialist with strong syndicalist leanings and a convert from a wealthy bourgeois family.[5] Weber took considerable interest in Michels's work on socialism and socialist parties and it is significant that Michels published widely in the *Archiv für Sozial-wissenschaft und Sozialpolitik*, although he could not at that time be considered as an established scholar. Michels's famous book *Political Parties* (which was based largely upon an analysis of the German Social Democrats) originated in a series of essays all of which had been published in the *Archiv*.

Michels belonged to a dissident group of left-wing socialists in Marburg with moderate anarchist views; though a convinced socialist, he soon became a bitter critic of the German Social Democratic Party. This may be attributed partly to the fact that he felt ostracized by the party, being an intellectual from a bourgeois background. Indeed, Michels was never fully at home with the German Social Democrats, even though he was a party member until 1907. His own passionately moralist approach to socialism as an ethical duty, which was combined, as it were, with a deep-rooted belief in fundamentalist democratic principles, was not shared by the bulk of party members. Neither were his leanings towards anarchist thought well received in a party in which pragmatic views prevailed and in which solidarity was considered obligatory. Admittedly, Michels was a moral fundamentalist (*Gesinnungsethiker*) and a syndicalist rather than an ordinary socialist. Both of these aspects of Michels's personality fascinated Max Weber. In some ways he saw in Michels an *alter ego* following paths which he forbade himself to enter upon, but which he would none the less have liked to follow. Hence a lifelong, asymmetrical partnership developed between the two men.[6]

Weber's and Michels's initial assessments of the German Social Democrats were not all that different. In 1906 Weber attended the Social Democratic Party Congress at Mannheim. His account to Michels of the proceedings was utterly devastating:

Mannheim was very depressing. I heard Bebel and Legien refer at least ten times to 'our *weakness*'. Furthermore this extremely petty-bourgeois demeanour, all these com-placent publicans' faces, the lack of dynamism and resolution, the inability to decide in favour of a 'rightist policy', as the way for a 'leftist policy' is blocked, or at least appears to be so. . . . These gentlemen don't frighten anyone any more.[7]

With considerable acuteness Weber observed that under the prevailing conditions the German Social Democratic Party was not a political force that could be taken seriously. It was neither prepared to opt for a constructive reformist policy nor willing to embark upon genuine revolutionary struggle against the established order, whatever its revolutionary rhetoric might suggest. The Social Democrats might have found considerable support for a reformist policy among the progressive sections of the liberal parties. This would, however, have required abandoning the policy of 'the revolutionizing of minds', that is to say, concentrating upon agitation to paint a rosy picture of the socialist revolution to come, while doing next to nothing to actually improve the workers' lot and not opting for a genuine revolutionary strategy, as envisaged at the time by Rosa Luxemburg, for instance. Weber was appalled to see that the party was unable to agree on any realistic political strategy, and that the Social Democrats indulged instead in a mixture of self-pity and utopian expectation that the capitalist system would eventually collapse virtually without their own help, resulting in a victory for socialism without a single shot having been fired.

According to Weber this was utter nonsense. In his view there were only two strategies open to the Social Democrats:

1 A reformist strategy which should aim at attaining gradual reforms in social and constitutional matters. This would require putting an end to the meaningless repetition of ritualistic formulas about the socialist *Endziel* (final goal).
2 Revolutionary struggle against the established system with no holds barred and regardless of the immediate consequences for those engaged in it. This was tantamount to a radical *gesinnungsethisch* (moral fundamentalist) approach, which, though perhaps impracticable, was at least honest and straightforward.

In Weber's opinion there were no compromises possible between these two ultimately mutually exclusive strategies.

It goes without saying that, while Weber respected the second alternative as a plausible one for those who sincerely believed in socialist ideas, he himself was in favour of a reformist policy. Not surprisingly he sought to establish personal contacts with some leading 'revolutionists' like Eduard Bernstein or Karl Renner. When in 1907 Roberto Michels argued in an article to be published in the *Archiv für Sozialwissenschaft* that strikes were justified whether they were won or lost, thereby partially following Rosa Luxemburg's argument that revolutionary mass strikes were paving the way for the eventual triumph of the working class by increasing working-class consciousness, Weber objected sharply. He considered this attitude to be a crude piece of 'success ethics': 'Syndicalism is either an idle whim of intellectual romantics and something for undisciplined workers who are not willing to make any financial sacrifice or else a *Gesinnungsreligion* [religious conviction] which is justified even if it never provides an ideal for the future that is "attainable".'[8]

In other words, in Weber's opinion it was not possible to refute anarchism on scientific or ethical grounds. provided that those who sincerely believed in its tenets were fully prepared to act regardless of whether it might have disastrous consequences for themselves. While he did not think such a heroic stance to be sensible, and advocated instead an evolutionary strategy, he fully respected those who thought that a genuine revolutionary struggle for a society should be conducted under whatever circumstances.

Seen from this vantage-point the Social Democrats did the worst possible thing. They tried to avoid clear-cut decisions regarding the two policy options open to them. Instead they immersed themselves and their followers in a social-ist utopia, merely reiterating the traditional socialist liturgy according to which capitalism would meet its deserved death in due course, whatever happened, and that eventually socialism would triumph. In fact this amounted to a quietist policy masked by verbal radicalism and revolutionary rhetoric. This policy in effect forestalled any constitutional reforms in Imperial Germany, since under the prevailing circumstances the bourgeois parties felt obliged to unite against the Social Democrats. Weber pointed this out perhaps most effectively in his essay on the Russian Revolution of 1905, written in 1906:

There is not a trace of plausibility in the view that the economic development of society, as such, must nurture within it the development either of inwardly 'freer' personalities or of more 'altruistic' ideals. Do we find the slightest hint of anything of the sort in those who, in their opinion, are borne forward to inevitable victory by 'material develop-ment'? 'Correct' Social Democrats drill the masses to perform a sort of spiritual goose-step. Instead of directing them towards the otherworldly paradise (which in Puritanism *also* showed respectable achievements on behalf of this-worldly 'freedom'), they point them to the terrestrial paradise and thereby turn the Social Democratic Party into a sort of shot in the arm for the existing order. They accustom their followers to a submissive attitude towards dogmas and party authorities, in other words to indulgence in the fruitless play-acting of mass strikes or the idle enjoyment of the enervating howls of their hired journalists, which are as harmless as they are, in the end, laughable in the eyes of their enemies. In short they accustom them to a 'hysterical wallowing in emotion', which replaces and inhibits economic and political thought and action. The only plant which can grow on this infertile soil, once the 'eschatological' age of the movement has passed and generation after generation has vainly clenched its fists in its pockets or bared its teeth at heaven, is that of spiritual apathy.[9]

In his analysis of the role of the Mensheviks during the Russian Revolution of 1905, he inserted some very unfavourable asides about the German Social Democrats: 'Their need to hurl abuse (at their opponents) is . . . politically futile, and, more importantly still, it stifles all changes for the better which might bring about a configuration which would provide the opportunity to embark upon effective political action.'[10] Neither Bebel nor Rosa Luxemburg escaped Weber's scathing criticism; he flatly rejected the former's intelligence, while being sceptical about the latter's political judgement. At the meeting of the Verein für Sozialpolitik at Magdeburg in 1907 Weber summarized his diagnosis of the German Social Democrats as follows: 'The party has lost all the revolutionary energies which it formerly possessed. Instead it has taken to mere grumbling and complaining.'[11] From such a political party, motivated as it was above all by self-pity, the bourgeoisie had nothing to fear whatsoever.

In 1908 and 1909 Weber conducted an intensive debate with Roberto Michels about parties and party organizations, and in particular about the German Social Democratic Party. Michels, who was working at what was to become his famous book on 'modern political parties', bitterly criticized the Social Democratic Party for having become an oligarchic organization which had effectively departed from the democratic path altogether. Weber took a radically different line. He was not worried about the fact that the German Social Democratic Party was about to become a bureaucratic mass party much like the American party machines. In any case he thought it useless to criticize this development, which was apparently inevitable and irreversible, from the vantage-point of a fundamentalist position, as Michels had done.[12]

Referring to Ostrogorski's studies on the American political system, Weber predicted that the German Social Democratic Party would turn into a 'ganz kommune Parteimaschine' – an ordinary party machine – in the American sense of the term. It would no longer be a threat to the existing social order. In due course it was bound to become a pragmatic working-class party pursuing reformist policies. This assessment of the character of the Social Democratic Party in Imperial Germany was matched by contempt for bourgeois fears about the alleged 'Red Peril'. Instead, Weber pleaded again and again for the Social Democrats to be given a fair share of influence and power in the political arena, whether in local government, in the federal states or at the level of the Reich. He welcomed the participation of Social Democrats in local government. Likewise he wanted the trade unions to be acknowledged as equal partners of the entrepreneurs and as the legitimate representatives of the workers' interests in all matters regarding industrial relations. He strongly condemned section 153 of the *Reichsgewerbeordnung* (the German industrial and commercial legal code) which made any intimidation of strike breakers even of an entirely peaceful nature a legal offence. This was, in his view, 'ein Recht für alte Weiber', a law fit only for old women. Likewise he argued against the patriarchal rule of management in the large plants of heavy industry.[13] He would have nothing to do with the authoritarian attitude of many German entrepreneurs *vis-à-vis* their employees. He had much the same contempt for the unions which refused to affiliate and denied their solidarity with the rest.

Instead Weber pleaded strongly for a liberal system of industrial relations in which the trade unions would be free to fight for the economic and social interests of the workers as best they could, as was the case in Great Britain at the time. Neither did he favour any semi-official arbitration boards designed to forestall or restrain strikes. It was the duty of the state to provide for a fair legal framework within which the unions and the entrepreneurs could conduct their struggle about wages and working conditions from roughly equal starting positions and without outside interference. Weber considered that the official government policy of hampering the growth of trade-unionism wherever possible by all sorts of legal and administrative measures would greatly impede the development of harmonious industrial relations in an advanced industrial society like Imperial Germany.

Late in 1912 Weber was actively engaged in assembling a group of progressive academics interested in social reform.[14] He planned to launch a Socialpolitische Vereinigung outside the Verein für Socialpolitik, since the latter was dominated by conservative academics. This new association was to revive public interest in social reform and halt the tendency towards reducing or even scrapping parts of the social welfare system which had come into being in the last decades. However, this new venture did not get off the ground, largely because a personal rift developed between Max Weber and Lujo Brentano over the issue of whether Social Democrats should be asked to join this new academic association from the start or whether it should restrict itself for the time being to rallying support among bourgeois academics and politicians, as Weber thought advisable for purely tactical reasons. This was all the more regrettable since Weber had otherwise consistently denounced the discrimination against scholars holding socialist convictions as was practised by the German academic community and, in particular, by the government authorities. He had, notably in the case of Michels, privately and publicly demanded that the ban against the *Habilitation* (qualification for university teaching) of scholars of socialist conviction be lifted. He had also offered publication in the *Archiv für Sozialwissenschaft* to socialist scholars wherever possible, though with limited success, since there were so few of them prepared to publish in a bourgeois journal. All in all Weber's attitude was straightforward enough; he wanted Social Democrats to be treated on an equal basis in all spheres of public life, and certainly he would have welcomed a policy ranging 'from Bassermann to Bebel', as canvassed by Friedrich Naumann in 1913, namely, the formation of a parliamentary coalition of all progressive forces in German society ranging from the Social Democrats to the National Liberals.

After the outbreak of the First World War Weber became a staunch supporter of Reich Chancellor Bethmann Hollweg's policy of 'reorientation', which proposed even-handed co-operation with the Social Democrats and envisaged constitutional reforms which would satisfy the legitimate demands of the working classes, though only after the end of the war. He welcomed the loyal attitude of the Social Democrats who rallied behind the government and joined the other classes in a common war effort, on the assumption that this was a defensive war.

During the First World War Weber's views on the Social Democratic Party mellowed a great deal; he tended to view their policies in a far more positive light than before, undoubtedly influenced by their loyal support for the government headed by Bethmann Hollweg during the early years of the war. The policy of the Social Democrats, or at any rate a large majority of the party, was largely motivated by feelings of national loyalty, but also by the expectation that the working classes would eventually be able to reap the benefits of this co-operation and become accepted as an essential part of the body politic.

Weber was strongly in favour of a policy placing the Social Democrats on an equal footing with the other political parties rather than treating them as outcasts, as had been official policy right up to July 1914. He thought it necessary to strengthen the fragile partnership between the working classes and the government which had developed as a consequence of the momentous events of 4 August 1914. Comparatively early on he recognized that the official policy of 'reorientation' did not go far enough, holding out vague promises of concessions to the working classes after the war as a *quid pro quo* for loyalty in matters related to the war effort. By the spring of 1916 Weber became one of the most outspoken critics of the Prussian three-class system of suffrage, and he effectively supported the Social Democrats' increasingly insistent demands for immediate electoral reform. Weber's public campaign against the existing electoral system in Prussia culminated in an article in the *Frankfurter Zeitung* late in 1917 in which he argued that, whatever else happened, suffrage had to be given to the soldiers returning from the war, echoing similar arguments which led in Great Britain to the Electoral Act of 1918.[15] Part of Weber's argument, though for obvious tactical reasons this was not explicitly stated, was that the Social Democrats could not be expected to remain loyal to the government indefinitely if there were no immediate reform of the Prussian electoral system.

The second issue where Weber joined forces with the Social Democrats was his determined opposition to far-reaching annexationist policies. Unlike the Social Democrats he did not oppose annexations on principle – in eastern Europe he was in favour of establishing semi-autonomous nation-states under the loosely defined overlordship of Imperial Germany. But he agreed with the Social Democrats that the war should be conducted as a defensive war and should not be carried on even a single day longer for annexationist objectives. He also rejected the policy of unrestricted submarine warfare which the German government had been considering since March 1916 and eventually declared in January 1917, thereby provoking the United States to join the Allies as an active belligerent. In Weber's opinion the entry of the United States into the war ended all hopes for a speedy conclusion of a negotiated peace of whatever sort. He now no longer hesitated to co-operate directly with Social Democrats in order to counteract the extremist propaganda of the German Fatherland Party. On 5 November 1917 he spoke jointly with the Social Democratic deputy Wolfgang Heine – albeit a member of the right wing of the party – during a public rally in Munich, 'for a peace of conciliation and against the danger of Pan-Germanism'. This rally had originally been scheduled for July 1917.[16]

During the later years of the war Weber's confidence in the reliability of the Social Democrats in matters of national interest grew steadily. On the occasion of the Stockholm Peace Conference which had been called by the Second International in May 1917, Weber even considered whether he should personally offer his assistance to Scheidemann, who was to become the head of the German delegation. Eventually he suggested that Scheidemann be accompanied by Dr Gutmann, one of his Russian friends. Admittedly Weber thereby hoped to bring his view across that 'if the German Social Democrats were to conclude a bad peace we will have the reactionary rule of the Pan-Germans after the war, and they [i.e. the Social Democrats] will lose all influence.'[17]

This particular example reveals Weber's increasing concern that under the impact of the Russian February Revolution the Social Democrats might drift further and further to the left. His essays on the revolutionary events in Russia published in January and February 1918 were to a large extent addressed to the Social Democrats in an attempt to immunize them against the revolutionary slogans emanating from Petrograd. Weber eventually went so far as to argue that the Soviet regime was actually nothing more than a rather ordinary military dictatorship and that Russian imperialism would soon resurface once again. Weber strongly pleaded with the Social Democrats and the leaders of the free trade unions for them to remain loyal to the German national cause; he considered this a matter of national duty, however bad the situation might still become. He publicly condemned the mass strikes of April 1917, and even more so the strikes of January 1918, even though he was himself furious about the outrageous manner in which the peace negotiations at Brest-Litowsk had been conducted. On the other hand he had a great deal of sympathy for the strikers' motives. He even defended the conduct of the leaders of the Social Democratic Party when they joined the central strike committee in Berlin in January 1918, in defiance of the law. Although they thereby publicly demonstrated their solidarity with the strikers, which could be seen as a flagrant violation of the joint national war effort, they actually brought the strike to an end without fuelling further unrest among the working class. In these weeks Weber privately confided that revolution was likely to develop if the war was not brought rapidly to a close, especially since there was still no indication that the constitutional reforms which were so long overdue would be implemented in the near future; instead, the conservatives in the Prussian parliament continued to fight the electoral reform tooth and nail.

Weber was fully aware of how difficult it had now become – since the rifts in the Social Democratic Party had resulted in a breakaway of its left wing – for the leaders of the Majority Social Democrats to maintain their policy of national loyalty, faced as they were with the organized opposition of the Independent Social Democrats, even though the suffering of the working classes had become almost unbearable given the steadily deteriorating economic conditions.

The crucial test for Weber's views on the Social Democrats came, however, with the outbreak of the Revolution in November 1918. Weber's initial reaction was negative in the extreme; in a violent emotional outburst he called the revolution an 'irresponsible bloody carnival' which dealt a death blow to Germany's few remaining chances of still obtaining reasonable peace conditions. He added, not without an element of tactical reasoning, that the Revolution was bound to destroy any chance of introducing socialism for many decades to come. He was enraged at the utter chaos allegedly created by the workers' and soldiers' councils. Only when he eventually joined the Heidelberg Workers' and Soldiers' Council as a representative of the middle classes did he realize that most of its representatives were actually respectable people who were working for the common good! He also had nothing favourable to say about the Rat der Volksbeauftragten (Council of People's Delegates), even though he had nearly been appointed Secretary of State for the Interior. A little later he had briefly been considered for the post of German Ambassador to Vienna. Admittedly Weber reserved most of his criticism for the Independent Socialist members of the Rat der Volksbeauftragten, in particular Haase and Barth, but the Majority Social Democrats fared little better, largely because he considered their policies as catastrophic in view of the necessity of achieving a tolerable peace. It was only somewhat later that he began to restrain his polemics against the revolutionary government. By January 1919, after the Independent Social Democrats had left the revolutionary government, he was prepared to concede that, while the Independent Social Democrats were irresponsible demagogues or, at best, utopian romanticists harbouring revolutionary dreams of a just society free of all violence, the Majority Social Democrats were 'honest people' doing their best under difficult circumstances.

Already by December 1918 Max Weber had demanded publicly that the middle classes ought to join forces with the Social Democrats in order to create a new democratic order. He participated in the foundation of a new, decisively liberal party behind which the bourgeoisie was to rally in order to put an end to the Revolution and to establish a parliamentary democracy. He actively engaged in the preparations for founding a local liberal party organization in Frankfurt, and became engaged almost from the beginning in founding the German Democratic Party, the first initiative having been taken in early December 1918 by Theodor Wolff and some prominent liberals in Berlin, notable among them being his brother Alfred. In a widely publicized speech at a public rally in Frankfurt on 1 December 1918 Weber pleaded for the middle classes to shake off the political apathy to which they had succumbed in the initial stages of the Revolution, and to participate in establishing a new democratic order jointly with the Majority Social Democrats.[18] Under the circumstances wholehearted co-operation with the Majority Social Democrats appeared to be the only viable line of action for the liberals and, indeed, for the middle classes as a whole. He stated emphatically: 'All honest, unreservedly pacifist and radical bourgeois democrats and Social Democrats could work side by side for decades to come until their ways eventually might have to part again.'[19] He also declared, in somewhat ambiguous terms, that his own views were 'very close to, if not identical with, those of many academically trained members of the Social Democratic Party'.[20]

In the following weeks Weber became deeply involved in the electoral campaign of the German Democratic Party for the National Assembly. He spoke at more than twenty public rallies, mostly in southern Germany. Here he argued again and again that the German Democratic Party, and indeed all progressive sections of the bourgeois classes alike, ought to co-operate with the Majority Social Democrats in a joint effort to establish a stable democratic order. In this context he went so far as to suggest that some degree of nationalization of the means of production might be unavoidable under the circumstances. In principle, however, he always stuck to his conviction that only a dynamic capitalism could rescue the German economy from utter ruin. He opposed all concrete socialist measures, arguing that this would be detrimental to the chances for the establishment of socialism in the future. The half-hearted and ill-considered nationalization policies of the Council of People's Delegates he considered absolutely futile, since they would endanger the economic recovery that was so desperately needed; besides they were merely playing into the hands of the Allied powers, who would find it easier to extract reparations from state-owned, as opposed to privately owned, industries.[21] He denounced the policies of the Rat der Volksbeauftragten, somewhat tongue in cheek, as 'digging the grave of socialism' and jeopardizing any serious socialist politics in the foreseeable future.

Weber's belief in the fundamental superiority of dynamic capitalism became evident once again when the German Democratic Party invited him to represent them on the second Commission on Socialization, formed in 1920. Weber rejected this request with unusual harshness:

At all meetings, *everywhere*, both private and public, I have declared 'socialization', in the sense now understood, to be 'nonsense'. We are in need of entrepreneurs (like Herr Stinnes or others of his calibre). I have said about the Law on Factory Organization: 'Ecrasez l'infame.' *From the standpoint of the possible future of socialism it is disastrous*. Politicians should and *must* make compromises. But I am by profession a scholar. . . . The scholar dare not make compromises to cover up such 'nonsense'.[22]

This statement reveals a considerable degree of self-doubt about whether such a rigid stance was justified. As a consequence of this step, Weber left the German Democratic Party and withdrew entirely from active politics.

Yet there remained an element of ambiguity in his attitude. He would not tolerate socialization in any form, but this verdict did not necessarily include Social Democratic Party politics. There was something more than tactical reasoning behind his recurring, although always ultimately rejected, thoughts of joining the Social Democrats – namely, a sympathy, in principle, with their efforts to win a position of equality for the proletariat within existing society.[23] But he remained a passionate adherent of a revitalized capitalist market economy, and it was only within these limits that he was prepared to support Social Democratic Party politics. He was always a fair antagonist of the socialist movement. He had the greatest respect for those Social Democrats who fought honestly for their socialist cause, however wrong he considered it to be. In this respect Weber's attitude differed substantially from that of the great majority of his contemporaries in Imperial Germany.

6

Roberto Michels and Max Weber: Moral Conviction versus the Politics of Responsibility

Roberto Michels (or Robert, before he renamed himself on emigrating to Italy) occupies a special position among the contemporaries of Max Weber in the social sciences. It is impossible to classify him unequivocally under any single heading among the tendencies within the social sciences of his day. As David Beetham rightly emphasizes, his significance as a scholar must be sought primarily in his remarkable capacity to co-ordinate and combine divergent theoretical positions.[1] Throughout his life, he also played the role of a mediator between the German and Italian social sciences and, in a sense, between Germany and Italy in general. Born into an upper-bourgeois Cologne family in 1876, he formed a special relationship with France and Italy at an early stage in his development. Having obtained a doctorate in history under Johann Gustav Droysen at the University of Halle, he went on to pursue extensive studies in history and the social sciences in France and Italy, where he came into close contact with syndicalist circles and became personally acquainted with Georges Sorel and Arturo Labriola.[2]

At the age of twenty-four, Michels joined first the Italian Socialist Party and then the German Social Democratic Party, becoming actively involved in Marburg with a group of socialist intellectuals of markedly anarcho-syndicalist coloration. As someone who had become a socialist on grounds of ethical and moral conviction, he found himself more or less on the margins of the German Social Democratic Party. Almost from the beginning of his involvement in Social Democratic politics, he criticized it from the perspective of a political strategy with syndicalist leanings, which owed a great deal to his firsthand knowledge of conditions within the Italian Socialist Party. His membership of the Social Democratic Party proved an obstacle to his *Habilitation* (qualification for university teaching) in Marburg. When, a little later, in 1906, he made a renewed attempt to obtain his *Habilitation*, in Jena, he was debarred on the same grounds during preliminary negotiations. As a result, Michels emigrated in 1907 to Turin, where he finally got his *Habilitation* with Achille Loria. Though he considered Italy his second home and felt 'at heart' an Italian, in his scholarly interests he remained primarily oriented towards the German scientific community. In Turin, he did, however, become acquainted with Gaetano Mosca and later also with Vilfredo Pareto. The writings of both men were to have considerable influence on his own work.

We do not know when Max Weber and Robert Michels first met. The first letter we have from Weber to Michels dates from 1 January 1906 and in it Weber responds very positively to a 'projected piece of work' by Michels. This is probably a reference to an article on 'German Social Democracy' which was published in the *Archiv für Sozialwissenschaft und Sozialpolitik* in the same year.[3] That article, however, had been preceded by an essay on 'The proletariat and the bourgeoisie in the socialist movement in Italy', for which Weber's support had certainly not been lacking; indeed it seems possible to attribute its publication essentially to his initiative.[4] One way or another, from the spring of 1906 onward an extremely close relationship developed between Michels and Weber, which was not equalled for intimacy and intensity in the rest of Weber's life. Michels confirms this retrospectively in an obituary for Weber, written in 1920: 'The writer had the good fortune of enjoying a close friendship with Max Weber for many years of his life, which, however, at the beginning of the First World War suffered a shock from which it did not completely recover after the war had ended.'[5]

Between Weber and Michels there arose what I have described elsewhere as an 'asymmetrical partnership', the effects of which on the development of the work of Michels – and indeed of Weber – in the social sciences were considerable.[6] As Wilfried Röhrich has so appositely remarked, where Michels was concerned, Max Weber took on the role of a critically questioning mentor, lending support to him in his scientific work with constant advice and critical appraisal.[7] But the full scope of his interest in Michels went far beyond this, extending, indeed, into an existential dimension. In a certain sense, Max Weber saw in Michels the personification of a conduct according to the ethic of conviction and in this respect his own *alter ego* – someone who, from premises which were in many respects identical to his own, tended to draw moralist consequences which he, by his rigorous, rationalistic self-criticism (corresponding to the postulate of the ethic of responsibility) denied himself. It is not by chance that Weber's letters to Michels contain the most spontaneous and direct expressions of his views on political, scientific and personal problems that we possess.

From the material at our disposal – despite the occasional obliqueness of its references – we may conclude that Weber was principally interested in Michels the socialist, or more precisely in Michels as a conviction socialist and, particularly, as a syndicalist who possessed close contacts with both German and Italian social democrats. We know from other contexts of the efforts Weber made throughout his life to encourage socialists to participate in the *Archiv*, in his attempt to find possible ways of breaking the monopoly of bourgeois social science. The young Michels was optimally qualified to present the problems of socialism and social democracy in the *Archiv* as an 'insider', that is to say, from the standpoint of a committed partisan. The fact that Michels's socialism denied him access to an academic career in Germany may have provided an additional motivation for Weber's overtures to him and the interest Weber took in his work. Whether or not this was the case, Weber argued vigorously in Michels's favour in the ensuing years and sought, wherever possible, to smooth a path for him. The refusal of a professorial title to Michels gave Weber occasion publicly to charge the *Kaiserreich* with allowing 'freedom of scholarship' only within boundaries defined by the limits of courtly tolerance; this, he said, represented 'disgrace and ignominy for a cultured nation [*Kulturnation*]'.[8] It was Weber who recommended Michels to Achille Loria, also a former student of August Meitzen, for a *Habilitation* in Turin. More importantly, however, he did his best to open the doors of the *Archiv* to Michels; almost all the more significant of Michels's writings in subsequent years first appeared in the *Archiv für Sozialwissenschaft*, particularly those articles that were later to be presented in a unified form in his famous *Political Parties*, published in 1911. In addition, Weber made efforts to persuade Michels to participate in the work of the Verein für Sozialpolitik (Social Policy Association). He enlisted him as an author in the *Grundriss der Sozialökonomik* ('Outline of Social Economics'), of which he had been editor since 1909. As early as 1908, he also began to press for Michels to become a joint editor, with Jaffé, Sombart and himself, of the *Archiv für Sozialwissenschaft*, despite the fact that this might have necessitated his own withdrawal from the editorial board. Only in 1913 was this ambition realized; however, Michels's editorship then came to an abrupt end after the entry of Italy into the First World War, essentially on account of political differences. Despite a subsequent bitter quarrel over an article Michels had published in a Basle newspaper arguing that Italy's entry into the war on the side of the Allies was justified, Weber continued to defend Michels against criticism from other quarters.[9]

Throughout these years, Weber continued to nurture the greatest expectations of Michels as a scholar. Yet he was never blind to Michels's weaknesses, the most serious of which, in his view, was a tendency to publish prematurely work that was more of a journalistic than a scholarly character, in which his arguments had not yet been sufficiently thought through. Weber's greatest hope of Michels was that he might produce a 'cultural history of the modern proletarian movement' in its ideological or, in Weber's own terms, its 'world-view' aspects. He repeatedly urged him to concentrate his efforts on a great undertaking of this kind rather than dissipate his talents in the production of essays and articles on current political questions. He considered such an under-taking to be 'an immense task, for which, to my knowledge, *only you* in the whole wide world, are fitted'.[10] Later still, he extracted from Michels the prom-ise of an article for the *Grundriss der Sozialökonomik* on the socialist movement. Michels promised to tailor the contents to guidelines laid down by Weber, but the article did not see the light of day until after Weber's death. For his part, Michels provided Weber with numerous contacts in socialist circles; this was how the Dutch anarchist Nieuwenhuis, for example, came to write in the *Archiv*.

Roberto Michels's early works are concerned predominantly with the Ger-man and Italian socialist movements and, at the same time, with the role of the socialist trade unions. It was his perspective as an observer steeped in the ideas of western-European-style syndicalism that inclined Michels to view the German Social Democrats critically. An attendant factor in the judgements he passed on them was, however, his own ethics of conviction, which led him to identify with the proletarian movement and to regard it as a fruit on the tree of capital-ism, destined in the end to receive its inevitable inheritance. His essay on party membership and social composition in the German Social Democratic Party, which was published in the *Archiv* in 1906, already makes unequivocal refer-ence to the points on which he diverged from the predominant political current within the Social Democratic Party, one particular instance of which was his view on the relative distance between party and unions, which he saw as a major cause of the weakness of the Social Democrats in Imperial Germany. He con-cluded, however, on the optimistic note that 'the German proletariat, the Ger-man wage labourers' represented the 'well-spring' of the German Social Democratic Party, 'a well-spring that was far from exhausted as yet'.[11] However, Michels grew increasingly disillusioned with the quietistic course steered by the leadership of the Social Democratic Party, which was revolutionary only in its language – something incompatible with his ethics of conviction. Furthermore, his frustration mounted at the impotent and isolated position of intellectuals within the party, where they were treated with distrust and a general lack of appreciation. This rapidly led him towards an increasingly critical assessment of the German Social Democratic Party.

For Michels, the quietism and purely verbal radicalism of the party were to be ascribed primarily to its leaders; thus he became a sharp critic both of the Kautskyan strategy of 'revolutionizing minds' and of the pragmatism of the trade-union leaders, who wanted no truck with a politics of revolutionary struggle involving the active participation of the unions, and were particularly opposed to the strategy of the political 'mass strike'. It was in this context that the problem of the gradual alienation of the Social Democratic leaders from the mass of the workers first posed itself for Michels; their step-by-step transition from a proletarian to a petty-bourgeois existence, and the shifts of position in politics and world-view which this engendered, seemed to Michels to have played a major part in producing an ossification of the leadership and a quietist political strategy, which paid lip-service to the classic revolutionary goals of the party, but did not pursue them in practice. Michels concluded that petty-bourgeois modes of thought had got the upper hand in the party.

On this point, Michels's views were very close to those of Max Weber, who, from premises that were to some degree opposed, had arrived at essentially the same conclusion, namely that a petty-bourgeois mentality predominated within the German Social Democratic Party. It may be presumed that Weber and Michels discussed their differences on this question at great length, both in conversation and, from the evidence which we have to hand, also in writing. Certainly, Weber made plans to visit Michels in Rome in 1906 for the Italian Socialist Party Congress, where he hoped to attend the sessions as an observer. In the end, nothing came of the plan, which had arisen out of Weber's lively interest in the political situation in Italy. He did, however, attend the Social Democratic Party Congress in Mannheim in 1906, where he witnessed the famous Strategy Debate on the political role of the unions. The debate ended, in effect, in a fundamental renunciation of the concept of the political strike and a rejection of the idea of a politically aggressive role for the trade unions. To recall the relatively extensive account of the proceedings he gave to Michels

Mannheim was very depressing. I heard Bebel and Legien refer at least ten times to 'our *weakness*'. Furthermore, this extremely petty-bourgeois demeanour, all these complacent publicans' faces, the lack of dynamism and resolution, the inability to decide in favour of a 'rightist policy', as the way for a 'leftist policy' is blocked, or at least appears to be so.... These gentlemen don't frighten anyone any more.[12]

Michels's immediate reaction to this letter is not known, though there can be little doubt that he too held the party's 'petty-bourgeois demeanour' essentially responsible for its belief that the 'way for a "leftist policy" was blocked. In Michels's view, access could be gained to what he saw as a desirable leftward course for the party, if necessary by employing the weapon of the political mass strike. Weber, by contrast, took quite the opposite view, bemoaning the failure of the Social Democrats to respond to prevailing social conditions by openly adopting a coherent revisionist line in alliance with the Progressive Liberals.

Instead the Social Democrats seemed to prefer to act as a force of 'inoculation', whose function was to protect and sustain the existing, semi-constitutional political order.[13] In his essay 'The German Social Democratic movement in its international context', which was published a year later in the *Archiv*, Michels took the German socialists to task in no uncertain terms for their political strategy, which he found wanting above all by comparison with the other European socialist parties of the Second International.[14] He referred with obvious disapproval to the 'universal acclaim' accorded to 'the relegation of the weapon of the general strike', at the most recent party congress in Mannheim, 'to the furthest corner of the party lumber-room' and pointed out that, 'perhaps with the exception of the Danish party, the German Social Democratic Party is the only one remaining within international socialism whose policy excludes the tactic of the general strike, as indeed it excludes any form of direct action, even including peaceful street demonstrations. And yet this is precisely the party with the poorest prospects of even the slightest degree of success, as far as alternative strategies are concerned.'[15]

In a similar vein, he registered with some bitterness the absolute irresolution and quietism of the German Social Democrats in relation to the measures that might possibly be taken in the struggle to prevent a European war. In this context, he quoted extensively from the statements of numerous socialist leaders from other parties. The conclusions he then drew on the state of the Social Democratic Party in many respects foreshadow the critique which today goes by the name of 'secondary integration'. For Michels, the condition of total impotence in which the German Social Democratic Party found itself had arisen not simply in spite of but indeed precisely because of its remarkably high level of organization. Although purportedly anticipating revolution, it could no longer claim to be a revolutionary party. Its 'purely verbal revolutionism, which lives in constant anticipation of the automatic catastrophe', was not matched by any will to revolutionary action. 'It is a characteristic feature of German Social Democracy that it assembles under its single umbrella the most flagrant of contradictions: revolutionary intransigence at election-time is ranged against the anti-revolutionary quietism of its general posture; high-sounding phraseology in its theory sits alongside a resigned compliance in its practice; its language is that of inflammatory prophecy, yet in its actions it is almost totally paralysed.'[16]

As far as their diagnosis of the condition of the German Social Democratic Party was concerned, Michels and Weber appear at this stage to have belonged more or less in the same camp. Both deplored the quietism of the Social Democrats' political strategy, bound up as it was with a purely verbal radicalism, whose ultimate goal was a mental disciplining of the masses and in which there was no place for the will to concrete political action. And Weber saw just as

clearly as Michels (who was possibly the first to bring the subject to his attention) that qualitative changes in the party's political strategy – among other
things, a weakening of its revolutionary *élan* – had been brought about by its
advancing bureaucratization. At the same time, he did point out to Michels that
this was a universal phenomenon, valid even for bourgeois parties; he referred
him in this context to studies by James Bryce and Maurice Ostrogorski on
American political parties.

Max Weber and Roberto Michels did, however, draw very different conclusions from their common diagnosis of the situation. Weber considered the process of bureaucratization in modern mass parties to be irreversible; what is
more, in the specific case of the Social Democratic Party, he did not particularly
disapprove of its effects. Quite the contrary, in fact, for he saw the increasing
bureaucratization of the Social Democratic Party as a guarantee against any
serious danger of revolutionary activity from that quarter. In the contemporary
context, he judged the bourgeois fear of the much-invoked 'Red Peril' to be
completely without foundation. It was during the debates of the Verein für
Sozialpolitik at Magdeburg in the autumn of 1907 that Weber expounded these
views, putting renewed emphasis on the disappearance from the party of any
will for revolutionary action – indeed, even for constructive reformist politics.
His statements were entirely in line with Michels's position; indeed, Weber
borrowed a number of Michels's own formulations. The German Social Democratic Party, said Weber, 'is today clearly in the process of transforming itself
into an enormous bureaucratic machine'. The long-term price of that transformation would, he maintained, inevitably be paid by those elements within the
party who were the bearers of 'revolutionary ideologies'. At the same time, he
denounced the 'petty-bourgeois physiognomy' of the Social Democrats, who
had, as he saw it, put 'lame, bombastically griping and grumbling debate into
the place of the Catilinarian energies of faith to which we have hitherto been
accustomed'.[17] This caustic use of public polemic was, however, too much for
Michels. Evidence of his vigorous letter of protest to Weber may be gleaned
from Weber's reply of 6 November 1907, which is all that remains of the
exchange. Weber's deliberations on the subject in this context are presented in a
mode that was very charactistically his own. He sets out the arguments both
from his own value-position and from the value-position which he assumes
would be adopted by the 'syndicalist' and partisan of the proletariat, Michels:

The crazy idea that a class party with alleged class ideals could ever become anything
other than a 'machine', in the American sense of the term, is the key issue. Therefore I
preach to my peers: 'you fools, the Social Democratic Party, whether parliamentary or
syndicalist, is not, and never will be, anything worse (from *your* point of view) than a
quite ordinary party machine.' As far as you are concerned, the conclusion would have

to be: *political* democratization is the only thing that is perhaps attainable in the foresee-able future, but this is not so insignificant an achievement. I cannot prevent you from believing that more is possible, neither can I force myself to do so.[18]

Disregarding the shared premise that both started out from, namely, a common perception of the absence of any propensity for revolutionary action in a German Social Democratic movement, whose radicalism was purely verbal, Weber here confronts central points of dissension between Michels and him-self. Michels was convinced in principle that a syndicalist strike strategy could gradually undermine the existing system, and that it could ultimately bring about the victory of the socialist movement. For his part, Weber respected Michels's view, but demanded that it be regarded as a position to be justified on grounds of ethical conviction, rather than as a realistic strategy that might expect to meet with concrete success in empirical reality. And when Michels declared his sympathy for the spontaneous revolutionary mass strike, a strategy that was being propagated at the time by Karl Liebknecht and Rosa Luxemburg and which he regarded both as a weapon of attrition to be employed against the existing social order and as a means of developing the revolutionary conscious-ness of the workers, Weber opposed him with some vigour:

It cannot possibly have escaped you that a *very* considerable proportion of all strikes (such as the defeated Hamburg dockers' strike) achieve the opposite of their desired effect, not only in the unions (this you would not mind) but as regards every kind of progress within the working-class movement, which they set back by years if not by decades. Their effect is exactly the opposite of what must be desired by anybody who measures the value of a strike by its contribution to the advance of 'socialization' or to the unification of the proletariat as a class or to whatever (provisional) socialist 'goals' you like. It is the most bizarre assertion that can ever be made to say, in the light of these experiences, that every strike works in the direction postulated by socialism, *ergo*, *every* strike is justified. And then there is this measuring of 'morality' by 'success'. Have you totally forgotten your Cohen? Surely he must have succeeded in curing you of *this* at least. Most particularly in curing Michels the *syndicalist*. The syndicalist M[ichels] ought to (is indeed compelled to) view the *conviction* which motivates a strike as 'proper' *in every case*; it is *patriotic* (patriotic to the class) – *ergo*, and so on. Yet what weakness is dis-played in this obsequious courting of success! And in this violation of the facts before you![16]

Michels, for his part, was in no way inclined at this stage simply to abjure his fundamentalist conception of democratic rule, which, though it owed much to Rousseau's idea of direct democracy, was also strongly influenced by anarchistic ideas of a society free from domination; neither was he prepared, as an alterna-tive, to embrace the pragmatic concept of democracy advocated by Weber. On the contrary, he continued to attribute the Social Democrats' unwillingness to engage in revolutionary action under the conditions of the Wilhelmine semi-constitutional system chiefly to a corruption of the revolutionary impulses that were proper to the proletariat as a class. Their leaders, he claimed, had led them into quietism and a thoroughgoing accommodation to the existing political system; that corruption stemmed from a progressive bureaucratization, and indeed from an oligarchization of the party's leading cadres. In the forefront of this process, as Michels saw it, was the steadily increasing distance of the leaders from what we would today call 'the grass roots'. What was more, he claimed, the leaders had sought to preserve their own positions through a gradual usurpation of power. The developing bureaucratic apparatuses had revealed themselves as wholly appropriate instruments for the attainment of this goal; at the same time, they themselves produced a further distancing of the leadership from the masses and from the proletarian milieu in general. Conversely, Michels also identified a need among the masses to subject themselves willingly to the leaders once these had been elected. As he saw it, all these factors together had caused the internal party process whereby opinions and conceptions were formed merely to degenerate into a struggle for supremacy among a small leadership elite, who used demagogic techniques to form and influence opinion among the mass of the membership.

The source of Michels's ideas in this context was Gaetano Mosca's theory of the 'political class', that class which holds political power in its hands once and for all. He also drew upon Vilfredo Pareto's theory of the 'cyclical succession of political elites', although he did not allow it to undermine his own radical-democratic position. The first cogent formulation of such ideas by Michels occurs in an essay on 'The oligarchic tendencies in society', which was published in the *Archiv* in the spring of 1908.[20] Most of the key terms, which make up the core of the book that he was to publish some three years later, *Political Parties* (*Zur Soziologie des Parteiwesens in der modernen Demokratie*), are to be found in this essay. Since, however, Mosca and Pareto were still expressly characterized as anti-democratic thinkers, Michels avoided any possibility of directly identifying his ideas with theirs.

Michels's and Weber's perceptions of the empirical facts regarding the Social Democratic Party overlap considerably; their interpretations, however, are diametrically opposed. To illustrate the asymmetrical relationship between their positions, in what follows two themes will be extracted somewhat arbitrarily from Michels's work which also play a central role in the work of Max Weber, although they do so in a characteristically modified form. These are, first, the role of bureaucracy as a means of 'self-defence', in other words, as an instrument for the stabilization of the rule of the 'political class' and, secondly, the interpretation of the relationship between the rulers and the 'ruled' as a relationship of domination.[21] There can have been no doubt how these two phenomena would be evaluated within Michels's political value-system; in his view, both tendencies were to be thoroughly deplored. It was his hope that to demonstrate simply the ways of their functioning might bring about an improvement in the situation they produced. Yet in no sense was he prepared to call into question the criteria by which he sought to assess modern society, and the socialist parties in particular, which he considered to be the true standard-bearers of the egalitarian idea and democracy. In particular, he did not wish to question the ideal of a democracy, which should be a direct democracy to the highest possible degree and immune from corruption by either power-seeking strata of representatives or oligarchies of leaders, an ideal that was very much alive in the anarchist tradition. He did, however, indicate that such an ideal was valid only as a yardstick against which reality could be measured; it was not to be regarded as a realizable postulate.

Max Weber's reaction to this line of argument was at once positive and extremely critical. He was convinced that Michels's radical-democratic perspective, which remained oriented towards the ideal of a more or less egalitarian democratic society of a socialist type organized along syndicalist lines, would inevitably come to grief when confronted with reality. He did not, however, in any sense deny the validity of Michels's perspective from the viewpoint of an ethic of conviction. Indeed, he showed great interest in it, though more as a thought experiment than anything else. In his response to Michels, he reiterates his belief that it is possible to sustain two antithetical perspectives – the one pragmatic and realist, the other moralistic – on the postulate of the realizability of a perfect socialist democracy even though the ultimate consequences of each display far-reaching discrepancies:

Your last piece of work in the *Archiv* is, however, considered *very* important by the people here; it has been mentioned to me in a number of different contexts. I found it thoroughly correct and commendable in its critical sections. But how much more resignation will you still have to put up with? Concepts such as 'popular will' and genuine will of the people do not exist for me any more. They are fictions. The same difficulties would present themselves if you tried to talk about a 'will of the shoe consumers' which was to determine the way the cobbler was to apply his skills. There are two possibilities. . . . Either

1　'My kingdom is not of this world' (Tolstoy) or syndicalism *taken to its logical conclusion*, which amounts to *nothing more than* the proposition that 'the ultimate goal is nothing, the movement everything' . . . a syndicalism which (of course) *you yourself* have not thought through to its conclusion! – or:
2　An *affirmation* of culture (i.e. culture that expresses itself objectively, in technical – or other – achievements) which goes hand in hand with an accommodation to the social

conditions underlying *all* 'techniques', be they economic, political or whatever (all of which would find their *most highly developed expression* precisely in collectivist societies).

In the latter case, all talk of 'revolution' is a farce. Any notion of abolishing the domination of man over man by whatever sort of socialist system or by however attenuated forms of 'democracy' is utopian. Your own critique in this matter does not by any means go far enough. The moment anyone who wishes to live as a 'modern individual', in the sense of having a newspaper every day and railways, electrical goods, etc., abandons the course of revolutionism *for its own sake*, that is, revolutionism without any goal, indeed revolutionism for which no goal is even *conceivable*, he necessarily *renounces* all those ideals which float before *your* eyes. You are a thoroughly honest chap and will yourself – as the [sober] sections of your article show – carry through the process of critical reflection which long ago brought me round to this way of thinking and stamped me, by virtue of that reflection, as a 'bourgeois' politician, at least for as long as the little that one *can* desire does not recede beyond the horizon.[22]

In the course of the following two years, Michels further elaborated the conceptions that he had begun to develop in his articles on the Social Democrats, and had first presented systematically in his essay, 'The oligarchical tendencies in society'. The piecemeal arguments developed there were now set down in coherent fashion in his *Political Parties*, the first edition of which was published in 1911.[23] Although we have only limited concrete evidence of his continuing discussions with Max Weber, they cannot have been without consequence for his work in this period. Michels himself expressly acknowledged Weber's influence in the preface to the second edition and, indeed, dedicated the first edition to him.[24] Michels complied only to a very limited extent with Weber's insistence that he should extend the basis of his analyses of modern parties by incorporating the available research on bourgeois parties; he did, however, in the more general sections of the book, take Ostrogorski's works on the subject into account. And he was clearly prepared to acknowledge, to a much greater extent than in 1908, the utopian status of that total direct democracy which had originally served as his normative guideline and which he had also judged to be a desirable form for the process of the formation of ideas within the party. He no longer regarded classical anarchism, which rejected on principle any form of centralization of power – including, of course, the formation of parties – as a logically imperative theoretical position.[25] In essence, however, his ultimate conclusion remained that of 1908. The conclusion to be drawn from his work, he claimed, was the practical maxim of continued struggle against the party system's structurally conditioned tendency towards the formation of oligarchies and, more generally, against all forms of domination.[26] The critical analysis of the 'deficiencies of democracy' presented by Michels aimed, by providing 'a clear and unembellished insight into the oligarchic dangers of democracy, if not to be in a position to prevent these altogether, then at least to be able to reduce them'.[27] For Michels, democracy still remained the 'lesser evil' by comparison with other forms of rule in general, and with pure aristocracy (as the classical form of oligarchic power) in particular.[28] Michels's critique of the democratic party system was not yet a product of right-wing thinking but of a radical-democratic position, which had its principal intellectual roots in the anarcho-syndicalist doctrine of a society completely free from domination. But contrary tendencies have a habit of coinciding in history, and indeed this is how things were to turn out in Michels's case.

When Roberto Michels dedicated his *Political Parties* to Max Weber, he did so in part in recognition of the many years of support he had received; in part, too, he was expressing his gratitude for the numerous suggestions and clarifications provided by Weber, largely during the period in which he wrote the numerous articles that formed the basis of the book. Weber's reaction to the work was by no means uncritical. He criticized it on a series of crucial points of detail, one of which was the concept of power (*Herrschaft*) employed by Michels. For one thing, he argued, the use of the concept was ambiguous; further, Michels had failed to recognize that all forms of social relations – even the most personal – were, in a sense, power relations (*Herrschaftsbeziehungen*).[29] The core of his interpretation may be viewed as diametrically opposed to Michels's roots in anarcho-syndicalism, in so far as Weber declared the idea of a social order free from domination – whatever form this may take – to be inconceivable. His criticism here runs along much the same lines as his earlier critique of Michels's position, which had condemned it as resting on idealist postulates that must necessarily come to grief when confronted with empirical reality.

Michels's arguments did, however, converge with Weber's own views on a number of central points: for example, in his emphasis upon advancing bureaucratization and its consequences for political parties and, by extension, for the formation of political objectives in general. The two authors were at their closest in their views on the function of political leaders, whose demagogic capabilities, directly corresponding to the masses' need for leadership (which Weber termed their 'submissiveness' (*Fügsamkeit*)), effect the submission of the masses to the system of domination. Weber's emphatic insistence that, in any political system, political decisions always rest in the hands of a few leading personalities is well known. The 'principle of the small number, that is, the superior political manœuvrability of *small* leading groups, always governs political action.'[30] His entire sociology of domination revolves around the question of the circumstances and the constitutional conditions that guarantee an optimum of capable political leadership. Weber's main argument for the parliamentarization of the constitution of Imperial Germany was that, in the pre-vailing circumstances, the parliamentary system represented the best possible way of selecting political leaders of proven ability. And, in the early stages of the Weimar Republic, his political demands culminated in a call for a 'leader democracy with a "machine"', as an alternative to the 'leaderless democracy' whose restoration in the course of 1919 seemed imminent despite all revolu-tionary changes.[31]

It would seem reasonable to raise the question whether Max Weber does not, at this point, display an affinity – if not in form then at least in content – both with Gaetano Mosca's theory of a 'political class' that has definitively taken over the role of political leadership and, more particularly, with Pareto's theory of the circulation of political elites. One might even take the view that Schum-peter's well-known theory of democracy, which he views as a competitive struggle between political leaders for the allegiance of the masses, and therefore for power, represents a logical extension of Max Weber's democracy theory as it might be developed from the standpoint of Pareto's circulation theory. There can be no doubt that Michels drew Weber's attention both directly and indirectly to the works of Mosca and Pareto. Already in his early article, 'Oligarchic tendencies in modern society', both authors are quoted extensively, and it is difficult to imagine that their theories played no part in the numerous conversations between Michels and Weber, whether in Heidelberg or Turin, even though, as far as I can ascertain, Mosca and Pareto are nowhere mentioned in the parts of the correspondence we possess. (Guilhelmo Ferrero, whom Weber considered insignificant and second-rate by comparison with Theodor Mommsen, is the only name occasionally mentioned.[32]) One looks in vain, however, for any explicit reference to the theories of Mosca or Pareto in Weber's work.

What does, however, emerge quite clearly from the comparison between Michels and Weber is the more or less absolute opposition between their inter-pretations of the empiricial material that formed the basis of Michels's *Political Parties*. Michels evaluated his material from a democratic fundamentalist stand-point, which regarded the principles of equality and popular sovereignty at the very least as binding value-standards for scientific judgement, though not always as maxims for political action. Weber, by contrast, increasingly came to judge the issues at stake primarily in terms of the questions of how effective political action (and, for him, this in practice meant effective political leader-ship) might be possible. He continued to hold all types of conviction politics (*Gesinnungspolitik*) in the highest regard, including the syndicalist variety so prominently expounded by Michels. (He did himself constantly feel tempted to let himself be swayed by a 'conviction ethic' rather than to maintain the sober rein on his own passions that his 'ethic of responsibility' demanded.) For Weber, however, such moralist politics remained unrealistic – even utopian – in the circumstances of the time.

It is not possible, within the limited scope of this chapter, to give a full exposition of this question here. We shall therefore restrict ourselves to two examples. In Roberto Michels's view, it was, first, demonstrably the case that the bureaucratization of parties and of the political system in general had, as a necessary consequence, resulted in a diminution in the quality of political leaders. In the first instance, he saw this simply as an effect of an increasing distance between the leaders and their own party membership, though it also resulted from an inevitable tendency among leaders to make the preservation of their own status their dominant political goal. Hence the vehemence of his declaration that 'the beginning of the formation of professional leadership' was to be seen as 'the beginning of the end of democracy'.[33] Max Weber, as we know, drew very different conclusions from the evidence of an increasing bureaucratization within modern parties. Not only did he consider the trend towards 'plebiscitarian democracy', which inevitably involved a substantial enhancement of the role of political leaders at the expense of the 'ruled', to be irreversible; he saw it also as a positive development, in that it served as a counterweight to the bureaucratization of the apparatuses of power.

Similarly, Weber viewed as fundamentally positive both the replacement of the older parties of notables by modern, bureaucratically organized mass parties and, with them, the rise of the professional politician who, of course, lives from politics, but also lives for politics. Particularly in the German political context of his day, he welcomed the demise of the older type of *Weltanschauungspartei* (ideology-oriented party) and its replacement by professionally led political parties, since only the latter appeared to have 'a chance of ever acquiring effective political power within the Wilhelmine political system'. From this point of view, the progressive discarding of a revolutionary programme within the Social Democratic Party, and its replacement by a realistic pragmatic policy involving a commitment to reforms in response to specific current problems, seemed to him a further positive development. Weber tended, to an extent, to judge the process of oligarchization identified by Michels within the Social Democratic Party – and within political parties in general – as part of a universal process of rationalization that extended to all spheres of life; in the medium term, he was inclined to emphasize the positive effects of this process, rather than the ultimate consequences it entailed for the liberal societies of the West.

In Weber's sociology of political parties (first formulated, at this stage in largely unsystematic form, in the years 1912–13) there is, however, evidence that he was by no means deaf to the objections raised by Michels over the question of the bureaucratization of parties.[34] To the extent that bureaucratization and the attendant trend towards plebiscitarian democracy afforded the leaders in the upper echelons of modern parties far greater practical chances of success in transforming political reality, Weber certainly welcomed both developments; on the other hand, he was equally aware of the danger that progressive bureaucratization might stifle political leadership altogether. Yet, rather than merely bemoaning the creeping growth of bureaucracy in the organization of power, Weber aspired towards a combination of the two opposing principles of charismatic leadership and bureaucratic organization, which he hoped would optimize the power of the party leadership to shape and form society. The power base of the great politicians, whose personal charisma made leadership their 'calling', was, he argued, independent and personal-plebiscitarian in nature; equipped with a bureaucratic organization, they would be able to realize their goals all the more effectively. This view finds paradigmatic expression in Weber's famous statement in 'Politics as a vocation': 'There is only the choice between leader democracy with a "machine" and leaderless democracy, that is to say, the rule of professional politicians without a vocation, i.e. without the inner charismatic qualities that make a leader.'[35] Weber's argument here displays parallels with the theory that he first developed systematically in his outline of the basic categories of social organization, in which modern plebiscitarian democracy is regarded as an anti-authoritarian variant of charismatic domination.[36] This later work marks a shift away from his own earlier interpretation of democratic rule as a value-rational variant of legal domination and towards a more strictly elitist or – if we may call it such – an 'aristocratic' conception of democratic rule. On the basis of observations of the party system and the transformations of the democratic system in the prevailing conditions of the twentieth century – observations which, to a great extent, he shared with Michels – Weber thus ultimately finds himself consigning the principle of popular sovereignty once and for all to the realm of mere fiction.

It appears perhaps only superficially paradoxical not only that Roberto Michels's subsequent development should have led him along the same road as Weber, but that it in fact took him a good deal further. It may indeed be impermissible to reduce an issue of such extraordinary complexity to a simplifying formula of this kind. The issue to which we are referring is, of course, Michels's conversion to Italian fascism, which involved an almost complete reversal of his political value-system. In chronological terms, Michels's conversion took place after the beginning of the First World War and thus lies outside the period in which it is possible to talk of the relationship between Weber and Michels as an 'asymmetrical partnership'. Michels's conversion would possibly, indeed almost certainly, have made irreversible the break between the two men, which had begun to heal somewhat after the end of the war. Yet there is a connection to be made with Weber, if only an indirect one, in so far as Michels justified his decision to support Mussolini and the Italian fascist *Führerstaat* by express reference to Max Weber.[37] Among other things, Michels was able to invoke Weber's explicit claim that the emotional attachment of the broad masses to the leader constitutes the specific characteristic of charismatic authority, and that the leader determines the content of policy on his own ultimate authority alone, while the assent of his supporters resides purely in their trust in the leader's charismatic leadership qualities as such, rather than in their concurrence with the particular objectives he lays down. For Weber, 'plebiscitarian democracy', which he views as the most significant among the forms of leader democracy, 'is, in its genuine sense, a type of charismatic domination which is concealed behind a type of a legitimacy formally derived from the will of the ruled and as a result of that will. The leader (demagogue) rules, in fact, by virtue of the devotion of his followers and their faith in him as a *person*.'[38] As I have demonstrated elsewhere, such a conception of democratic rule, according to which the 'recognition' of the leader's qualities by his followers to a large extent takes on a formal quality, yet is at the same time expressly claimed to be essential in principle, was certainly by no means immune from possible reinterpretation along anti-democratic lines.[39]

The perpetuation of an element of 'recognition by the ruled' in the form of democratic elections, already formalized to an excessive degree in Weber, was declared by Michels, as it was by Carl Schmitt, to be dispensable. That recognition could, Michels argued, find equally adequate expression in forms other than democratic elections within a constitutional parliamentary system. More precisely, it could, he said, be much more directly articulated in the form of popular acclamation than could ever be possible within a system of parliamentary representation. Indeed, Michels went so far as to characterize the former type of 'recognition' of the leader as imperfect and impure:

under charismatic leadership, the masses delegate their will in conscious admiration and veneration of the leader, in a form which appears almost as an unquestioned and voluntary sacrifice. In democracy, by contrast, the maintenance of the act of delegation of the will sustains the appearance of a will which remains potentially in the hands of those who delegate it to their elected leaders.[40]

Pushing to its radical ends a reasoning which Weber had already elaborated in rudimentary form, in so far as he held that charismatic leaders do not simply consider themselves 'the electors' mandatory', but rather create their following by virtue of their own specific demagogic qualities, Michels came to the conclusion that true political consensus could only be achieved through the elimination of the election of parliamentary representatives, since such an election constituted an act of falsification of the popular will. Weber's theory of charismatic leaders who attract a following outside the sphere of parliament and parties by virtue of their personal demagogic capacities could be adapted with relative ease to suit Michels's ends: 'Charismatic leaders . . . make themselves masters of the body politic independently of, or even contrary to, the traditional methods of conferring the authority of the state upon individuals. . . . Their power rests on the worship which their personality inspires and is circumscribed by it.'[41] This was the line of argument that led Michels in the end to defend the rule of Mussolini expressly by referring to the 'tipologia politica di Max Weber, il saggio di Eidelberga'.[42] Analogously, at the same time he cast doubt on the possibility of considering the principle of the 'selection of leaders' – a principle much vaunted by Weber – to be a 'specific characteristic' of democracy alone. It should rather be interpreted, he maintained, in the light of Pareto's theory of the circulation of elites. The principle according to which the leaders 'never gave way to the masses, but only ever to other new leaders' seemed to him fundamentally valid for all political systems; there was nothing exceptional in this regard about parliamentary democracy.[43]

It would, of course, clearly be inappropriate to attribute Michels's shift towards fascism even indirectly to Max Weber's influence. At the very most, Michels might be seen to have taken just a shade too literally Weber's advice on the necessity for him to take stock of reality and revise the convictions of his fundamentalist conception of democracy. Yet indications of an inclination towards proto-fascist ideas are to be found at a relatively early date in Michels's work, for example in his 1908 article 'Homo Oeconomicus and co-operation', where Michels declares that 'the age of individualism in the economic sphere' is today to be regarded as 'definitively at an end'.[44] In his view, forms of co-operative organization of economic activity were advancing to replace individualism on all fronts. Taking co-operative organization as the lowest common denominator, he was able to produce that hypothesis through a sweeping amalgamation of the socialist movement of worker co-operatives in both production and distribution with the co-operative societies of the lower middle classes and the prevailing tendencies towards the formation of trusts and cartels, within which he saw private capital as being transformed into 'social or impersonal capital'.[45] The signs of the time pointed, he maintained, towards a continuing transformation of the existing system of market-oriented competitive capitalism, and towards a growth in the 'co-operative organization of social production to the exclusion of free competition'.[46] In other words, in predicting the rise of a 'corporatively organized capitalism', Michels's work may be seen in a certain sense to foreshadow the idea of a corporate state, which was later to be propagated by Italian fascism. The advance of what he called 'co-operative' forms of social organization (we might equally term them 'corporative' forms) seemed to Michels to have deprived the Marxist theory of classes of much of its interpretative power; above all, since 'the tendency to form oligarchies reveals itself in that class with exactly the same vigour as in all the other classes of society', the mass movement of socialism seemed to him inevitably doomed to founder.[47]

Michels's work on co-operative organization certainly offers numerous points of departure for his later defection to the fascist camp, with its promise of a future society where producers would live together in relative harmony under the aegis of the openly oligarchic rule of charismatic leaders, a society in which the historical contradiction between labour and capital would increasingly lose all meaning. In this sense, his relationship with Max Weber can in no way be seen as the sole cause of that defection. We may note also that Max Weber, not surprisingly, found this very essay on 'Co-operation' superficial and vague and did not hesitate, even though he was perfectly aware of Michels's sensitivity to criticism of too direct a nature, to write to Michels in all frankness that, 'as a scholarly essay', it had been decidely below his 'usual standards', since 'it was vague, sidestepped a number of issues and failed to clarify any problem'.[48]

Although Michels had already left both the Italian Socialist Party and the German Social Democratic Party by 1907, we should none the less avoid dating his renunciation of socialism and of his radical-democratic standpoint too early (as Röhrich in particular is inclined to do). In Michels's article on August Bebel, which was published in the *Archiv für Sozialwissenschaft* in 1913, he still shows a substantial degree of sympathy with the socialist workers' movement.[49] Although his enthusiasm for Bebel had clearly waned by comparison with earlier years, he still saw in him the genuine representative of the wishes of the proletarian working class of Germany.[50] In this context, he referred, among other things, to the opinion expressed by Bebel that those elements 'who attacked him as an opportunist, and rallied to the standard of radicalism, or even of anarchism, within the party', most usually 'tended suddenly to re-emerge a short while later on the most extreme right wing of Social Democracy, if not indeed within the bourgeois camp'.[51] In a sense, Michels himself fell victim to the same fate. The ultimate reasons for Michels's political transformation lie outside the field of the present study, since I am concerned here only with an interpretation of his work in its relation to Max Weber. However, a twofold observation may appear in place here. On the one hand, Michels's biography serves as an example of the political dangers inherent in an adoption of political positions on the grounds of conviction alone. We may also conclude, on the other hand, that the same danger emerged to a certain extent from Max Weber's all too radical formalization of the substance of democratic rule, as it appears, for example, in his sociology of domination; it was for this reason that Michels could, after all, continue to consider himself a disciple of Max Weber even after he had become an apologist for Italian fascism.

PART III

The Development of Max Weber's Theoretical Ideas

7

Max Weber on Bureaucracy and Bureaucratization: Threat to Liberty and Instrument of Creative Action

The analysis of social consequences of bureaucratization was one of Max Weber's main preoccupations throughout his scholarly work. His famous essay on *The Protestant Ethic and the Spirit of Capitalism*, probably the best known of his works in the English-speaking world, ends with an almost apocalyptic vision of the eventual 'mechanized petrification' of Western individualistic societies, directly inspired by Nietzsche's Zarathustra.[1] For capitalism, despite its origins in religious world-views (*Weltbilder*) of a specific individualistic character, appeared to him to be inevitably allied to the forces of rationalization and bureaucratization, and, if not inhibited by counter-forces of some sort or another, might well end in the creation of a completely ossified social order in which there would no longer be any room for individual initiative, let alone a sophisticated personal culture like the one which developed in the West. Weber's thinking was dominated by the problems likely to be generated by this secular process of bureaucratization which he observed to be proceeding, at least for the time being, with irresistible force on all social levels. He considered capitalism and bureaucratization to be the two genuine revolutionary forces of the present age, which would gradually replace all traditional forms of social organization throughout the world, albeit with varying speeds and different patterns. Capitalism and bureaucratization were, in his opinion, the main promoters of the secular process of rationalization which, even though it was perhaps not irreversible, was obviously the dominant trend of our time.

This observation would appear to be corroborated by the history of the great world religions. Almost without exception, an evolutionary process can be discerned from primarily magic or charismatic forms of religious belief, which are specifically 'otherworldly', to progressively routinized as well as institutionalized forms of religious activity less and less at variance with secular reality. Eventually, not just in the case of the 'Protestant ethic' but everywhere else too, religious world-views became dispensable inasmuch as their influence on the social conduct of the people in everyday life tended to weaken, while institutional forces and material interests increasingly determined their actions and intellectual outlook. These ideas about the inevitable routinization and formal rationalization of all religious world-views were embedded in a specific notion of the course of universal history. This notion provides the background to Weber's elaborate attempts to assess correctly the nature and functioning of bureaucracies, both past and present, on the various levels of societal life, notably within the political and economic spheres, but also in the cultural and educational sub-systems of advanced industrial societies. However, Weber was not just a passionate adversary of bureaucracy, as can be said of many critics of modern civilization, all of whom were influenced in some way or another by Nietzsche's incisive condemnation of modernity as the beginning of the end of humanity and individual greatness. On the contrary, Weber thought it naïve to assume that under the conditions of modernity one might simply opt for an alternative sort of non-bureaucratic society, particularly if the likely consequences of such a line of action were rationally taken into account. In his view, there was no room for alternative ways of life. Weber did not think it at all possible to sustain the level of civilization and culture reached in modern industrial societies without widespread recourse to the bureaucratic techniques of social organization. A mere negation of bureaucratization and its concomitant phenomena, in particular industrial capitalism, would not just appear to be a futile attitude for anyone who accepted the standards of modern civilization. It would also be wrong on ethical grounds, being little more than a moral stance devoid of all practical significance. Rather, modern man must face reality. In other words, we have to put up with the fact that we live under social conditions increasingly determined by bureaucratic institutions of all kinds.

Weber's own attitude towards capitalism and rationalization was, not surprisingly, rather ambivalent. Weber was confronted here with an insoluble antinomy. First, the modern techniques of bureaucratic organization were infinitely superior to all traditional forms of social organization, namely the types of patrimonial or honorific (*Honoratioren*) administration. He considered it a fact of life that advanced industrial societies could no longer do without bureaucratic techniques. Second, Weber welcomed the techniques of bureaucratic organization for moral reasons as well. Rigorous rationalization of one's own life-conduct in order to maximize the chances of achieving one's personally chosen goals appeared to him an essential element of a moral code of behaviour in consonance with the 'ethic of responsibility'. In order to do this, the use of bureaucratic techniques was not only perfectly legitimate but ethically prescribed whenever these appeared useful for attaining such goals. The rigorous rationalization of one's own social conduct in accordance with certain ultimate objectives, associated with a proper assessment of the social conditions under which one would have to operate, was, in a way, for Weber the ultimate objective of any human being seeking personal self-realization. On the other hand, Weber was all too aware of the fact that bureaucratization and rationalization were about to undermine the liberal society of his own age. They were working towards the destruction of the very social premises on which individualist conduct was dependent. They heralded a new, bureaucratized and collectivist society in which the individual was reduced to utter powerlessness.

Weber's position was thus essentially an antinomical one. He simultaneously welcomed and opposed the modern rational techniques of social organization associated with the emergence of bureaucracies on all levels of society. He emphasized throughout his work the specific advantages of bureaucratic techniques for the achievement of rational conduct in social affairs, but he was quick to point out that the process of bureaucratization was bound to have adverse effects on a liberal social order built around the principles of individuality and personal self-realization. To put it another way, Weber's intentions went far beyond merely providing precise descriptions of empirical bureaucratic phenomena; rather he aimed at systematically assessing the inherent properties of bureaucratic types of social organization, as contrasted with possible alternative ones. However, he did not stop there. He wished to draw attention to precisely those aspects of bureaucratic rule which were of particular significance if viewed from the above-mentioned vantage-points, namely (a) as a means of achieving one's objectives in the best possible manner and (b) as a form of social organization with a high degree of efficiency, though with possible adverse consequences for a liberal social order geared to providing a maximum of freedom and individual initiative.

Weber's well-known method of ideal-typical analysis, which drew upon all relevant historical evidence available, therefore went far beyond formulating empirically tested generalizations. On the contrary, it was intended to produce an interpretation (albeit hypothetical) of certain aspects of social reality which emphasized precisely those elements which, within a given socio-historical context, would affect, either positively or negatively, ultimate cultural values.

Max Weber's ideal-typical systematization of the problems of bureaucracy and bureaucratization proceeded essentially on four levels:

1 The assessment of the specific properties of bureaucratic institutions as pure types, i.e. as if they were operating in a social context without modifying or countervailing forces at work, that is to say in a semi-static social context.

2 The analysis of the inherent dynamism of bureaucratic institutions, again assuming a social context in which there are no countervailing tendencies at work. In other words, bureaucratization is seen here as a sort of self-propelling process in time, which is apparently irreversible and which, if allowed to continue uninhibited, would eventually result in the complete ossification of the social system within which it develops.

3 With the help of this epistemological apparatus Weber then sets out to assess the specific properties of bureaucratic institutions, positive or negative depending on the vantage-point, in comparison with possible alternative types of social organization.

4 Eventually, at an even more elevated epistemological level, bureaucracy and bureaucratization are used as cornerstones in a substantive theory of history, albeit of a purely hypothetical nature. At this level the historical process is conceived of as an eternal struggle between 'charismatic' innovation and bureaucratic 'rationalization', as Runciman puts it,[2] or, as I have described it elsewhere,[3] as an eternal struggle between the creative forces of charisma and rationalization, the latter being firmly allied to bureaucratization as the most effective strategy for achieving a formal rationalization of social interaction at all levels of society. It certainly appeared that the latter was in the stronger position. Indeed, Weber believed that in his own time routinization and bureaucratization had, at least for the foreseeable future, gained the upper hand over all charismatic types of social organization. Fundamentally, however, the outcome of this struggle was still open. In a way rationalization and charisma are antinomical concepts; reality oscillates between these extreme modes of social organization.

Let me briefly discuss the meaning of the concept of bureaucracy on these four levels, starting with Weber's description of 'bureaucracy' as a type of social organization. To quote his own definition:

The purely bureaucratic form of administrative organization, that is the monocratic variety of bureaucracy, is, as regards the precision, constancy, stringency and reliability of its operations, superior to all other forms of administrative organization. Its operations are calculable both for the heads of the administrative machinery and for those who are affected by it. Owing to the intensity and the scope of its operations, it is capable of being applied to all kinds of administrative tasks. Hence it is, in a purely technical sense, capable of attaining a maximum of efficiency and therefore, in all respects, formally the most rational form of exercising authority over human beings.[4]

It is for this very reason that wherever the co-operation of human beings must be organized on a permanent basis the specific techniques of bureaucratic administration are superior to all other traditional forms of administration.

The particular strength of bureaucratic administration is due, among other factors, to the fact that those who operate the administrative machinery and those who own it are kept rigorously apart. In contrast to many traditional political systems, the task of administration no longer forms part of the public functions of specific honorific classes, entitled to a share in the exercise of public power because of their personal or social status. It becomes the exclusive domain of a particular profession, the civil servants or, in the non-governmental sphere, the managerial staff (*Privatbeamten*). They operate in accordance with a system of formal regulations, within precisely fixed functions (*Zuständigkeiten*), and in so doing are subjected to the permanent control of their superiors. They are expected to devote their full energy to the fulfilment of their obligations, but they have to operate strictly according to rules and must never let personal motives, emotions or inclinations influence their decisions. In return the bureaucratic personnel are often given a privileged status, in comparison with their social environment. The way in which they are remunerated for their work also ensures their dependence upon the bureaucratic institution and prevents considerations of personal gain from influencing how they carry out their duties. Impersonal performance of prescribed duties is expected from them, not individual initiative or subjective reasoning.

The hierarchical structure of a bureaucratic institution and the subjection of all its operations to formally rational rules and regulations has, according to Weber, a series of crucial advantages, namely universal applicability to whatever sphere of social interaction, predictability and, above all, a maximum degree of efficiency. All its operations, from top to bottom, can be geared to the rational attainment of specific objectives, since in principle everything depends only on formal regulations and the specific orders of superiors. As Weber himself puts it: 'The fully developed bureaucratic mechanism compares with other organizations exactly as does the machine with non-mechanical modes of production. Precision, speed, unambiguity, knowledge of the files, continuity, discretion, unity, strict subordination, reduction of friction and of material and personal costs – these are raised to the optimum in the strictly bureaucratic administration.'[5] Indeed, in fully developed institutions the chances of implementing particular measures instigated by those in superior positions are optimal. They guarantee not only regularity and efficiency of operation, but above all formal rational implementation in accordance with the original intentions of those who control them. They are, in a way, perfect instruments of effective rule, in particular under the conditions of mass society.

This very fact, however, accounts for the tendency of bureaucracies to mushroom. They possess an inherent drive to extend their control of those societal affairs within their sphere of activity even further, eventually taking virtually everything into their grasp in order to eliminate any sources of irrational or unpredictable social conduct. The demand for maximum formal rationality and maximum efficiency requires that nothing should be left to chance. Therefore, bureaucracies tend to subject everything to their control, unless there are countervailing forces at work. They tend to sweep anything aside that stands in the way of their inherent tendency to extend their sway over ever wider segments of social reality. It is largely because of their *Amtswissen*, that is to say their 'official knowledge', associated with recourse to governmental power, that they tend to make everyone comply with their will. This dynamism was considered by Weber to be a social force of a semi-dependent nature, once the process of bureaucratization had got under way.

It is at this point that we reach the third level of Weber's analysis of bureaucracy, namely its evaluation not only as a perfect instrument of administration and rule, but also as a potential threat to leadership and individual initiative and therefore as a danger to individual freedom. To be sure, neither the modern state, nor its subsidiary institutions, nor modern capitalist business can do without bureaucracy, least of all modern 'mass democracy'. But at the same time it contains the seeds of their eventual decline, or alternatively their ossification. In a way the gradual restriction of individual initiative and competition lies at the heart of the matter, if seen from a substantive-rational as opposed to a formal-rational point of view. First, the more fully developed bureaucratic systems are, the more their operations become strictly impersonal: bureaucracy's specific nature emerges the more perfectly the more it is 'dehumanized', the more completely it succeeds in eliminating from official business love, hatred and, above all, purely personal, irrational and emotional elements which escape calculation. Second, all bureaucratic institutions tend increasingly to subject the personal conduct of all the individuals within their reach to formal-rational regulation of their own making, if only in the interests of a gradual perfection of their administrative performance. Third, bureaucratization inevitably tends to create a new, privileged 'class' of bureaucratic office-holders, which is separated from the mass of the population by upbringing, specialized education and training, as well as security of employment and guaranteed regular income. Djilas's 'new class' is indeed foreshadowed in Weber's ideal-typical analysis of modern bureaucracy. Worse, this 'class' is prepared to serve virtually any master, whatever his origins and whatever his objectives.

The most serious aspect of it all, however, according to Weber, is that bureaucratic organizations tend to stifle all creative leadership. Bureaucracies are totally unable to bring forth leaders. All their operations are supposed to be pursued according to strictly formal-rational rules without the least regard for personal preferences or value-attitudes. Bureaucratic institutions, or, for that matter, bureaucratic officials, therefore preclude rather than encourage the development of genuine leadership qualities among their members. Bureaucratic institutions, if left to themselves, are not only self-perpetuating but also averse to all innovation or change which is not in line with their own intentionalized regulations. Routinization and, eventually, ossification are therefore always looming on the horizon.

These observations lead to the fourth level of ideal-typical conceptualization, namely the specific properties of bureaucratic institutions as compared with other types of social organization. As has already been pointed out, Weber deliberately accentuated the hierarchical as well as the impersonal features of bureaucratic institutions, because he believed that through them the social as well as the psychological conditions of modern man would be drastically altered with significant consequences for the future of mankind. Seen from this vantage-point, Weber's theory of bureaucracy was an exercise in defending humanity. His ideal-typical conceptualization of bureaucratization as an irreversible process was meant to be a sort of self-denying prophecy that should help to prevent precisely the sort of outcome it forecast. At this level of Weber's analysis, bureaucracy is no longer regarded merely as a technical instrument for the implementation of rules and the exercise of power, but as a form of social organization. It is seen as being, or at least forming the core of, a particular type of social system, since its instrumental rational principles pervade the latter throughout.

Weber subsumes the 'pure type' of a bureaucratic social system under the heading of legal, or rather formally legal, domination within the frame of reference of his well-known theory of 'three pure types of legitimate domination'. This typology was intended to encompass all possible forms of legitimate domination, and it was construed by taking account of their typically different moral foundations as seen from the perspective of human beings subjected to them. Weber found three pure types of legitimate domination, namely legal domination, traditional domination and charismatic domination. On this last, highest level of ideal-typical conceptualization, bureaucracy is the key feature of a particular sort of culture, and the consequences of bureaucratic organization extend far beyond the spheres of politics and economics.

The universal predominance of bureaucratic techniques of domination as well as a submissive mentality are perhaps the most conspicuous feature of the pure type of legal domination, if considered in its most fully developed version. The pure type of legal domination ideally involves an omnipotent administrative organization, subjecting all spheres of life to its activities. It is based upon a legal system which operates according to formally enacted, codified laws and regulations which are purpose-orientated rather than based on moral norms of some kind. Its operations are therefore calculable and predictable throughout. It does not allow for any significant individual initiative, lest this upset the system even to the slightest degree. Ideally its legitimacy rests exclusively on the assumption that all its laws are legal to the extent that they have been enacted in a formally correct way; there are no subtantive standards of justice or legitimacy.

The essential features of this type of legitimate rule are highlighted by contrasting them with the other two types, traditional and charismatic rule. Charismatic rule in its pure form, unlike legal rule, is highly creative and capable of initiating innovative social processes of substantial magnitude. In its initial stages charismatic rule is highly effective, inasmuch as it usually motivates the leader's followers from the inside out. They are supposed not only to lend full support to the leader but also to rationalize their own conduct in accordance with the ideals spelt out by the leader. Charismatic rule is also, however, extremely unstable and susceptible from the start to routinization. Traditional domination, in particular its patrimonial version, is halfway towards legal forms of government, to the extent that authority is ascribed to a particular person in accordance with generally accepted traditions. As a rule, however, various social groups, in particular the landowning classes, tend to have a share in the actual exercise of power, especially at the local and regional levels of politics. Even in the case of pure patrimonial rule where the master has succeeded in monopolizing the legitimate right to exercise power, he is constantly confronted by the danger of the administrative apparatus being appropriated by particular groups with an elevated status in society, be they aristocratic landowners or patrimonial servants.

In contrast to both charismatic rule, aided by followers personally devoted to the master, and to the various sub-types of traditional rule with more or less developed bureaucratic machineries, formal legal rule relies entirely upon bureaucracies which operate totally according to the principles of instrumental rationality. This method of government is infinitely more efficient. Frictions and conflicts can be reduced to a minimum, and all energies geared to achieving an optimum effect. However, the impersonal nature of legal rule, associated with the progressive elimination of all forms of individual activity, creates conditions which will eventually precipitate its failure, or more often its petrifaction. While all social interactions become more and more uniform, the incentives for innovation of any kind are gradually lost. A climate develops which no longer allows for the emergence of dynamic leaders. It is also no longer able to react flexibly to challenges, external or internal. Therefore petrifaction or destruction, from outside or, less likely, from within, is the ultimate outcome.

The ideal-typical theory of legitimate forms of domination was not meant to be an evolutionary scheme of history leading from charismatic forms of rule in the early stages of historical development to traditional forms of government, be they patriarchal or patrimonial in character, on to the modern forms of legal and, as regards their governmental techniques, bureaucratic rule, although some traces of such a conception can still be found in the earlier versions of the 'three pure types of legitimate domination'. On the contrary, all these forms can be observed in empirical reality alongside one another in various stages of development and frequently in the most diverse combinations. History in its entirety consists of a theoretically unlimited number of such processes, each initiated by charismatic breakthroughs of some sort with enough momentum to accumulate the energies needed to get new social movements going; however, the charismatic ideas that provide the impetus for these movements are soon subjected to routinization. Eventually these movements will crystallize into formal legal systems which are ultimately geared to little else but their own reproduction.

In a way, Weber's fascination with and at the same time his fear of bureaucracy, as a particular form of social organization with a lasting impact on all those subjected to its control, is the central theme in most of his sociological writings. Did he, however, think that Western societies were doomed by the seemingly irreversible advance of rationalization and bureaucratization? To some extent this would appear to be so. Though he considered history to be in principle an open-ended process, Weber believed that in his own time all the social indicators were pointing towards the predominance, and the eventual triumph, of formal legal domination as a result of its ever more perfect administrative techniques. Deploring the German passion for bureaucratic solutions in politics, he exclaimed late in 1918:

The lifeless machinery [of modern industrial production] is solidified human spirit. Only for this reason does it possess the power to force men into its service ... as is experienced in modern factory life. Solidified human spirit is also the living machinery of bureaucratic organization, with the assignment of its functions to a multitude of specialized experts, its rigid regulation of competence and its hierarchical pattern of obedience to the respective superior authority. The bureaucratic organization is, together with the lifeless machinery, about to produce the iron cage of future serfdom in which men will have to live helplessly, like the fellahin in ancient Egypt, if they consider an efficient, that is to say rational, bureaucratic administration, which also provides for their needs, as the only and ultimate ideal that is to determine the nature of their own government.[6]

But this is only half the story. In fact, much of Weber's work is devoted to mobilizing resistance to the universal trend towards bureaucratization. Throughout his writings he pointed out again and again the threat to a liberal order created by insufficiently controlled or checked bureaucratic institutions. In so doing he deliberately reformulated his own ideal-typical models, and not merely for the sake of argument, into sets of diametrically opposed pure types, in order to highlight the respective properties of the social institutions and world-views in question in a clear-cut manner. This he did from the point of view of whether they might contribute to bureaucratization by stifling individual initiative or alternatively provide a maximum of dynamism, creativity and leadership. Most important in this respect is perhaps the sharp distinction which he drew between the leading politician on the one hand and the civil servant on the other. While civil servants must attend to their duties and implement orders regardless of whether they think them right, politicians must quit their office whenever they are prevented from achieving their personal objectives, at least in essential matters. The antinomy between political leaders gifted with charismatic qualities who are expected to give a lead to their followers and rally the people behind their policies, and civil servants who are called upon to implement those policies in a formal-rational manner, could indeed not be greater.

Antinomical interpretations of a similar, if not always quite as pointed, quality also turn up in Weber's theory of capitalism, in particular the market economy. The ideal-typical antimony between a liberal market economy in which everything is left to individuals' ability to do their best and a centrally directed economy is highlighted in the strongest terms. The bureaucratic welfare state appears as a combination of these two types of social organization; it accepts the market economy but seeks to alleviate its consequences for the workers who cannot sell their labour according to market conditions. In his own day Weber himself was an advocate of far-reaching social reforms, but he was careful to support forms of social legislation which would interfere as little as possible with the struggle between trade unions and employers. In principle, of course, a competitive market economy was definitely preferable to any sort of centrally directed economy (although most modern market economies in his day left much to be desired if measured against the yardstick of Weber's pure type of market economy). However, in Weber's view it was unlikely that any modern market economy would survive for any length of time if it did not provide a certain degree of social welfare and, above all, allow the working classes to thrash out freely their differences with the employers as well as to have a share in the running of political affairs. Weber certainly did not propose the total abolition of social-welfare institutions, in fact quite the reverse. But he sought to show that these had to be paid for in terms of a reduction in the formal rationality of the economy. In advanced industrial economies social-welfare institutions or social legislation were required to restore the equilibrium between workers and employers, thereby re-establishing the conditions under which individual initiative could still be effective on the shopfloor, such as in the trade-union movement. On the other hand Weber was acutely aware of the fact that a highly developed system of welfare institutions might well undermine individual responsibility, especially if it were left to the state to sort out labour conflicts and wage disputes without the full participation of workers and employers. Occasionally he argued this case forcefully, even perhaps a little carried away by his own rhetoric. For example:

In American 'benevolent feudalism', in Germany's so-called 'welfare institutions', in the Russian factory constitution – everywhere the iron cage of future serfdom is ready. We just have to wait until the slowing down of technological and economic 'progress' and the triumph of 'rents' over 'profits', associated with the exhaustion of remaining 'free' soil and remaining 'free' markets, finally makes the masses ready to accommodate themselves in it.[7]

Perhaps the most striking example of Weber's dualist approach to the analysis of social reality is, however, the antinomy between market economies and planned economies (the latter comprising most versions of socialist economies). In the second case the means of production are *de facto*, if not *de jure*, controlled (or, as Weber put it, borrowing a phrase from Marx, appropriated) by a particular bureaucratic class, and the social product tends to be distributed according to schematic formulas. In the first case both are regulated by the formally free interplay of the market-place. Weber was not blind to the disadvantages of absolutely free competition in the market, and indeed was very much aware of the limitations of the market economy under the conditions of advanced capitalism. None the less he was very definite on one point: all socialist systems, at least so long as they were based on a centrally directed economy, were bound to stimulate bureaucratization far more than any capitalist system would ever do. The dynamism of the capitalist market economy was the one factor which could keep the expansionist tendencies of bureaucracy in check, at least for the foreseeable future. Similarly he argued that it is only the businessman and the private entrepreneur who are capable of matching the inside knowledge and hance the institutional power of the governmental administrations.

On the other hand, he had no patience with any sort of final solutions for effectively doing away with bureaucratization. He dismissed in harsh terms the intellectuals' cult of the irrational, be it in the form of romantic anarchism, revolutionary attitudes for their own sake, or intellectual cults like those of the Stefan George circle. There was no way of getting rid of bureaucracy altogether, since its services were indispensable in all advanced mass societies. But it could be kept in check by sensible social and political institutions, and a dynamic political system.

Indeed, Weber was definite about the need to maintain as much dynamism in modern industrial societies as possible, by whatever means this could be achieved. A viable market-orientated capitalism was, in this respect, infinitely preferable to any alternative system, particularly centralized socialist ones. On the political level he held that parliamentary institutions with the power to set up investigating committees with statutory powers would be a suitable means of keeping the governmental administrations under control. What seemed much more important to him, however, was the development of suitable institutions to provide effective leadership. His own ultimate suggestion was 'plebiscitarian leader democracy'. An institutionalized combination of the two competing forces, namely charisma and bureaucracy, might – under modern conditions – come nearest to a solution to the problem of how to cope with the perennial danger of bureaucratization and solidification of social systems.

It is perhaps Weber's greatest achievement that he succeeded in assessing the character of modern bureaucratic institutions both in the instrumental-rational perspective of their specific capabilities and in the substantive-rational perspective of the seemingly irreversible impact of bureaucratization as a rationalizing force as well as a threat to open societies like our own and indeed to the future of mankind as a whole.

8

Ideal Type and Pure Type:
Two Variants of Max Weber's
Ideal-typical Method

The development and systematization of an ideal-typical method of analysing and presenting sociological and historical knowledge is one of Max Weber's enduring achievements. This is so despite the fact that disagreement persists about the logical status and epistemological function of this method, with the result that its value is still hotly debated. While social scientists tend towards a detached and often highly critical assessment of Weber's ideal-typical method (although this position is currently being revised), historians, in so far as they use typological methods at all, have found it most useful, sometimes in conjunction with the older typological methods of Jacob Burckhardt.[1] In some respects H. Stuart Hughes put things in a nutshell when he observed, twenty years ago, that Weber's methodology marked the point of greatest coincidence between the approaches of sociology and history.[2] In recent years, social scientists are taking more notice of Max Weber inasmuch as he offers ways of incorporating a historical dimension into sociological research and developing macro-sociological theories so as to lead them out of the dead end of the purely empirical approach suggested by logical positivism. Conversely, Marxist-Leninists are prepared now to discard the conventional assessment of Weber's methodology as an expression of the irrationalism of late bourgeois imperialism which can be found, for example, in Jürgen Streisand's *Studien über die deutsche Geschichtswissenschaft* published in 1965.[3] Despite the fundamental opposition between Max Weber's ideological position and Marxism, Marxist-Leninist scholars are recognizing it as an approach which is, at least in parts, compatible with Marxist typological methods.

This essay pursues two objectives: to point out the key features of Max Weber's ideal-typical method; and to show that it underwent substantial change after about 1913. It will also become clear that, despite their very different – sometimes diametrically opposed – epistemological aims, interesting parallels exist between Max Weber and Karl Marx. These parallels could provide the point of departure for further study. In his major essay 'Die "Objektivität" sozialwissenschaftlicher und sozialpolitischer Erkenntnis', Max Weber had already emphasized the proximity of his ideal-typical method to Marx, whom he refers to here as 'a great thinker'.[4] Weber describes Marx's theories on the objective process of history as 'by far the most important example of ideal-typical constructions', although he does not discuss them in detail.[5] Although Max Weber subsumes Marx's theory of history as a particular variant of 'ideal-typical construction', from a Marxist viewpoint this is obviously not, or at least not immediately, acceptable, since it implies that Marx's laws of the historical process have only a hypothetical status, or that they are at best only partial theories which cannot claim, taken by themselves, to be objective, let alone universally valid. Nevertheless, Marxists too might find it useful to examine what Weber and Marx have in common in this respect, as a more careful analysis of Marx might reveal.

First, however, I shall return to the methodological problems of historiography. Compared with theories based on the epistemological programme of logical positivism, Weber's ideal-typical method has the fundamental advantage for historians that it systematically incorporates the dimension of 'understanding'. This is done in two ways: (1) in the sense of understanding the actions of individuals, or groups of indivdiuals, who are the subject of historical contemplation, that is to say as a hermeneutical device, and (2) in the sense of an 'interpretative' integration of the subject area which is the object of understanding into overarching patterns of meaning. (The latter factor, incidentally, relates it to typologies or theories of a Marxist stamp, although Weber intended it to have a completely different – namely a purely nomological, not a substantive – status.) Integration into overarching 'patterns of meaning', to repeat my own phrase, entails an *interpretation* of the subject areas which are descriptively comprehended, by means of the ideal-typical models, from certain relevant viewpoints, or, as Weber expressed it in his early methodological studies, from the vantage-point of their 'cultural significance'. This can easily be illustrated by reference to an example selected at random. Let us take the ideal type of 'bureaucracy'. Here precisely those elements are consistently emphasized which are of particular importance from the vantage-point of the potential threat posed to Western liberal civilization by the universal process of progressive bureaucratization in all areas of life – for example, the strictly hierarchical structure of bureaucracies, the deliberate elimination of individual initiative and its replacement by strict subordination to bureaucratic regulations, the high value placed on discipline, and so on. In other words, it is those features of bureaucratic organization which are stressed precisely because they lead, potentially or actually (at the level of concept formation this distinction is immaterial), to the repression of responsible behaviour and individual initiative and to the eventual emergence of a society of thoroughly conformist 'professionals'.[6]

Initially Weber did not hesitate to describe his 'interpretative' method (i.e. subsuming social phenomena under ideal types constructed in this way) as establishing a 'value-relationship' in keeping with Rickert's neo-Kantian theory, but he distinguished it sharply from the passing of 'value-judgements'. As he saw it, 'value-judgements' could be avoided precisely because 'value-relationships' only establish an interrelation between certain social phenomena and certain ideal values, while they do not explicitly evaluate them in any way. The information is supplied which enables an evaluation to be made on a rational basis in the light of certain 'ultimate' concerns. In the case selected here as an example, this could be either an affirmation of bureaucratic techniques or, conversely, a rejection of them in line with certain instrumental-rational or value-rational viewpoints in the context of value-positions of a principally meta-scientific status. Weber himself assumed that as a rule any such evaluation amounted to a conflict between different, if not competing, ideal values which claim equal allegiance from the individual.

For Weber, the 'purpose of ideal-typical concepts was to accentuate not the generic similarities between cultural phenomena, but their differences'.[7] This also holds true for the various ideal-typical constructions which are to be found in Weber's work, although, as we shall see, their emphasis changes and the epistemological goals they serve undergo a certain displacement.

This provides a first answer to those critics of Weber's methodology, notably Pfister and Janoska-Bendl, who argue that his ideal-typical method is ambiguous and that he presents a large number of ideal types of varying epistemological status without distinguishing them clearly from each other.[8] Weber was obviously not interested in standardizing the construction of ideal-typical concepts or models. On the contrary, the conceptual terminology he chose permits a whole range of variations in the formation of ideal-typical concepts, according to the specific epistemological goal they serve.[9]

At first glance, this is difficult to understand. According to Weber, ideal types are basically nomological in nature; that is, they do not possess reality in any sense – as is the case with Platonic ideas or Hegelian concepts – nor do they have a normative status of any sort. In principle, ideal types can be constructed at random, although it is obligatory to make full use of all relevant empirical information; it is intended to achieve the greatest possible conceptual clarity by accentuating those aspects which are seen to have particular significance from a specific vantage-point (which may be affected by personal preferences, be they of a value-oriented or an instrumental nature). This accentuation is seen to be value-neutral because ideal types are considered no more than instrumental in achieving the clearest possible conceptual understanding of given circumstances in the light of 'ultimate' viewpoints. They are intended to measure the discrepancy between a particular segment of empirical reality and the constructed norm, not to provide a direct representation of reality. In other words, ideal-typical constructs are always perspectival. This means that they cannot be used to attain a 'holistic' understanding of the world; rather, their theme is a theoretically limited number of segments of reality.

In comparison with conventional conceptualizations of the world-historical process, as proposed by the classical philosophy of history, this epistemological programme may sound modest. However, the range of ideal-typical concepts Weber developed on this methodological basis in his sociological work is extraordinarily wide. In many cases they come close to universal-historical schemes of the historical process as such.

Basically, two categories of ideal types can be distinguished in Weber's methodological writings:

1 structural types – i.e. constructs which represent structures (they may be either ideal or material in kind);
2 types of social change – i.e. constructs which represent historical processes in time.

In both cases the formation of ideal-typical concepts ranges over a wide spectrum and the ideal-typical constructs differ widely in the scope of their applicability. In other words, we are dealing with ideal types of very different degrees of aggregation and complexity.

Weber's historical and sociological work contains a wide range of ideal-typical structural models (to introduce a term which he himself did not use, but which is perfectly compatible with his own approach). The range extends from ideal-typical constructs which attempt to encapsulate the significance of particular historical formations, such as 'the West' or (to take an example Weber refers to himself in his essay on 'Objectivity in the social sciences') 'the Renaissance', right through to constructs of comparatively limited scope and complexity such as 'party of notables', 'the state', 'legal domination', and so on. A large number of phenomena which are empirically relatively diffuse and, as a rule, appear in a wide range of different modes are subsumed under a rationally constructed, internally consistent concept which deliberately accentuates those aspects which carry significance in a wider interpretative context. The ideal type of 'the state' is, above all, distinguished from a large number of otherwise comparable institutional bodies by its 'monopoly of physical violence'. Legal domination ideally represents rule according to formally enacted regulations, which need not have any substantive foundation at all; the merely formal nature of its basis represents its specificity. A 'party of notables' is distinguished by a particular pattern of restricted representation, limited to a socially elevated group which, on the grounds of exercising important social functions, claims the right to speak for the people as a whole. This strategy of accentuating significant aspects renders the ideal-typical method particularly suitable for interpreting historical reality from a specific vantage-point which, of course, may differ from context to context. The ideal type of bureaucracy, for example, emphasizes above all its superior efficiency compared to other types of social organization; on the other hand, bureaucratic institutions are inherently hostile to individual initiative and accordingly they pose a threat to freedom, especially if seen in a universal-historical perspective.

At a first glance, ideal types of social or ideal structures are relatively static. As we shall see, however, this is not necessarily the case – for example, when they are arranged in pairs or even in systems. Besides, they often have to be seen as directional types, that is to say they embody an ideal-typical trend which unfolds their inherent principles of construction in an ever purer form. Bureaucracies, for example, tend to progressively extend their scope to ever wider areas of social life if no opposing factors prevent them from unfolding their inherent principle ever more fully. 'Legal domination' will eventually eliminate all substantive elements which may be embodied in an existing legal order, because such fundamentalist elements in principle merely tend to disturb the smooth operation of the formalistic procedures which ideally establish its 'legality'. This may demonstrate that ideal-typical structural models are by no means static, although they are composed in a way which precludes the inclusion of any temporal components. On the contrary, Weber often uses pairs of ideal-typical concepts constructed in a dichotomic form, precisely in order to demonstrate that the respective dominant principles of organization or social structure tend either to encourage or, conversely, to hinder change. The ideal-typical 'capitalist entrepreneur', for example, is a source of extreme dynamism, while the ideal-typical capitalist *rentier* who lives on fixed interest-bearing securities represents a thoroughly conservative stance, as all his economic interests point to the maintenance of the status quo.

However, special attention must be given to those ideal types which represent typical social processes, thereby themselves directly arriving at the typical conditions under which social change may take place. They range from ideal types representing various forms of conduct of individuals or relatively homogeneous groups which are likely to have significant social consequences, either dynamic or static, through to explicit ideal-typical models of historical processes (which, however, differ widely in their scope). In his essay on 'Objectivity in the social sciences', which is, incidentally, still close to historicist conceptualizations, Weber observes: 'Developments can also be reconstructed in an ideal-typical manner; and those reconstructions can be of considerable value.'[10] As already mentioned, Weber considered Marx's theory of history to be an 'ideal-typical developmental model' of this type. Much the same could be said about the essays on *The Protestant Ethic and the Spirit of Capitalism*. Weber based his interpretation of the emergence of modern, capital-intensive, market-orientated capitalism (that is to say, not capitalism as such) on an ideal-typical developmental model of a similar nature. To be more precise, he used it as a means of explaining why this new type of economic activity, closely associated with a specific life-conduct and geared specifically towards capital accumulation and increasing profits, emerged among bourgeois entrepreneurs and gradually developed into a revolutionary force which irresistibly supplanted the economic systems predominant in traditional societies, where life-conduct was dominated by tradition and social status, and economic activity was geared to maintaining a certain lifestyle in line with the social role of the respective social groups, rather than to maximizing production and economic expansion.

It should be mentioned in passing that Weber by no means intended this thesis to be a comprehensive explanation of the development of capitalism as a new economic formation of potential – and increasingly real – revolutionary quality. Rather, it was meant to be an ideal-typical reconstruction of a particular segment in the history of the genesis of modern capitalism, namely the inter-relationship of economic activity and the value-oriented life-conduct of the entrepreneurial class in nascent capitalism.

A comparison of this model with Marx's theory of 'primary accumulation' would certainly be productive. Another case in question is Weber's developmental model of a secular process of 'rationalization' in the West culminating in the modern, 'demagicized' technical civilization of our present age, assisted among other factors by modern rational science. This is also, certainly, a 'developmental construction' of universal-historical proportions. Here too it would be misleading to consider this attempt to interpret a sizeable segment of universal history from a particular vantage-point, namely the perspective of a progressive advance in formal rationality, as a substantive reconstruction of history – such as had been attempted by the philosophy of history – although this misunderstanding is rather common. Rather, the ideal-typical model which poses a steady advance of formally rational forms of social interaction throughout time serves merely as a guide through the complexity of historical reality. In fact at every juncture in the historical development of Western culture things could also have taken a different turn, and they frequently did, at least partially. The ideal-typical model of rationalization is constructed around the idea that rationalization will win through because of its inherent dynamics, but all the same it is an 'open' model that neither claims inevitability nor can be expressed in evolutionist terms as a substantive reconstruction of the social history of the West *per se*.[11]

This observation is corroborated by the fact that in Weber's late work the ideal type gradually takes on a new, far more formalized shape. Starting with *Über einige Kategorien der verstehenden Soziologie* (1913),[12] and culminating in the 'Kategorienlehre' of *Economy and Society*,[13] Weber turned away from this sort of ideal-typical, unilinear reconstruction of certain culturally specific sequences of the historical process. This shift in the meaning of ideal type is linked directly to the development of a formal-rational variant of ideal types constructed according to criteria of 'functional rationality' (*Richtigkeitsrationalität*) – or, in other words, according to the full adaptation of forms of social action to the functional requirements which will ensure the fullest attainment of the objectives pursued. By 1913 Weber clearly gave preference to functionally rational (*richtigkeitsrational*) ideal types over other possible variants of ideal-typical constructions, although there existed a multiplicity of different versions in the earlier essays, notably in 'Objectivity in the social sciences'.

In Weber's view, social conduct is in accordance with the criterion of functional rationality – or, as he puts it, *Richtigkeitsrationalität* – when it is oriented exclusively by considerations of how the means available, in order to achieve a particular end, can be put to optimum use without the intervention of value-rational or other fundamentalistic factors of a subjective nature; or, in other words, when social conduct accords with the principles of rational science and is exclusively oriented by instrumental-rational considerations.[14] That is to say, he wishes to give special consideration to those forms of social conduct which are ideally adapted to the formal conditions and technical means which will ensure the fullest implementation of its objectives. In this context Weber explicitly points out that for developing general concepts of sociology the type of functionally rational conduct (*Richtigkeitstypus*), seen in a purely logical sense, represents only one instance of the construction of ideal types, whereas there is always the possibility of constructing ideal types according to value-rational positions of diverse sorts. Similarly, he argues that functionally rational action (*richtigkeitsrationales Handeln*, sometimes simply abbreviated to *Richtigkeits-typus*) stands at the opposite extreme to empirical reality, where highly diverse mixtures of subjectively motivated actions (that is, actions predominantly based on irrational and subconscious grounds) are the rule. Weber regards this dichotomy between the type of 'correctly rational action' and subjectively motivated types of action as 'entwicklungsdynamisch von der höchsten Bedeutung',[15] as highly significant in respect of its potential for initiating 'dynamic development'. The type of *Richtigkeitsrationalität* takes as its theme precisely those aspects of social reality which may speed up social change as a result of superior social organization or formal-rational efficiency, in contrast to those aspects which really belong to the *Geltungssphäre*, the sphere of subjective values.

In Weber's early methodological essays this difference is not clearly expressed. The dichotomy of value-rational action and functionally rational action (*richtigkeitsrationales Handeln*) is not systematically unfolded before 1915, although we encounter the distinction between formal and substantive rationality already in *The Protestant Ethic*, although only fleetingly. Beginning with the 'Introduction' to the *Collected Essays on the Sociology of Religion* and the 'Zwischenbetrachtung'[16] this dichotomy rises to a prominent position in Weber's thought. Here he distinguishes systematically between 'formal rationality' (i.e. purely instrumental rationality oriented towards specific goals) and 'substantive rationality' (i.e. rationality oriented towards 'ultimate' and binding material values, which determine its direction and intensity). From now on Weber is interested in bringing out as clearly as possible the tension which exists between instrumental-rational organization in social reality and the potentially multiple forms of 'substantive rationality'. Accordingly, he increasingly opts for constructing systems of ideal types which are informed by the principle of *Richtigkeitsrationalität*, that is to say, an optimal adaptation to the functionally rational conditions of social action, and not by subtantive ideal values.

This shift of emphasis in the formation of ideal types is also expressed in a change in nomenclature. In the essay *Über einige Kategorien der verstehenden Soziologie*, Weber argues, somewhat surprisingly, that if ideal types are constructed in accordance with functional rationality (*Richtigkeitsrationalität*), the ideal type becomes in fact a (pure) type which is formed by a reductionist process from a set of factual observations ('eine empirisch zum "reinen" Typus sublimierte Faktizität den Idealtypus bilde').[17] In these somewhat obscure passages the notion of 'pure type' turns up in his sociology for the first time. In his later work Weber exclusively used the notion of 'pure type', although he himself was not aware of the fundamental break this represented with his earlier methodological position.[18] Sometimes he added 'ideal type' in brackets to 'pure type' in order to make it easier for the reader. This was justified only inasmuch as the 'pure type' may be considered a special variant of the ideal type. But Weber actually assigned to it a different epistemological function.

The ideal-typical casuistry or, to be more precise, the casuistry of 'pure types' as presented in an extremely formalized way in *Economy and Society*, deliberately accentuates the dimension of 'formal rationality' or 'instrumental rationality': it is the main principle which informs the construction of these 'pure types'. The perspectival dimension, or, as Weber initially expressed it, in accordance with Rickert, the function of establishing 'value-relationships' via the construction of ideal types, was relegated to a secondary position without, however, losing its significance. In the 'Soziologische Kategorienlehre', the chronologically latest section of *Economy and Society* written in 1920 (Weber actually intended to rewrite the whole work along the same lines), Weber embarks upon a casuistry of 'pure types' which, in line with the principle of *Richtigkeitsrationalität*, are constructed in such a manner as to unfold the relevant principle inherent in each case in the purest possible form. These 'pure types' differ from the usage of ideal types which we find in Weber's writings before 1918 in that as a rule they are arranged in groups which are linked with one another in a complementary, dichotomic or hierarchical relationship, each representing an ideally altogether different principle. Accordingly these pure types are deliberately constructed in such a manner as to conform to the extreme pole within a wide spectrum of alternative forms of social action, social conduct or social institutionalization. A telling example is the ideal-typical dichotomy between the 'responsible politician' who acts in principle on his own initiative only, and the civil servant dependent throughout on directives from the bureaucratic apparatus,[19] or, as I have already mentioned, between the capitalist entrepreneur and the capitalist *rentier* whose income derives from fixed interest-bearing securities, and which is accordingly decoupled from economic conjunctions.

A particularly interesting, and highly controversial, example is the dichotomy between the pure types of 'market economy' and 'planned economy' which is presented in considerable detail in *Economy and Society*. Weber systematically sets these two economic formations against one another, as being fundamentally different in their composition and their respective economic and social consequences, and then relates them to other dichotomous typologies such as '"formally" free versus unfree labour', and 'money economy' versus 'barter economy'.[20] In the context of the presentation in *Economy and Society* of systematically conceivable 'pure types' of economy which can be inferred from history, we find among other things a critical discussion of the different variants of a 'rational' socialist order which seemed systematically possible at that time. Combined with this is an incisive analysis of the capitalist system which, it seems to me, is considerably indebted to Karl Marx's *Das Kapital*.[21] The 'pure type' of capitalism – provided that it corresponds fully to the principle of 'formal rationality', that is, allows no value-rational modifications such as welfare institutions or legal limitations on the formally free marketing of labour – proves to be a pitiless 'cage of serfdom'. In this respect Weber's typological model is in no way less harsh than Marx's assessment of early capitalism.[22] Weber uses the twin pair of 'market' and 'planned' economy, together with a typology of the possible variant organizational forms of 'labour' and economic performance, as an instrument for a systematic reconstruction of all the known forms of economic systems since antiquity. At the same time it provides an assessment of the relative 'social costs' of any particular type of economic system or labour organization which may be chosen from a spectrum (in many respects empirically infinite) of practical options from a vantage-point which is unequivocally committed to the ideal of the free individual who can take responsibility for his or her own creative actions.

This is even more obvious in what is probably the best-known example of a multidimensional model comprising a system of several 'pure types', namely the 'three pure types of legitimate domination'. Since a rather more detailed account of this typology was given elsewhere in this volume, it may suffice merely to pinpoint the essential aspects relevant in this context. It distinguishes between legal, traditional and charismatic domination, each of which has its own specific claim to legitimacy. In the case of legal domination legitimacy rests on formally enacted rules; in that of traditional domination it is based on the 'sanctity of good old custom' and prescription; whereas in the case of charismatic domination the source of legitimacy is the charismatic quality of a leader which is inherently unstable, although it can be recast in an institutional form (institutionalized charisma). Each one of these 'pure types' of legitimate domination refers to a particular source of legitimacy which is opposed to that of the other two. It is claimed that these types together cover all conceivable forms of legitimating the exercise of power. The 'three pure types of legitimate domination' are, in a way, a typological reconstruction of universal history seen from a specific angle, namely how permanence in the exercise of power may be secured and in what modes it may be considered legitimate by the subjects. We are therefore no longer dealing merely with a reconstruction of a particular segment of the historical process from a certain vantage-point, as was the case, for instance, with Weber's essays on *The Protestant Ethic and the Spirit of Capitalism*. Rather, this is a model, claiming comprehensive validity, of real or potential historical reality as it presents itself from a specific perspective.

Moreover, this model is by no means as static as it would appear at first sight. Each of the three 'pure' types of legitimate domination has its own immanent dynamic which tends towards the full unfolding of itself and, in the course of doing so, eventually effects its own cancellation. Charismatic domination is typically unstable and attains permanence only through routinization and appropriation of the ruler's original charisma by a ruling class. Traditional domination is constantly exposed to erosion by routinization of the substantive principles from which it draws its legitimacy, and ultimately routinization lays the foundation for the emergence of a system of purely legal domination. Legal domination tends gradually to eliminate all those value-rational principles which initially justified it, by purely pragmatic regulations; if this goes on for a long time the system eventually will stagnate and ultimately becomes petrified; thus it is ripe for a 'charismatic revolution', a charismatic 'breakthrough' which will wipe out the network of formalized patterns of social interaction and bureaucratic institutions and install a new, value-oriented social system.

It would be wrong, however, to interpret this as a circular model of the course of universal history. It should be realized that in empirical reality only mixed versions of legitimacy of domination exist, that usually different types of legitimacy are superimposed upon each other in the most diverse forms. Precisely for this reason, this typology permits constant social change to be interpreted from viewpoints which on the one hand are informed by our knowledge of the entire history of mankind, and on the other are oriented by contemporary interests which are related to value-attitudes of various kinds.

Ideal-typical constructs composed of a plurality of 'pure types', such as the 'three pure types of legitimate domination', possess a new quality compared with the usage of ideal types in Weber's earlier work. They transcend the dichotomy which exists between 'structural types' and 'types of social change' as they are presented theoretically in Weber's early methodological essays and applied to specific historical phenomena, in particular in his writings on the social and cultural history of agrarian societies in antiquity, and in *The Protestant Ethic*. The systems of 'pure types' to be found in *Economy and Society* are in principle structural models which lack the dimension of historical time, or incorporate it only formally, while abstaining from giving it any historical specificity. Nevertheless in these types precisely those aspects of social order or systems of domination are accentuated which tend to inject dynamism, or conversely stagnation, into the system, thus affecting the process of social change positively or negatively. Moreover these systems of 'pure types' are also in principle perspectival – that is, they are constructed in the light of the ultimate cultural aspects of the historical process, even though 'value-relationship' is largely replaced by functional rationality (*Richtigkeitsrationalität*). The value aspect comes into play not in the construction of the individual 'pure types' but rather in the manner in which they are related to one another, forming a systematic whole. In the final analysis, these ideal-typical concept constructions are informed by the principle of eternal struggle between different hierarchies of 'ultimate' values and the institutional concretizations they have found in the course of history. It is no accident that these dichotomous or pluralistic systems of 'pure types' consistently emphasize the dialectical contrasts or rather the antinomic structure of social reality. The 'pure types' connected with one another to form an integrated system are informed by specific value-attitudes which, in turn, are in constant conflict with one another. This may be illustrated by an example. The capitalist system is based on the formal principle of the greatest possible efficiency achieved by a maximum of formal rationality. This forms an insoluble contrast to the substantive principles of equality and human dignity. Weber therefore assigned to capitalism substantive irrationality, while in terms of formal rationality the system of capitalism is not surpassed by any other type of socio-economic organization.

Last but not least these systems of 'pure types' are themselves subject to historical change; all ideal-typical constructs may become antiquated, so that the creation of ever new ideal-typical constructs becomes necessary (that is to say: 'die Vergänglichkeit *aller*, *aber* zugleich der Unvermeidlichkeit immer *neuer* idealtypischer Konstruktionen'). This is true for all historical disciplines, as Weber had pointed out as early as 1905 in his essay on 'Objectivity'.[23] The fruitfulness of ideal-typical constructions for historical research is obvious, although only rarely have attempts been made to write universal history with such a wide horizon as that presented by Max Weber. In a way his typology of 'pure types' may be seen *in nuce* as a theoretical model of universal history of enormous scope which is limited only by the level of historical knowledge available in his time.

9

Rationalization and Myth
in Weber's Thought

Of all the thinkers of our age Max Weber perhaps described and analysed in the most systematic fashion of all the departure of the modern world, especially of the West, from all magical and mystical forms of *Weltanschauung*. The theme of *Entzauberung* or the 'disenchantment' of the world as a secular process pervades the whole of his sociological work like a leitmotiv. The progressive rationalization of all social relationships together with the increasingly expansive bureaucratization of all social institutions appeared to him to be an inevitable fate at least for his own contemporary world. Certainly his personal attitude to the problem of rationalization always remained ambivalent: on the one hand he greeted continuing rationalization as a precondition for the optimal possible social action which is oriented to ultimate ideal values and thus as well for maximum individual self-realization; on the other hand he complained that in the course of the increasing rationalization and bureaucratization of all social relations the sphere of personal creative action and thought became more and more constricted and that thereby the room for life-conduct based on ultimate personal values became progressively smaller. But there appeared no prospect of ever really escaping this state of affairs, or at least to pretend there was one was feeble and insincere. Instead, the individual was called upon in all intellectual honesty to confront the basic fact 'that he is fated to live in an age that is ignorant of God and in which prophets are unknown'.[1] The obligation to rational life-conduct in respect of one's ultimate personal ideals in life, the objective demonstration of the validity of which is in the final analysis impossible, remains the only unquestionable certainty.

As Günter Dux put it, if Weber 'perhaps proclaimed the end not of religion but of a material religiosity many millennia old',[2] then this did not occur in the name of a positivist belief in science and progress as the legitimate heirs to conventional forms of religious or mystical world-views. On the contrary, Weber was only too aware of the limits of scientific cognition. He was fundamentally sceptical of the possibility of regaining by means of modern rational science the lost certainty about the meaning of historical reality, in much the same way as this had found a rather more pessimistic resolution in ancient theogonic myth and then a more or less mainly positive one in the salvational certitude of Christian eschatology. Already in his famous essay on 'Objectivity in the social sciences', dating from the year 1904, he had written:

The fate of a cultural epoch which has eaten from the tree of knowledge is to have to recognize that we cannot discern the *meaning* of world events from even the most complete evidence that their investigation provides, but that we must be able to create it for ourselves, that 'world-views' can never be the result of advances in empirical knowledge, that in other words the highest ideals which motivate us the most can only ever take effect in conflict with other ideals which are just as sacred to other people as ours are to us.[3]

What is more, to a certain extent the problem of meaning is further accentuated by the achievements of modern empirical science. Science may indeed assist in accounting in rational form for the ultimate reasons behind one's action, but the individual's choice between competing ideal values is thereby rendered even more difficult and subjected to even more rigorous self-examination. In spite of all the achievements of science, individuals are left to themselves in the end in questions concerning their own value-orientations in view of competing world-views and diverse 'ideal and material interests'. They are required in all intellectual sincerity – almost the last substantial relic of Enlightenment thought – to play out in their own hearts the relentless conflict between competing ideal values, in a situation of extreme intellectual solitude, or even if need be to 'sacrifice the intellect' and, fully conscious of the irrational nature of their own actions, to give themselves over to an explicit religious doctrine or to an absolutely valid principle, or even just to one that is held to be absolutely valid, no matter how flagrantly this may contradict everyday reality.

Personality for Weber is based in the final analysis on the consistency of one's inner relationship to ultimate values and life-meanings. How to make the choice between alternative ideal values, or even between alternative ethical viewpoints such as are represented by the ethics of responsibility on the one hand and by the ethics of conviction on the other, cannot be determined by any sort of formal rules. Here science can accomplish even less. 'For specialist science is concerned with technique and teaches technical methods. But, wherever values are at issue, there the problem is projected on to a completely different spiritual plane inaccessible to all science.'[4] The ethical standpoint Weber had in mind and which he required of every individual living in the 'disenchanted' world of our present age tended to aim for a maximum of tension between ultimate ethical or even extra-ethical norms prescribed for individuals and everyday reality; it was to some extent, in his own words, a sort of 'hero ethic' which places 'fundamental demands on a person to which he is generally incapable of doing justice other than at exceptional highpoints in his existence'.[5] This obligation to be relentlessly candid with respect to the ultimate reasons behind one's own desires and actions and at the same time the consciousness of the intractability of value-conflicts, which require the realization of ideals only at the cost of other ideals often held to be equally binding, can be looked upon as the most radical form at all conceivable of an individualistic and, if it is permissible to speak thus, 'spiritually aristocratic' material ethic of values, even if only partially formulated.

In the theory of the individually responsible, active personality existing within a complex network of material and ideal interests and yet still oriented towards final ideal values or world-views, the spheres of values and of empirical reality, of what is and of what ought to be, undergo as it were a reconciliation which is in practice realizable only in a particular context. This is at the core of his scientific work and, to a lesser degree, of his political work as well. The origins of this theory in a Christian religiosity of radical Protestant conformity, combined with idealism's view of personality and with the nihilistic destruction in the work of Nietzsche of all material religion in favour of the self-realization of great personalities, seem to be unmistakable. This explains at the same time why Max Weber remained comparatively distant from all conventional mythological thought in its religious just as much as its cultural and, ultimately, political forms. Not incidentally, the concept of myth plays merely a subordinate role in his sociological writings, although mythical forms of secular behaviour are repeatedly mentioned, notably in connection with the rise of world religions, as an important variety of a religious thought operating mainly through symbolic means.[6] The transposition of the meaning of historical events on to an anthropomorphically conceived divine cosmos characteristic of classical mythology ran somewhat counter to his own conception of how religious modes of thought developed from the prolific intermixture of the divine and the secular that originally existed, right up to the dichotomy of an omnipotent god on the one hand and of the human world on the other, which as such was beyond salvation, if it was not completely depraved already. Although in his discussion of the eternal conflict between alternative values and competing world-views, formulations would always flow from his pen which owed something to ancient mythology, he confronted mythological thought and to a certain extent every form of myth in general with scepticism, if not complete rejection. For the symbolic representation of alternative

world-views or life-ideals in mythological form, not to mention their symbolic identification with the action and thought of 'deified heroes',[7] resulted in
his opinion in a concealment of the fundamental conflicts of values and
accordingly in a dilution of the ultimate existential choice between different
ideal values. Indeed, one can ask whether Max Weber did not himself hover
on the threshold of mythological modes of thought with such a radical conception of the role of the individual as a completely self-dependent mediator
between quite separate spheres of reality. It may be after all that the famous final
section of 'Science as a vocation' could point to such a conclusion, stating as it
does that the individual is capable of living up to 'the demands of today' only if
'everyone finds and obeys the devil who holds the fibres of his very life'.[8] But
this question should not be pursued further here.

Myth and magic appear in Weber's writings on the sociology of religion as
important early precursors of religious world-views. Peculiar to both, however,
is the fact that they are really of an archaic nature only. The breakthrough of
revolutionary forms of religious behaviour in world history was in Weber's
view achieved in every case through great prophetship with its characteristic
conjoining in one unitary salvational doctrine of religious norms and radical
demands made of a religious discipleship. According to Weber, it was methodical life-conduct in the service of religious duties imposed by a charismatic
prophethood and a doctrine of otherworldly salvation which demanded that
the faithful go beyond the confines of everyday routine that made possible the
extraordinary social effects of the higher religions, namely Judaism and subsequently Christianity. The culmination of this development was reached with
Puritanism. Its doctrine of salvation, ultimately and not incidentally closely
connected with the Old Testament tension between the omnipotence of a
single God and the wickedness of the faithful, and its extremely pointed dogma
of predestination, permitted the rise of that 'great rationalism of systematically
ethical life-conduct',[9] the revolutionary consequences of which changed
society, and which Weber never ceased to admire. Beside the rise of modern,
production-intensive, market-oriented capitalism, it was above all else the
principle of 'rationalization of life-conduct' not just in the religious sphere but
in particular also in the innerworldly sphere, with its wide-ranging secular consequences, that is owed largely to Puritanism. In this respect, as a summation of
his universal-historical analysis of world religions in 1920, Weber could testify
of Puritanism: 'It was here that this great process in religious history of the "disenchantment" of the world reached its conclusion, which began with ancient
Judaic prophetism and, in conjunction with Hellenic scientific thought,
repudiated every magical means of finding redemption as superstition and
sacrilege.'[10]

With the 'innerworldly ascetism' of Puritanism, and thereby the systematic rationalization of the whole of personal life-conduct in pursuit of stringent otherworldly religious ideals in stark contrast to everyday routine, a threshold of world-historical significance, as it were, had been crossed, from which Weber would have viewed it as intellectually false to want to retreat. Mythical forms of world-views which strove to reconcile the characteristic tension between the 'transcendental' and everyday reality by symbolical means were thus for him quite unacceptable. This circumstance can be graphically demonstrated at the level of his personal biography.

To begin with it can be asserted that although according to his own admission he felt 'religiously neutral' he was certainly deeply indebted to Puritan religiosity. He once expressed this condition eminently clearly to Adolf von Harnack in a text which dealt with the problem of assessing Lutheranism: 'the fact that our nation never, in *any* form, underwent the education of rigorous asceticism is the source of everything that I find odious in it (*as well as in myself*)' (emphasis added).[11] The extent to which Weber frequently identified, not with the religious strictness of Puritanism, but rather with its rationalization of life-conduct in the service of otherworldly life-ideals that are considered irrevocable, as was embodied in perfect form in Puritan theology, could hardly be greater.

This also determined Weber's attitude to such political or spiritual tendencies that saw in the establishment of a new myth or the revitalization of traditional myths a way out of the problems of the present. Of interest in this connection is the controversy with Stefan George and the George circle, which reached a climax in the summer of 1910 in the sense that Weber's postulate of the rationalizing force of the Protestant ethic was itself made a target for the criticism of modern rationalistic culture by a student of George's.[12] Through the intercession of Gundolf it even led to several meetings between Weber and Stefan George. Max Weber had great personal respect for Stefan George as a writer operating with the emotive means of expression of a sensually composed diction of great expressive power, yet his claim to have a prophetic mission and a natural gift for leadership seemed just as arrogant as his literary exertions directed towards creating a myth of a humanity in need of renewal. Although, as he stressed, 'Stefan George and his students . . . in crucial issues presumably in the final analysis' served 'other gods' than he did himself, this did not prevent Weber from expressly conceding them the right to hold such an intellectual opinion, although this amounted to the creation of new mythical thought renouncing modernity. Yet in the end there was a world of difference between the two men.[13]

Weber certainly had a far greater interest in forms of political myth formation which were geared towards direct socio-political consequences. As we have already seen, he counted the *Communist Manifesto* among those texts which created a powerful political myth. Historically perhaps the most significant form of such political myth creation, Sorel's theory of the general strike, is not in fact directly mentioned anywhere in Weber's work. But Weber did take syndicalist ideology in all its forms to task when it was expounded to him by Roberto Michels in 1909.[14] As an attitude founded in the ethics of conviction which is well aware of the empirical improbability of really causing a social upheaval with anarchist techniques of action, yet which nevertheless persists in the belief that the existing system is so unjust that one is compelled to fight against it without regard to considerations of what is politically realistic, the syndicalist doctrine was respectable although, in Weber's personal view, dubious; any mythological elevation of syndicalist strategy, perhaps in the form of an idealization of the general strike as Sorel intended it, would have seemed to him an inappropriate intermingling of the normative sphere with that of responsible politics, at least in so far as the 'myth of the general strike' is used as a power source of the revolutionary movement. Syndicalism was, as Weber ventured, 'either an idle whim of intellectual romantics and ... undisciplined workers ... or else a religion of conviction which is justified even if it never provides an ideal for the future that is "attainable"'.[15]

Incomparably more severe was Weber's verdict on that form of political myth formation which at the start of the First World War adopted the 'ideas of 1914', which, in opposition to the ideals of 1789, intended to inflate the German authoritarian traditions of Prussian-German convention into an ideal of a naturally attuned, 'organic' and thus more human way of life and therefore at the same time to create a myth of the world-historical superiority of the Prussian-German authoritarian social model. Weber saw in this little more than pathetic literary verbiage which sought to avoid reality.[16]

The efforts of the publisher Eugen Diederichs in a series of conferences at Burg Lauenstein in Thuringia in the early summer and autumn of 1917 to kindle a revitalized German national consciousness which would be oriented essentially towards romantic standards of life belong to a similar category. These aspirations tended to be extremely anti-rationalist, anti-modernist and anti-capitalist, and at the same time to be committed to organic state theory of the sort that ever since Adam Müller had never completely disappeared from the history of German political ideas. It was Diederichs who propagated a symbiotic combination of a spiritually aristocratic, largely secularized Protestantism and the idea of an authoritarian state with a German nationalist slant. He made conscious use of mythological formulations such as the 'coming of the Third Reich' and the 'myth of the unredeemed God' who was to find salvation through the revolt of men of intellect against the prevailing materialism and egalitarianism and through the resumption of spiritual pursuits, in such a way that the German Reformation would reach fruition.[17] Max Maurenbrecher in particular added a political note as he called for a revival of the idea of the German state derived from the spirit of German idealism and German Romanticism which would prove itself far superior to the 'democratic individualism' originating in the Enlightenment. At the conferences in Burg Lauenstein Weber did not pass over any opportunity of rigorously opposing political mythologizing such as this. Similarly he criticized the anti-rationalist preconceptions of the Youth Movement which was also pursuing alternative mythological designs to bourgeois-capitalist society.[18]

Finally reference may also be made to Max Weber's address 'Science as a vocation', which represents at the same time a critical dialogue with the irrationalist tendencies in large sections of the organized German student body, and indeed in the intelligentsia in general. This address was delivered, as we now know, as early as 7 November 1917 to the Federation of Liberal Students (Freistudentischer Bund) in Munich.[19] Weber's categorical assertion that science was not capable of providing the justification for values but could only assist the individual in 'giving an account to himself of the ultimate meaning of his own conduct' was given an equally cool reception as his criticism of the expectant attitude of students who looked to their professors as 'leaders' rather than 'teachers', despite the fact that it was precisely the latter group of people who definitely did not have a calling for suggesting or even providing solutions to questions of values. Even less well received was Weber's polemic against 'the modern intellectualist romanticism of the irrational',[20] which in the revival of mythical thought hoped for salvation from the sobering rationalism of science, which refused to provide answers to the genuinely vital issues facing mankind. Erich Kahler, a student of Stefan George, in a book on *The Vocation of Science* that was deliberately bent on controversy, later explained what a generation of students inclined to neo-romantic modes of thought really wanted to hear from Max Weber.[21]

On the other hand, Weber reached the remarkable conclusion in the very same lecture that at the end of a 'process of disenchantment continued over thousands of years of Western civilization'[22] the 'struggle between the gods of various orders and values' was none the less still going on, perhaps 'demystified' and divested of its mythical manifestations, yet basically continuing in exactly the same way. What is more, Weber's interpretation points to the conclusion that it was precisely the process of the progressive disenchantment of the world through science that brought into even sharper relief the conflicts between alternative value-positions or world-views.[23] Weber himself reached the prophetic-sounding conclusion that 'many old gods, demystified and thus in the shape of impersonal forces, are rising up from their graves. They strive to gain power over our lives and again they resume their eternal struggle with one another.'[24] It almost seems as if he meant by this that humanity after a thousand years of emancipation from mythical forms of ontological validation had returned to its initial condition – namely, a return to mythological ways of thinking and conversing, although maybe on a higher level. Or, to put it another way, mankind had reached the end of a universal 'process of rationalization and socialization' in which Max Weber was inclined to discern the fundamental motive force behind the development of the Western world, and that another open-ended process was about to be begun which would again be propelled by mythical forces, though perhaps on a higher level.

To answer this question it is necessary to examine more closely what theoretical status the idea of rationalization as the basic central motif in Western history actually possessed in Max Weber's work. Earlier interpretations were in the main unswervingly ready to view the rationalization concept as the axis of universal-historical development along which as it were a unilinear reconstruction of all past history right up to the present could be unfolded.[25] However, Weber repeatedly was quite explicit in pointing out that in his ideal-typical constructions, not to mention his studies on the sociology of religion, he never had as his sole object the development of a substantive theory of history or even just of a general model of the course of Western history. At best he regarded as feasible only hypothetical systematizations with the help of which certain culturally significant characteristics of the historical process could be portrayed with a high degree of accuracy. These words of caution have been largely ignored by the great majority of interpretations of his work. None the less, many of his texts, particularly from the early period up until about 1913, including the older sections of *Economy and Society*, admit at least in part of such a reconstruction of Western history.

It seems, however, that Weber's interest in a reconstruction of segments of past reality on the basis of ideal-typical process models, a classic example of which can be found in *The Protestant Ethic*, progressively declined and that, accordingly, even the studies of the great non-Christian world religions were pursued no longer just from the point of view of functioning as a negative test case for the propositions of the Protestantism thesis. 'Disenchantment' eventually turned out to be a cultural phenomenon that was definitely not unique to the Western tradition but common to all forms of religious or spiritual movements originally initiated by great prophetship or natural charisma. Similarly, the sequence that can still be observed throughout the older parts of *Economy and Society*, from charismatic through traditional to legal or bureaucratic forms of social or political organization, is no longer presented as the quintessence of one and the same historical process but is merely retained as a tendential, almost purposeful procedural form which can occur essentially in the most diverse historical formations and in the most varied of epochs, even including the modern period, and can even be empirically authenticated. In the later versions of the 'three pure types of legitimate domination' the order of types of domination is hence reversed. Charisma is no longer an ideal-typical scheme for the justification of spiritual, religious or political domination, characteristic of the early forms of human social order; instead it becomes a universal category. Charisma is now viewed quite simply as the source of creative action oriented to personal ideal values of an otherworldly kind. In the same way the concept of rationality takes on a new dimension; indeed, greater emphasis is increasingly given to the notion that rationalization is possible in relation to highly diverse ideal values or religious world-views and accordingly that it can no longer be claimed only for the type of formal rationality specific to the West which results in an instrumental-rational subjugation not just of nature but also of social institutions.

This new dimension of a systematic concept formation no longer consistent with the developmental ideal types predominant in his earlier works was not fully unfolded throughout Max Weber's later work but was plainly recognizable all the same. A clear realization of this fact is certainly somewhat impeded by the patchwork nature of the texts in the editions available to us nowadays.[26] This will be outlined only briefly here, first in relation to the concept of 'charisma' and then in relation to the concept of 'rationalization', which is divested of its characteristics as a theory related to a particular period of history and instead is promoted to the antinomical conceptual twin of charisma.[27]

At the end of the chapter on 'Political and hierocratic domination' – a text already committed to paper before 1913 and still solely concerned with historical manifestations of religious charismatic forms of domination – Max Weber speaks of 'the Age of Enlightenment belief that, if allowed to run its course unrestrained, with the help of divine providence and because the individual knows his own interests best himself, relatively speaking at least, individual reason must produce the best possible world: the charismatic transfiguration of reason ... is the last guise assumed by charisma on its fateful course.'[28] Here charisma appears as a phenomenon of the past which seems to be definitively superseded in modernity. In other chronologically later passages this verdict is tempered; here Weber states instead that through the progressive rationalization and bureaucratization of every aspect of life the significance of charisma is increasingly restricted. In later sections of *Economy and Society*, particularly in

the chapter on 'Types of domination', charisma is in fact still assigned principally to a pre-rationalist age as a form of political or religious domination, but it
is ascribed the quality of a revolutionary force which, in contrast to the 'equally
revolutionary force of *ratio*, could be a 'transformation from within, which,
born of misery or of rapture', entailed 'a transformation of the main orientation
of convictions and action and a completely new orientation of all attitudes to
every individual life-form and to the "world" in general'.[29] At the same time
Weber considered a reorientation of charisma away from domination to be
suited to providing the basis for an empirical justification of a novel, non-
dogmatic theory of 'plebiscitarian leader democracy'.

In the end it is charisma and rationalization which in general, as dichoto-
mously interrelated forces, constitute social change. Charisma (which according to Weber's sociological theory to some extent occupies the position of both
Judaic prophetship and Puritan asceticism, oriented to imperative otherworldly
norms, in the prehistory of the modern world) is assigned the role of the innovative element within the historical process; it represents as it were the point
where personality is imposed on to the empirical process of history. Rationalization, on the other hand, either operates as instrumental-rational adaptation
to pre-existing values, interests and circumstances which can be designated as
binding, or else operates circuitously by way of the intellectualizing of the cognition of reality itself. Here as a rule it uses the instruments of bureaucratic
organization for the optimum fulfilment of its respective objectives.

The concept of rationalization likewise undergoes a more differentiated
interpretation in Weber's later work; it frees itself from every historical reification such as appears particularly in the interpretation of Western history as a
unilinear process of 'disenchantment' of a quasi-evolutionist nature. Rather
there is an increasingly precise elaboration of how there can be, and indeed was,
rationalization in pursuit of the most diverse ideals and that such rationalizations tended as a matter of course to come into conflict with one another.
Charismatic domination can and does as a rule make use of bureaucratic techniques in order to maximize the effect of its actions, just as was the case with
Judaic prophetism, Weber's great typical example of rationalization of life-
conduct effected by charismatic gift of grace in the light of definite ideals; it demands an adjustment of its adherents' life-conduct according to rational
principles in line with its own ultimate objectives, just as indeed may be the case
with bureaucratic forms of domination. It turns out that rationalization of life-
conduct in line with purely instrumental-rational maximalization of personal
behaviour which takes given circumstances into account is really only a border-
line case of rationalization, namely 'formal rationalization'. The 'formal
rationality' thus achieved can by all means and as a rule does tend to be in

conflict with a multiplicity of possible forms of 'material rationality', which is oriented to definite material ideal values or ideal interests more closely specifiable only in the concrete historical instance.

With the distinction between 'formal' and 'material' rationality, the more explicit and clearly expounded historical unequivocalness of the concept of rationalization in Weber's earlier writings, and with it also the concept of 'disenchantment', essentially disappears. This is why it thus appears impossible to view the essence of Max Weber's sociological theory as an evolutionistic reconstruction of past history, whether it be that of the West (as Schluchter suggests) or else of world history in general (as argued by Tenbruck). It attempts to be this only in the sense of a theory for the meaningful interpretation of what is basically a plurality of histories, though at the level of knowledge about the whole of the past history of mankind. Acting as the implicit guiding thought in this undertaking is the question of how freedom, as a precondition for the self-realization of the personality, is possible at all in a society dominated by the constant rivalry between material and ideal interests, but also in a world increasingly assuming the form of an 'iron cage' of future serfdom.

At this point the discussion has turned full circle. Max Weber's theory of rationalization and 'disenchantment', as a central problem of history in general, is to be understood in the final analysis not as a theory to explain the triumph of modern rational thought over myth, magic, charismatic irrationality and traditionally legitimated orders, but as a fundamental phenomenon of universal history. Even major manifestation and movement which occurred first as phenomena explicitly outside everyday routine is subject to the process of 'disenchantment' and rationalization. If 'disenchantment' can mean many things, according to whether it is spiritual or material ideals from which the rationalization of personal life-conduct or of the social order results, then the theory of rationalization presents itself in a new light. In principle, rationalization cannot point to any means of escape from the fundamental irrationalities of reality, and modern science is capable of doing this least of all, according to Weber. Rather, these irrationalities are only displaced on to a more deep-seated level of reality where they emerge in even sharper relief: 'Yet, wherever rational empirical cognition has systematically completed the disenchantment of the world and its transformation in one causal mechanism, the conflict with the moral postulate that the world is a divinely ordained cosmos or somehow oriented to meaningful ethics will surface again all the more forcefully.'[30] No matter how sublime the development of an innerworldly culture, such as one formed out of the accumulation of a purposively guided selection of cultural assets, may become, it will provide no help out of this dilemma.[31] Rather, it appears that there always exists a plurality of possible rationalizations in the sense of relevant alternative world-views – alongside and in competition with that apparently or genuinely purely instrumental 'formal rationality' responding solely to the sheer pressure of adaptation, which ultimately represents a reification of long since institutionalized innovatory forces, although for its part it owes its existence to a combination of creative charisma and material rationalization in keeping with the former's chosen objectives.

Seen in such a perspective, Weber's initially so peculiar statement about the 'many ancient gods' who, 'demystified and thus in the shape of impersonal forces', recommence their 'eternal struggle' makes sense once again.[32] In institutionalized form, in the shape of bureaucratic political or social movements, the individual is confronted by just that multiplicity of competing forces which people of earlier epochs not infrequently tried to explain in mythological terms. In spite of his basic affirmation of the principle of rational life-conduct as an essential element of a personality which is at peace with itself, and notwithstanding the fact that the secular process of modernization and rationalization put the world at the disposal of man's whim, in the sense that it made the world causally explicable, Weber considered the insurmountable tension between supra-mundane ideals, whether they be articulated in magical, mythical or religious forms, as an essential fact of human existence. His attitude may be described as that of a thinker who has as it were thought through the principles of the Enlightenment to their ultimate conclusion and freed them from all naïve hopes in the all-powerful force of rationality as a purely emancipatory factor. This made him adopt a stance in the end which, although in principle on the side of rationality, still systematically included the whole range of the irrational and thus also the various forms of mythical thought as possible components of reality.

Personally Weber regarded a return to a mythological understanding of the world, in the sense of an abandonment of the stringent rules of rational science, to be impracticable; but, whether it was a question of delineating those twilight regions from which all human conduct derives its motivation and in which scholarship not least of all finds its own basic intellectual inspiration, it was not just coincidence that from his pen flowed images which originated in ancient mythology. His work cannot in any case be viewed as the final triumph of the Enlightenment over the various mythical world-views, despite his prescription that, precisely in a world where the struggle between competing world-views is conducted through new 'disenchanted' forms of an impersonal nature, it would be feeble to seek refuge in the mere sham of an anti-intellectualist irrationalism, even if this were to seek to legitimate itself in some form or other as the renaissance of myth.

The Two Dimensions of Social Change in Max Weber's Sociological Theory

The growing interest in Max Weber's sociology which is observable today must be due, among other things, to the fact that it explicitly or implicitly encompasses the historical dimension of social reality, even in its purely theoretical elements. It may well be said that his sociological theory derives its strength from the fact that it is unfolded against the backcloth of universal history. Weber's writings are full of important insights based upon historical observations. His ideal-typical conceptualizations are of considerable value for historical research, and, indeed, they were meant to be so. However, there is still considerable confusion about Max Weber's notion of social and historical change, although this issue is central to his sociological thought. In part this is due to the fact that Weber never presented his views on the historical process in a systematic manner, for methodological reasons which I have discussed elsewhere.[1] Instead we find in his work a great variety of ideal-typical reconstructions of particular segments of universal history which he considered to be significant from a present-day vantage-point, given the fact that modern individualistic society was at risk of being overwhelmed by the twin forces of bureaucracy and formal rationalization. In this respect, mention must be made, in particular, of Weber's socio-economic studies on antiquity, his studies on *The Protestant Ethic and the Spirit of Capitalism*, his famous treatise *The City* and, above all, his *Sociology of World Religions*. Furthermore, the first section of *Economy and Society*, the casuistry of the system of 'pure types', which deliberately transcends historical reality inasmuch as all direct references to the dimension of historical time have been eliminated, may be seen as a formalized model of the various politcial and social formations to be found in universal history.

Usually Weber's notion of the historical process is described as an essentially unilinear model of the progressive unfolding of the rationalist culture of the West or, as Wolfgang Schluchter put it more recently, a 'developmental history' of Western culture, which is characterized, above all, by the progressive rationalization of all forms of social interaction and the increasing 'disenchantment' of all otherworldly value-attitudes. However, it should be kept in mind that Max Weber had consistently refused to develop a substantive theory of universal history, such as had been done by many social scientists before him and, indeed, after him. Although it may be said that his work contains many elements of a subtantive theory of world history or, at any rate, of the history of the West, we intend to show that this was not at all Weber's intention. On the contrary, his historical sociology deliberately abstained from developing a substantive scheme of universal history, or of Western history. Instead, Weber intended to develop systems of ideal types, and of 'pure types' which would allow the meaningful interpretation of social processes, both past and present, from the vantage-point of particular 'ideal values', thereby establishing their *Kulturbedeutsamkeit* (cultural significance).[2] Hypothetical extrapolations about the future of Western culture condition the way in which the phenomena are analysed without any substantive evaluation.

It would appear in the debate about Weber's notion of world-historical development conducted by Wolfgang Schluchter, Friedrich Tenbruck, Wilhelm Hennis and, more recently, Günther Roth that this aspect of Weber's theoretical position has not been paid sufficient attention. It would appear that in this debate a neo-evolutionist, a neo-idealist and perhaps an anthropological interpretation of his work are all at loggerheads with one another. Wolfgang Schluchter, the main exponent of the neo-evolutionist position, has undertaken a wide-ranging reconstruction of Weber's notion of Western history which focuses, in particular, on his *Sociology of World Religions*. Although Schluchter takes considerable care to steer clear of older evolutionist theories (which had been heavily criticized by Weber himself), he nevertheless defines Weber's sociology as a 'social history of the West' which must be seen as a 'partial theory of evolution, with a realistic intent'.[3] Its essential theme is, according to Schluchter, the emergence of the modern rationalistic world civilization which stands out from all other known historical civilizations because it succeeded in mastering nature by means of modern rational science. Schluchter does not contend that Weber's historical sociology is concerned only with the history of Western rationalism. But its essential theme is, in his view, the emergence of rational forms of social interaction, notably rational science, cultural systems based upon the principle of rationality and, last but not least, a rational capitalist economy. This is true, he argues, even, or rather especially, when Weber deals with non-Western cultures, notably the great non-Western world religions, such as Hinduism, Buddhism or Judaism. In this context Schluchter emphasizes above all the role of 'material' rather than specifically religious interests, referring to Weber's famous dictum that 'not ideas, but material and ideal interests, directly govern men's social conduct'.[4]

Schluchter does not deny that the 'world-views' created by the great world religions guided the actions of men on to fundamentally different paths. But he stresses that these 'world-views' are not just independent variables but largely dependent upon economic and social factors. In order to substantiate this interpretation he again refers to a rather late text, namely the Introduction to the *Collected Essays on the Sociology of Religion*. Here Weber does indeed speak of a reciprocal relationship between a particular 'world-view' and the 'economic ethics' (*Wirtschaftsgesinnung*) derived from it on the one hand, and a particular socio-economic order on the other.[5] This line of reasoning is clearly directed against Friedrich Tenbruck's attempts to reformulate Weber's theory of Western culture in a neo-idealist manner. On the basis of a new critical interpretation of the texts (which, however, did not fully stand up to the criticisms which followed) Tenbruck objected to the view that Weber must be seen primarily as a theorist of the process of rationalization of the modern world, as had been argued *inter alia* by Reinhard Bendix.[6] Rather than considering rationalization and bureaucratization of social institutions as Weber's main interest, he emphasizes Weber's continuing interest in the autonomous role of ideal, particularly religious factors. Accordingly he argues that it is not *Economy and Society*, as has conventionally been seen to be the case, but the *Sociology of World Religions* which forms the very core of his work, and it is in these essays that Weber's notion of the process of world history is expressed in a definitive form. It is not the process of rationalization as such, and certainly not in its reduction to the developmental history of modern Western civilization, which is, according to Tenbruck, his main theme; rather it is the original, innovative role of religious ideas, followed by their gradual rationalization and disenchantment due to the immanent logic of rationalization to which all religious doctrines tend to be subjected in the course of time. 'By discovering religious rationalization Weber brought reason back into history, or, to put it another way, restored the unity of human history which had been destroyed by the impact of scientism and modernization.'[7] In the course of working on the history of Western world religions Weber had come to see world history in a new perspective; he had arrived at the conclusion that mankind had reached the end of a process of rationalization which had lasted 3000 years. In a way this thesis merely amounts to the turning upside-down of the traditional rationalization thesis rather than its refutation.

Yet another interpretation has been put forward by Wilhelm Hennis, who in doing so revives a line of reasoning already to be found in the work of Siegfried Landshut and Karl Löwith. Hennis argues that Weber's universal-historical studies have one central theme, namely which type of human being is likely to thrive best in a particular socio-economic and cultural system. Indeed, Weber always tended to focus on the question which types of life-conduct (*Lebensführung*) are favoured most under particular social and economic conditions, and which not. This implies, of course, that different societies practise different forms of social selection or, rather, give preference to certain types of human beings. This social mechanism normally operates quite independently of the policies of governments; rather it is dependent on the socio-economic and cultural conditions in a given society which influence the individual life-conduct of most if not all of the individuals belonging to it. This interpretation, which may rightly be called an anthropological one, objects on principle to all reconstructions of Weber's sociological theory in either an evolutionist or a teleological form, since this would result in falsifying the key dichotomy between 'personality and life orders' ('die Persönlichkeit und die Lebensordnungen'). In order to substantiate this view Hennis put considerable effort into a new interpretation of Weber's earlier writings which are still primarily historical in nature. Yet it seems that although this approach touches upon an important aspect of Weber's thought it is not likely to provide us with the key to a comprehensive interpretation of his promised sociological thought.[8]

It would appear that none of these approaches can fully do justice to Weber's intentions in his sociological analyses of the world-historical process or, to be more precise, his analyses of significant segments of the past. Nor do they give a satisfactory answer to the question whether social change is brought about in history primarily by ideal and religious factors – to put it in Weber's own terminology, 'other-worldly' (*ausseralltägliche*) events – or by socio-economic conditions, in other words, the dynamics of social stratification and institutional structures which tend to condition people's actions.

In his earlier writings at any rate Weber himself seems to have been rather ambiguous on this point. In his studies on agricultural labour east of the Elbe from the early 1890s Weber suggests that it was the advance of the capitalist mode of production which undermined the traditional agrarian economy in these regions dominated by a closed landed aristocracy. This resulted in a progressive deterioration of the standards of living of agricultural labour, and induced the workers of German nationality to move to the industrial centres, leaving their jobs to Polish migrant labourers. In short, the irresistible advance of capitalist modes of production, enforced by overseas competition, destroyed the traditional patriarchal pattern of labour relations in the East Elbian regions which had been in existance for centuries and had been based upon a convergence of the economic interests of workers and landlords, replacing it by formally free labour with the inevitable consequence that class conflict was from now on a dominant feature of social relations. At the same time, however, Weber pointed out that the ideal motive of obtaining a greater degree of freedom likewise played an important role as an independent factor inducing agricultural labour to seek a new livelihood by migrating to Berlin, to the industrial regions in the West, or possibly even overseas. In *Die Agrarverhältnisse im Altertum* Weber came the closest ever to using a Marxist model of explanation. The system of land division and the modes of production largely based upon enslaved labour appear to determine the course of events, whereas human will and human action are entirely conditioned by these material factors. In the famous study on *The City* in antiquity and early modern Europe the key question is whether and how formally free labour had gradually emerged as an entirely new form of social organization, and, in this connection, where and under which conditions an autonomous urban bourgeoisie developed. This is the central theme around which he assembled an enormously rich mass of historical evidence. Without being in any way an evolutionary scheme, *The City* culminates in an analysis of the city of medieval central Europe which, owing to a political confraternization of the burghers – the so-called *conjurationes* – had won independence from their former territorial landlords. Economic interests appear to have played a dominant role as well. Urban liberties, whether usurped or generously granted by territorial rulers, were largely respected on economic grounds, but occasionally ideal motives came to play a role too. Religion is assigned a subordinate role; Weber took care to emphasize that the city saints were worshipped largely in order to provide legitimacy for the newly acquired urban liberties. On the other hand Weber assigned particular (and, on the grounds of historical evidence, undue) weight to the role played by conspiracies or revolutionary actions by the burghers against the territorial rulers, be they kings, princes or ecclesiastical powers. The idealist theme of emancipation from feudal patronage is, according to Weber, an independent variable at work in history, notwithstanding the overriding importance of economic interests. In *The Protestant Ethic and the Spirit of Capitalism*, by contrast, the accent is clearly placed on ideal or, to be more precise, on religious motivations which are singled out as innovative factors of the first order which initiate secular social change. The economic ethic of unceasing work, stemming from the inner-worldly asceticism of the Puritans, must, according to Weber, be considered the most important, if not the only root from which modern[9] market-oriented industrial capitalism grew. Only later – partly in response to the widespread criticism of his thesis as too onesided – did Weber qualify and indeed modify this view, which he himself regarded as a refutation of Marx's theory of historical materialism (not, perhaps, entirely justified if we bear in mind that in his theory of primary accumulation Marx argued in part on surprisingly similar lines).[10]

In Max Weber's studies on Hinduism, Buddhism and Judaism (he never paid detailed attention to Islam) we find a far more complex interrelationship of religious and socio-economic factors. Here too, Weber sees the origins of these secular religious movements as belonging to the realm of 'otherworldly' (*ausseralltäglich*) events. Religious virtuosity and individual charisma, partly arising from magic, partly allying themselves with it, play a decisive innovative role. In his studies on Hinduism and Buddhism, for instance, he addressed himself explicitly to the problem of whether religious factors are an independent variable. He pointed out that a merely economic explanation of the emergence of the Hindu caste system or the origins of the doctrine of karma was not enough. He argued that both were created by a rational system of ethical thought – the *dharma* doctrine – but not at all by economic conditions of whatever sort.[11] However, the manner in which these religious impulses were being transformed into religious movements must be attributed primarily, if not exclusively, to socio-economic factors. This is the case in particular as regards the process of institutionalization and the gradual development of clearly defined dogmatic systems to which these religious movements are irresistibly subjected in the course of time. It is in this institutionalized form that religious doctrines exercised enormous influence on the social system around them. As Weber put it, they often determined the developmental path which a particular culture was to follow for centuries. In the case of Hinduism, for instance, in Weber's opinion, the role of the brahmins, the Vedic caste of intellectuals, was predominant: they exercised a decisive influence. Likewise in the case of Buddhism it was the small class of Chinese bureaucratic literati which determined the future course of events.

On the basis of these findings it would appear impossible to resolve definitively the controversial issue of how far Max Weber regarded ideal and religious factors as independent or, in the final analysis, as decisive variables in the historical process. He persistently emphasized the key role played by individual action oriented by 'otherworldly' (*ausseralltäglich*) ideas, religious or otherwise. Yet at the same time he argued again and again that the life-conduct of individuals is largely determined by socio-economic conditions beyond their control; the average person at any rate has little choice other than to adapt his or her life-conduct to the prevailing social and economic circumstances; conformity to given conditions and traditions is likely to be the individual's normal reaction. However, one may break out of this pattern by choosing rationally to orientate one's conduct of life by 'otherworldy' ideals of some kind. Historical experience shows that the 'world-views' created by religious movements served such purposes, in conjunction with other institutional and economic factors pointing in the same direction.

This shows clearly that Weber did not come down on the side of an idealist interpretation of history, however veiled, as Tenbruck would have it; rather he eventually opted, after a good deal of uncertainty, for a two-dimensional model of social change. On the one hand he deliberately emphasized such types of social change as are initiated by the innovative deeds of great personalities whose actions originate in 'otherworldly' value-attitudes of a most stringent nature. On the other hand he repeatedly pointed out that social processes are largely determined by rigid institutional structures, be they social, economic or even ideal; individuals are usually helpless against them, and, as a rule, their life-conduct is largely determined by them, if only because invariably their economic interests point towards adaptation and conformity with the given social order. It was only late in his life that Weber succeeded in definitively formulating his views on the two alternative forms in which social change operates in history, in a passage inserted by him in 1920 into his 'Einleitung in die Wirtschaftsethik der Weltreligionen' (as already mentioned): 'Interests (both material and ideal), not ideas, directly govern human action. But the world-views created by "ideas" very often set the points of the rails along which the course of action proceeded, propelled by the dynamic of interests.'[12]

This is to say that social change is initiated by actions which may be motivated by 'ideal' or by 'material' interests. Idealist motives enter into the arena only in an indirect way; they determine the direction in which a given social system will develop further, driven forward by inherent dynamics of its own. In the following pages I shall try to reconstruct this two-dimensional model of social and historical change in a systematic manner, with reference to Weber's later works (which belong to the same period as the passage just quoted).

Max Weber's sociology abounds in dichotomies in the construction of ideal types and ideal-typical classifications. It is not difficult to find equivalents to the dichotomy of 'ideal' and 'material' interests, which, as we have seen, essentially determine the course of human action. 'Value-rational' and 'instrumental-rational' action apparently form a similar pair of dichotomic concepts which directly correspond to the former. 'Value-rational' action is oriented by sub-stantive value-attitudes which in principle are of a 'non-everyday' nature; ultimately such values originate in charismatic action of some sort. 'Instrumental-rational' action conversely is always conditioned by the prevailing situation and tends to take full account of the economic institutional constraints which limit it. The means by which a given objective will be obtained in the most likely manner are calculated rationally, if necessary by referring to the methods and information provided by rational scientific knowledge. But this way of calculating the means tends to restrict the choice of goals as well, inasmuch as instrumental-rational action will always try to make sure that the desired goal will be achieved; this, however, requires that the particular goals must be within reach, in practical terms. It follows from this that instrumentally oriented action will always favour adaptation to given social conditions, rather than challenging them. As Weber puts it himself, instrumental-rational action always results in a 'deliberate adaptation to given situations in terms of self-interest'.[13] To put it otherwise, instrumental-rational action always gives preference to 'formal rationality', that is to say it always seeks optimally to exploit the rules and regulations of an existing social system.

On the other hand, value-rational action is oriented by 'non-everyday' or 'otherworldly' values which are regarded subjectively as absolutely binding; therefore considerations conditioned by the concrete situation and the chances of success in view of exterior factors are of secondary importance. In the final analysis, value-rational or, as it might be called also, 'substantive-rational' forms of social conduct are always induced by charismatic value-attitudes, or else by charismatic deeds which confer a concrete meaning upon such value-attitudes and provide them, in the shape of the followers devoted to these values, with an institutional embodiment in society. In contrast to instrumental-rational action, all charismatically oriented types of social action are, in a specific sense, directed by the inner self of the acting person, or, as Weber puts it, they are 'innengeleitet'. Charisma manifests its revolutionary power, which amounts to a challenge to everyday reality, 'from within, from a central *metanoia* [that is to say 'fundamental change'] in the conduct of the followers'.[14]

The impact of these two alternative types of social action upon a given social order is altogether different. Charismatically directed action is an innovative force, and potentially it may induce innovation, and even revolutionary change of world-historical magnitude. By contrast, instrumental-rational action is primarily oriented by material interests and inclined to operate within the restraints of the given situation in order to ensure optimal success. Therefore it fosters progressive routinization – and eventually 'formal' rationalization – both of dominant 'world-views' and of existing social systems: it is the essential driving force behind what Weber occasionally describes, in shorthand so to speak, as 'die Eigengesetzlichkeiten', that is to say the immanent laws of development to which institutions are subjected, regardless of whether they embody 'ideal' or 'material' interests or a combination of both. This may be illustrated by reference to a famous passage in *The Protestant Ethic and the Spirit of Capitalism* where Weber argued exactly along such lines. Modern industrial capitalism, it is stated there, once it has become established in an institutionalized form, no longer requires the inner driving force stemming from ideal or religious value-attitudes because the dynamic of material interests in itself guarantees its steady advance.[15] As religious movements become institutionalized in the course of time, with groups of intellectuals declaring themselves the movements' spokesmen and the author-ized interpreters of their doctrines, similar processes of rationalization can be observed. The religious virtuosi who provide the initial charismatic impulses are usually soon replaced by an institutionalized priesthood which ensures that the doctrine which they teach to their followers is interpreted and progressively unfolded in a consistent, that is to say, 'rational' manner. However irrational their content, such religious messages are gradually transformed into a traditionalist doctrine, and as this is further unfolded in a systematic manner by the intellec-tuals who are considered its authoritative interpreters it eventually becomes a thoroughly rationalist system of thought which has its direct correlation in the institutionalized body administering the religious doctrine to the rank and file of the followers in a rationalized form.

As can be deduced from these observations, instrumental-rational and value-rational action represent two entirely different or, to be more precise, antagon-istic principles. They correspond to two equally antagonistic forms of life-conduct. To put it briefly, the former is ruled by the principle of adaptation to given reality, the latter determined by value-attitudes which as a rule derive from 'non-everyday' beliefs. It is possible to elaborate this two-dimensional model of social change further, on the basis of Weber's later writings, notably the casuistry of 'pure types' which we find in *Economy and Society* and those pas-sages of his essays on the *Sociology of World Religions* which are at about the same level of development of his sociological thought. The figure reproduced over-leaf may be helpful in further elucidating this argument.

We consistently find in Max Weber's sociological work two fundamentally different notions of how social change may come about. Although in empirical reality we find them almost always operating in conjunction with one another, they are qualitatively different and have entirely different social consequences. 'Ideal interests' which have their roots in particular 'world-views' lead to value-rational action. They correspond to a form of life-conduct (*Lebensführung*) which is guided by substantive values and strives to see the social order recon-stituted accordingly. The individuals involved will attempt to rationalize their life-conduct in such a way as to maximize the chances of this being done. This amounts to challenging given 'everyday' reality.

The systematic rationalization of the social conduct of individuals and groups in view of certain 'ultimate' or 'otherworldly' ideas usually leads to an enormous accumulation of social energies which at a certain point in time may become strong enough to break the routine of everyday life and give birth to entirely new social developments. It goes without saying that this may happen in extremely diverse ways, and on all levels of social life, and may take rather different forms, extending from a 'retreat from the world' to restless 'inner-worldly' activity. However, it may bring about the initial impulses for social innovations of considerable magnitude or, to put it another way, induce social change of substantial proportions.

The two dimensions of social change

value-rational change	*instrumental-rational change*
otherworldly world-views	innerworldly world-views
ideal interests	material interests
substantive-rational life-conduct	formal-rational life-conduct
value-rational social action	instrumental-rational social action
charisma, leading to substantive rationalization	routinization, leading to formal rationalization
amounting to: challenge to given social order on the basis of various forms of otherworldly life-conduct ranging from extreme asceticism to restless innerworldly activity	amounting to: adaptation to given social order; progressive forms of realization of its immanent principles via routinization and rationalization

This dimension of social change, however, is confronted throughout with another one, which in many ways would appear to be even more formidable, namely change which is initiated not by innovative social action but rather by the immanent dynamic of institutions and socio-economic systems. In the course of time they tend progressively to unfold those principles on which they are based – Max Weber often put this in metaphorical terms: he called it the *Eigengesetzlichkeiten*, that is to say the 'immanent dynamic' of institutions or structures. 'Material' – or 'substantive' – interests, which often originate in socio-economic constellations of a particular kind, and 'instrumental-rational' action correlate with one another, and both with a purpose-rational type of life-conduct, that is to say the life-conduct expected by and demanded from 'pro-fessionals' or, as Weber put it in Nietzschean terms, the *Fachmensch*, whose behaviour is determined by the mechanisms of institutionalized systems, such as the purely formal-rational structures of modern industrial society. This type of life-conduct lies at the root of the process of routinization and eventually the formal rationalization of social systems. It will become dominant, unless there are no countervailing forces to prevent it. It is governed by the principle of optimally adapting to given conditions and conforming with the immanent principles of establishing institutions and structures. Because of this orientation this type of life-conduct is bound to foster the process of routinization or formal rationalization of institutions and social systems. It is this type of human conduct in particular which is cultivated by bureaucratic institutions.

This two-dimensional model of social change may be seen as a synthesis of the 'idealist' and 'materialist' notions of change discussed above; furthermore, it takes into account Hennis's observation that Max Weber was above all interested in one issue, namely the likely consequences of different forms of life-conduct in history. It would appear that there is much to be said for the view that Weber always posed the question of what impact 'world-views' or 'ideas' have on social systems, seen in a world-historical perspective. More complex is the position regarding those interpretations which argue that Max Weber had been concerned above all with the analysis of the secular processes of rationalization and routinization, phenomena of the greatest importance for our understanding of the present world. In fact Max Weber was interested in the interrelation of both dimensions of social reality; the first concerns those types of personal life-conduct which are governed by value-rational or by substantive-rational principles that in the final analysis are based on value attitudes, which in turn derive their normative power from charismatic sources of some sort. The second refers to those *Eigengesetzlichkeiten* (internal dynamics) which govern the development patterns of institutions and systems; these always point towards progressive routinization and formal rationalization.

It goes without saying that the stuff of history is full of phenomena of the latter variety. In the realm of actual historical events routinization and rationalization, either of religious, philosophical or aesthetic doctrines or of social and political institutions, are predominant, while charismatic revolutions or value-oriented breakthroughs are the exception. Accordingly Weber's sociology is very much concerned with the former. Even so, his main interest was reserved for those *Weichenstellungen* (switching of tracks) which initiate new developmental paths in historical reality owing to the impact on history of 'world-views' which owe their initial formation to value-oriented individual action, usually by charismatic personalities. Weber's essays on *The Sociology of World Religions*, the casuistry of 'pure types' in *Economy and Society* and his political treatises all revolve around the key question of how and under which conditions such *Weichenstellungen* came about or are likely to occur. Likewise he was passionately interested in assessing to what degree they were effective in actually changing the direction of the course of history. In this context, strong personal leadership – not only in a religious or a political sense, but in all spheres of culture – is assigned a key role in providing the impulses that may eventually lead to entirely new developments. Max Weber proceeded from the key observation that in the known history of the world, historical developments (which, at first sight, seem by necessity to follow their own immanent dynamic) could be redirected on to revolutionary paths when, and only when, individuals or groups of individuals develop strict, ethically regulated ways of conducting their lives in the service of ultimate, 'non-everyday' ideals. As a rule these ideals stand in stark contrast to everyday reality, thereby posing a challenge to it. This, however, is tantamount to saying that significant social change will always be just around the corner. For if these individuals orientate their life-conduct by these 'non-everyday' ideals without reservation, while exercising asceticism in other fields of human activity, they will accumulate considerable social energies which eventually will break the mould of 'everyday' reality. It was this feature which in Weber's opinion distinguished ancient Judaic prophecy and Puritan asceticism from other comparable religious movements; they mark decisive points at which tracks were switched in the course of history, setting in motion those forces that eventually brought about modern industrial civilization.

For Max Weber, this by no means implied a devaluation of other religious systems. On the contrary, he was fascinated by Hinduism and Confucianism, those Asiatic religious creeds whose highest goal is innerworldly perfection, to be found in a dignified and aesthetically consummate personal life in which the individual has come to terms once and for all with the imperfections of the world as it is. The parallels with attitudes expressed by present-day Western intellectual elites were already self-evident to Weber. In later years he occasionally toyed with the idea of whether he should not embark upon a similar path, as is indicated in the 'Zwischenbetrachtung' in the *Collected Essays on the Sociology of World Religions*, which may be read as a (however sublime) self-confession on the part of Weber, and also in occasional talks with Georg Lukács.[16] However, in principle he still identified with the personal ideal of a rigorous, innerworldly, disciplined life-conduct in the service of ultimate ideals: 'The notion that through plain conduct addressed to meeting the "demands of the day" one may achieve salvation, which lies at the heart of all that makes up the specific significance of the "personality" in the West, is alien to Asia. This is as foreign to Asian thought as the pure factual rationalism of the West which tries hard to discover the impersonal laws that govern the world.'[17]

Accordingly the developmental path of Western culture forms the perspectival focus of Max Weber's universal-historical studies.

There can be no question that the future of Western culture was central to Weber's interest. Max Weber's reconstruction of the history of Western civilization, as a process of progressive rationalization and disenchantment of Western culture, associated with the development of a rational science, a rational relationship of man to nature (being the precondition for its progressive subjection to human control), and the creation of a rational state, must be viewed as the very essence of his sociology. The rise of modern industrial capitalism and its rapid expansion over the globe, associated with the inevitable destruction of all pre-modern socio-economic systems, and the growth of bureaucratic forms of social organizations in all spheres of life were, in his view, irreversible. In this context he was particularly concerned about the impact of the twin forces of formal rationalization and routinization upon the personal life-sphere of the individual. They apparently posed a mortal danger to any form of life-conduct oriented towards 'non-everyday' ideals. If we take into account the fact that Weber assigned to this type of value-oriented life-conduct a fundamental significance as it affected the very chances of genuine innovation in the course of time, it immediately becomes clear why he thought that the eventual triumph of these forces would be tantamount to the ossification and petrifaction of society. To put it another way, Max Weber was, in a way, the prophet of the expansion of Western civilization over the whole world and of the triumph of modern industrial capitalism over all traditional socio-economic formations. However, at the same time he was painfully aware of the fact that this triumph carried with it the seeds of its eventual downfall. For, as the 'ideal interests' from which capitalism had originally derived its strength *vis-à-vis* all traditional societies progressively weakened in the course of time, there arose a real danger that this society's fate might be the same as had befallen late antiquity.

This being said, it should be noted that this was perhaps not the whole of Max Weber's message. Certainly his views about the developmental path of world history, or at any rate of the history of the West, must not be pressed into a unilinear evolutionist model, regardless of whether this follows the tracks which are determined by 'ideal interests' or those determined by 'material interests'. It will have to be admitted that even Weber repeatedly expressed himself in a manner which would suggest that he had indeed intended this, even though he never formulated in a systematic way what might be called a scheme of universal history, or even of the history of Western civilization. For this reason it is not surprising that there have been repeated attempts to reconstruct Weber's theory of the developmental path of Western civilization against the backcloth of world history in a linear manner, with rationalization providing the thread of this teleological scheme and modern industrial society the final goal. This was done in a solid, if not always convincing manner, for instance by Günther Abramowski.[18]

Friedrich Tenbruck suggested an alternative approach, namely to give proper attention to the key role which Weber assigned to religious beliefs and religious world-views in the process of history. All the same he shares the view that Weber, once he had discovered that progressive 'disenchantment' was the decisive feature of Western history, developed a comprehensive analysis of processes of rationalization in all spheres of life.[19] Wolfgang Schluchter is far more circumspect in his own attempt, to reconstruct Weber's universal-historical thought as a 'developmental history of the West'. He postulates neither a deterministic nor a strictly continuous evolutionary process towards modernity. Even so, in his view Weber's sociology reaches its culmination in a theory of our own rational world civilization. It was the result of many different evolutionary steps forward, a process in which religious world-views had played an important role, though within the context of particular socio-economic structures.[20]

Paradoxically, however, nowhere in Weber's work do we find a systematic exposition of his views on the history of Western culture, although he constantly refers to bureaucratization and rationalization as its central theme. He presented his views regarding the future of the individualist societies of the West only in segmented form. Nor was he consistent on these matters. But it was certainly not his aim to develop yet another evolutionist model of the history of Western civilization or, indeed, of universal history, adding one further example of this specimen which had been abundantly represented in European literature ever since Hegel. Admittedly, in his early work Weber had still been strongly influenced by the copious nineteenth-century literature employing models of social evolution of various sorts, but in his own methodological writings he had worked hard to steer clear of all the evolutionary theories enumerating various stages of the development of human society which had been current at the time. This is illustrated by his devastating critique of Stammler,[21] and also his uncompromising rejection of, for example, Lamprecht's cultural history.[22] Recently, Günther Roth has drawn attention to this point, adding a rejoinder that we should hesitate to impute to Max Weber a unilinear evolutionary model of universal history culminating in present-day Western civilization.[23]

However, it will have to be admitted that Weber's early writings on the social history of antiquity, on the origins of modern industrial capitalism and on the city in ancient and medieval history broadly follow, if not always explicitly, an evolutionist scheme of some sort. Likewise the earlier sections of *Economy and*

Society, notably the chapters on the sociology of domination and the sociology of law, are organized according to a teleological model of the historical process pointing towards an even greater dominance of rationality and formal legality. Although this teleological model is introduced with reservations which qualify it as hypothetical, it is nevertheless presented in a quasi-objective manner. According to this model, magic 'world-views' and charismatic or patriarchal forms of domination – political, religious or ideological – were predominant in the early stages of known human history. As time went on, they were subjected to routinization and demagification. Eventually they gave way to modern rational and bureaucratic forms of domination which are based upon a purely formal legal system which can be reconstructed at will and enlists the support of rational science. If this developmental path is projected into the foreseeable future, the overwhelming pressure of advancing bureaucratization will, or at least might, result in a petrifaction of modern culture. In such contexts Weber did not always avoid the trap of formulating the uniqueness of Western culture in such a way as to let it appear in a fatalistic light, with a ring of finality.

Weber's intensive studies of the great world religions other than Christianity, which he had embarked upon by 1915 with enormous vigour and passionate interest, helped him to transcend this vaguely evolutionist notion of universal history which, however tentatively he had presented his respective findings, inevitably created a misleading impression of unilinearity and teleological conceptualization. Initially he had turned to the study of the great oriental world religions in order to further corroborate his thesis on the origins of capitalism and to demonstrate even more strongly the singularity of Western individualist culture. However, a more thorough and more intimate study of Hinduism, Buddhism and Confucianism soon carried him far beyond his original intention, even though its framework was never fully cleared away, not even when he prepared the *Collected Essays on the Sociology of Religion* for publication early in 1920, shortly before his death.

For one thing, Max Weber fully recognized the great religious achievements of Asian and, in particular, of Indian religious thought throughout the centuries: 'There will be found but few ideas beyond the confines of practical interests whose origins cannot be sought in India.' Similarly he observed: 'it can be assumed that in the realm of reflection about the question of whether the world and human life are meaningful there is absolutely nothing which had not been thought about in Asia long before [Christianity].'[24] Moreover, Weber soon discovered that the difference between the Western tradition and the Asian cultures which did not experience a process of gradual 'disenchantment' of religious beliefs and a formal rationalization of culture according to the Western model was not just one of rationality versus magic, irrational charisma and superstition, but one of radically different modes of rationalization. In fact, Weber was far from simply discarding Hinduism and Buddhism as irrationalist and backward religious creeds. On the contrary, he was fascinated to find that Hinduism and Buddhism were in fact thoroughly rational systems of thought, if judged according to their own ethical premises. Although Hinduism represented an absolute contrast to the innerworldly ethics of Protestantism, it was, on its own terms, a consistent value-rational system of thought; during the course of many centuries its ethico-religious principles had been transformed by the brahmin caste into a rational doctrine which was both coherent and stringent if seen from the vantage-point of the first principles of Hinduism. Weber admired brahminism for its immanent rationality, by the standards of its own premises, and he emphasized the fact that it shunned all irrational ways of seeking the salvation of the soul. In his opinion, the doctrine of karma had been successful throughout Asia precisely because of the rational manner in which it had answered the eternal question of how to find peace and salvation for the individual, by preaching contemplation and 'otherworldly' asceticism.

In principle, the pattern of social change initiated by ideal impulses operated here also, although the practical consequences were acquiescence in the conditions of life as the ultimate path to individual salvation. Strong 'non-everyday' beliefs induce the individual to adopt a particular life-conduct which, if taken up by larger groups and exercised for generations, eventually accumulates enough strength to serve as the basis for a new world civilization. It is only in contrast to the perennial restlessness of the Puritans that these oriental religions appear to be agents of social stagnation *per se*. Certainly they rationalized the life-conduct of their followers in such a way as to lead them away from restless economic activity. But all the same they represent typical cases of social change of significant dimension being induced by 'other-worldly' beliefs.

In view of these findings it would appear advisable to exercise caution in assigning to Western civilization a qualitatively higher status than to the Far-Eastern cultures. Admittedly Weber put special emphasis upon the singularity of Western development, in comparison with that of the Far-Eastern cultures, and he did so even in very late texts, as the Introduction to the *Collected Essays on the Sociology of World Religions*.[25] But it would seem questionable to deduce from this, as Schluchter does, that Weber valued modern Western rationalism more highly than other rationalisms not only because his own vantage-point was a European one but also on substantive grounds.[26] Admittedly Weber argued that those cultural phenomena which developed 'on Western ground' represent 'a general developmental trend which would appear to be universally valid and

significant'.[27] This remark obviously referred to the fact that Western civilization was about to conquer the whole world. But the usual caveat is not absent
here either: 'at any rate as we ourselves would like to think'.[28] In Weber's texts
such statements (which can be sustained only in the context of a substantive
philosophy of history) are always clearly marked as meta-scientific.

However, it would certainly not be possible to argue that Weber considered
the Western and the oriental cultures in principle to be equal. His personal
choice was unequivocal: he identified unreservedly with the Western cultural
tradition. He repeatedly pointed out that his aim was to establish the dis-
tinctive character of Western culture by comparing it with other world
religions (which, incidentally, he intended to supplement with analyses of
Egyptian, Mesopotamian, Zarathustrian and Christian religious creeds).[29]
However, his study of the Protestant ethic is by no means merely a contrasting
model against which his theories about the origins of capitalism and the
Western type of rationalization might be verified and described in more precise
terms. As has been shown above, he discovered here patterns of rationalization
of life-conduct on religious grounds which corroborated his view that social
change may spring from such 'ideal' sources, though in practice they become
effective only in conjunction with 'material interests' that often take on
institutionalized form.

Furthermore, in his studies of the oriental world religions Weber became
more and more aware of the fact that rationalization can mean very different
things in different contexts. Rationalization was by no means absent or insignificant in the Far-Eastern civilizations, yet it operated from entirely different
premises and accordingly it had a totally different impact upon the social fabric.
Up to then, Weber had talked, in comparatively objective terms, about the
process of rationalization which, owing to the dynamic of mature capitalism
and the advance of bureaucratization associated with it, as well as the progressive intellectualization of all 'world-views', was about to dominate more and
more spheres of life. Now he began to qualify this observation; it was not
'rationality' but 'formal rationality' which was the decisive element in the 'iron
cage of future serfdom', which appeared to be the eventual fate of Western
civilization so long as there were no countervailing forces to prevent it.

At about the same time Weber began to distinguish sharply between 'formal'
and 'substantive' rationality, both in the late sections of *Economy and Society* and
in his studies on the sociology of world religions. As I have explained above,
'formal rationality' refers to 'instrumental-rational' action which tends to adapt
to prevailing circumstances. 'Substantive rationality', by contrast, refers to a
rationalization of life-conduct oriented by certain 'ultimate' or 'otherworldly'
ideals.[30] Accordingly 'rationality' can mean many different things, depending

on the given situation; this implies, however, that there exists – or at any rate there can exist – not just one but a plurality of 'rationalization processes' in history. This was clearly Weber's own view. He pointed out that 'rationalizations of the most varied character have existed in various spheres of life and in the most diverse sectors of culture'. However, he considered it decisive 'which particular sectors are rationalized, and what direction this process will take'.[31]

It could be argued that for Weber the differentiation between various types of rationalization, depending on different value-orientations, was not an altogether new departure. Already in *The Protestant Ethic* it is said that 'life can be "rationalized" from altogether different "ultimate" viewpoints and in altogether different directions.'[32] However, in 1905 this statement carried no particular weight, inasmuch as the singularity of the type of 'rationalization' stemming from Puritan religiosity appeared to be beyond doubt; surely it was there to stay, whereas the other varieties of 'rationalization' were inevitably receding into the background. When Weber re-edited the essays on *The Protestant Ethic* in 1919, he found it necessary to add a rejoinder which emphasized the importance of this statement (which in the 1905 version had been rather a marginal comment, but which by now had gained a new significance): 'All studies devoted to "rationalization" ought to begin with this plain sentence.'[33] Weber had good reason for doing so; for by then he had arrived at a more differentiated position which distinguished between 'formal' and 'substantive' rationality. Western culture did not represent the only case of rationalization of all spheres of life, but rather a special variety of rationalization, although of the greatest cultural significance, namely 'formal rationality' (it could also be said to be 'technical rationality', although nowhere does Weber use this term). Therefore he now considered it necessary to emphasize the antinomical character of the concept of 'rationality', and to point out that 'rationality' is a meaningful term only if it is related to a particular vantage-point. With hindsight he ascribed to the essays in *The Protestant Ethic and the Spirit of Capitalism* above all the intention 'to demonstrate that "rationality", although it appears to be an unequivocal concept, may in fact mean very different things'.[34] Certainly this had not been his original objective when he wrote these essays. Rather we see here a new intonation of the theme of 'rationality', which is at variance with much of what he wrote in his earlier works. It indicates that Weber no longer believed rationality and rationalization to be unambiguous guidelines for reconstructing segments of historical development, let alone of the history of Western culture in its entirety. Admittedly, the consequences of his new insight nevertheless did not receive a full implementation in his late work. But it should be noted that by 1919 Weber considered it greatly important to advise caution with regard to applying the concept of 'rationality' to social phenomena without any prior investigation of its actual meaning in a given context and in relation to a given system of 'ultimate' ideal values.

The distinction between formal and substantive rationality shows up also in the *Sociology of Law*, as applied to the different legal systems to be found in history. However, as is indicated by the heading of section 5 – 'Formal and substantive rationalization of law: theocratic and secular law' (in *Economy and Society* this heading is only incompletely reproduced) – they were still related to different historical formations.[35] Substantive forms of legal proceedings and accordingly substantive rationalization of law are described as typical features of theocratic law in its various historical variants. With the triumph of Roman law, however, substantive law and substantive legal proceedings appeared doomed, even though Weber was prepared to concede that even today the universal advance of formal law had been slowed down at times 'by demands for substantive justice on the grounds of class interests and ideology'.[36] But the trend of the time pointed in the opposite direction. 'Inevitably the notion must expand that the law is a rational technical apparatus, which is continually transformable in the light of expediential considerations and devoid of all sacredness of content.'[37] In Weber's view, this was 'unavoidable destiny'.

Now Weber considered that the evolutionist resolution of the antinomy between substantive and formal law suggested in the *Sociology of Law* was no longer tenable. He began to emphasize more and more strongly that the antinomy between formal and substantive rationality cannot be dissolved into a sequence of historical stages; it is a fundamental antinomy which exists in all societal formations, even the modern bureaucratic ones. In the context of a passage discussing different types of market-oriented money economies written in 1920, Weber made this point unequivocally clear: 'Formal and substantive rationality, by whatever standard the latter is measured, are always in principle separate things, even if in many (and theoretically, although on totally unreal premises, even in all) cases they may coincide empirically.'[38] Any inquiry into social institutions and historical developments will have to take account of both these aspects of rationality which may be conditioned by ideal values of very different, even antagonistic, nature.

The differentiation of the notion of rationality had important consequences for Weber's understanding of the developmental history of Western culture. Up to then he had described the development of Western culture, albeit hypothetically, in quasi-objective language; the process of rationalization, propelled by the immanent dynamic of the capitalist system, but also by the progressive intellectualization of all world-views, appeared irreversible. Rationality appeared to be the ultimate stage in world history; it was bound to triumph over all its rivals. Now this proposition had to be reformulated, namely as the progressive accumulation of *formal* rationality. This was all-important, inasmuch as formal and substantive rationality were governed by entirely different principles. On account of the fundamental dichotomy between formal and substantive rationality which did not lose its momentum in the course of time, the notion of the process of Western development had to be seen in a new light. The discovery of the fundamental antinomy of formal and substantive rationality[39] relativized the theoretical model of rationalization which had served as a theoretical backbone to Weber's universal-historical studies. It cleared the way for a wider, comparatively more differentiated notion of universal history. Now history was the embodiment of a plurality of competing processes of rationalization, directed either by the immanent dynamic of material conditions and institutional structures, or by ideal interests which draw their energy from otherworldly and subjectively absolutely binding ideal values anchored in particular world-views which have found a concrete base in the life-conduct of social groups. These world-views are in a perennial struggle with one another. This was true for rational Western civilization of Weber's own day just as much as for former historical formations.

Let us recapitulate. We find two different dimensions in which rationalization of social systems operates. On the first plane rationalization is governed by material interests; for this reason it is usually steered into the realm of formal rationality, because instrumental-rational adaptation to the regularly recurring circumstances of given reality is likely to be the most effective form of social conduct. On another plane, however, rationalization is governed by ideal interests which in turn are determined by otherworldly, that is to say 'non-everyday', ideals which may be so stringent as to induce individuals to adopt a methodical lifestyle in order to live up to these ideals as well as they can. In other words, this second type of rationality is governed, in Weber's terminology, by substantive considerations which usually are at variance with the principles of formal rationality. In Weber's opinion substantive and formal rationalization can coexist for long periods of time, but in principle they are in insoluble conflict with one another.[40] The very fact that they have entirely different roots guarantees that in principle there exists at any given moment in history a plurality of potential developmental paths. To put it another way, universal history is in principle open, notwithstanding the prediction that, under given circumstances, formal rationalization and bureaucratization are likely to be triumphant. But the possibility that at some point in the future substantive rationality might provide sufficient social energies to give a new turn to the developmental path of Western civilization could no longer be entirely ruled out.

PART IV

The Rediscovery of Max Weber

Max Weber in Modern Social Thought

In his famous treatise *La Sociologie allemande contemporaine* Raymond Aron stated that Max Weber was certainly the most important German sociologist of his time.[1] Today this would appear to be an obvious thing to say, as there is a worldwide resurgence of interest in his work.[2] At the time, however, this was anything but an established fact. Certainly he was acclaimed by the German sociological profession, and beyond it by historians, social scientists and philosophers, as a thinker of great originality and intellectual power. Yet it is a matter of considerable dispute whether he had a substantial intellectual following among the still fairly small group of sociologists during the Weimar period. It should be remembered that at that time sociology had not yet been fully accepted as an independent field of inquiry within the academic system. Certainly it is fair to say that during his lifetime Max Weber had not established a 'school' in the classic sense, even though he had been one of the founders of the Deutsche Gesellschaft für Soziologie and had exercised considerable influence upon its operations in its early years. It may also be said that he had no direct heirs among the sociologists of the 1920s and the early 1930s, although men like Joseph Schumpeter, Karl Löwenstein, Karl Mannheim or Karl Jaspers continued to be strongly influenced by his ideas.

So far we have few satisfactory accounts of the development of the social sciences in Germany either in the 1920s or under National Socialism, except, perhaps, Georg Lukács's rather onesided account *Die Zerstörung der Vernunft*, first published in 1925.[3] All we have is a great variety of essays and personal recollections, whereas systematic research is still in its initial stages.[4] There are but a few monographic studies or general assessments.[5] So far Raymond Aron's account written in 1935 and reprinted in 1950 (a much needed German edition was published three years later) has not yet been surpassed.[6] This circumstance makes it somewhat difficult correctly to assess the influence of Max Weber on social thought in Germany in the period preceding Hitler's rise to power. One point, however, can no longer be disputed. Contrary to a widely held view, during the Weimar Republic Max Weber was the most cited and, if this criterion is used, the most influential sociologist in Germany.[7] This may, however, lead to false conclusions, inasmuch as there are almost no attempts at a systematic reconstruction of the major themes of his sociological work. It should also be realized that, since much of his work was published only posthumously, the time span for a proper reception of his ideas has been very short indeed, as Rainer Lepsius pointed out recently.[8]

The common belief that Max Weber had found no significant following at all in his own time, after his premature death in June 1920, was, in part, a myth which was perhaps unintentionally produced by the Heidelberg Circle which had gathered around Marianne Weber and Karl Jaspers in the 1920s. Both Marianne Weber and Karl Jaspers, the latter in a most influential and impressively written book *Max Weber: Politiker, Forscher, Philosoph* first published in 1932, described Max Weber as a personality of outstanding rank who never found the acclaim which he deserved, either among his fellow academics or from the public at large. Jaspers put this in rather lofty terms: 'After Nietzsche, man had found, at any rate up to now, his last and definite personification in Max Weber.' ('Er hat seine vorläufig letzte grosse Gestalt in Max Weber gehabt, die Gestalt unserer Welt, die in so reissendem Tempo sich verwandelt, dass die besonderen Inhalte der Weberschen Welt trotz der Kürze der Zeit schon vergangen sind.')[9] In Jaspers's view there were few, if any, other thinkers around who were worthy of and equal to this great man.

In fact, Weber's work received considerable attention both within professional sociology and in adjacent fields. As late as 1934, according to a survey conducted by the American sociologist Earle Edward Eubank, he was rated one of the great, if not the greatest, sociologist by his colleagues in Germany.[10] In this respect, at least, he was certainly no outsider, as conventional wisdom would have it. The impressive number of scholars who contributed to the *Erinnerungsgabe für Max Weber*, published in 1923 by Melchior Palyi in two volumes, also indicates that Max Weber certainly was not forgotten, but was – at any rate for the time being – a key figure in contemporary German social thought.[11] Although Max Weber's sociological theory found its way into the major textbooks of the day only in a fragmentary and sometimes distorted form, social scientists, whether they favoured his ideas or not, found it imperative to devote a great deal of their scholarly attention to Max Weber's major themes, either critically assessing or positively acclaiming them.

Moreover, important aspects of Weber's work received considerable attention and explicit evaluation in major studies by scholars in neighbouring disciplines. Already in 1928 Bernhard Pfister had written a major study of Weber's theory of ideal types, which correctly assessed the latter's methodo-logical position as an attempt to build a bridge between formal sociology, as represented by Karl Menger, and historicism, as represented by Gustav Schmoller.[12] Others followed suit. Alexander von Schelting published in 1934 his analysis of what he called Max Weber's *Wissenschaftslehre* (theory of scientific knowledge), a term which, though unsatisfactory, is still in common usage.[13] Joachim Wach incorporated Weber's contribution to the theory of understanding into his pioneering study *Das Verstehen*.[14] Karl Löwith wrote a masterful account of Max Weber's relationship to Karl Marx; he found that Marx's theory of alienation had a direct equivalent in Weber's idea of dis-enchantment, that is to say the increasing isolation and insignificance of the personality in a world full of bureaucracies.[15] Likewise Siegfried Landshut drew attention to the points of coincidence between Marx's and Weber's theories, strongly regretting, however, that the latter, in retaining a dubious stance of objectivity, had failed to draw adequate conclusions from his findings by opposing the capitalist order directly as a system which ought to be superseded by a new order of society.[16] Carl Schmitt took Weber's theories of parlia-mentary government and charismatic leadership as a point of departure for his own political theory which, however, pointed in an altogether different direction.[17] Schmitt's functionalist conception of parliamentary politics, associated with his preference for personal-plebiscitary rule, was directly based on premises to be found in Weber's writings. However, deviating from Weber's own intentions, he used this to substantiate a radical refutation of liberal democracy. His theory of decisionism also owed a great deal to Weber, although it negated the essential ethical premises of Weber's thought, in par-ticular the moral obligation to choose between different values in a rational manner and with the utmost degree of honesty. Among historians Otto Hintze ought to be mentioned as one who adapted Weber's ideal-typical method to historiographical usage. His universal-historical studies of European constitu-tional history since the seventeenth century match Weber's thought both in scope and in the decisiveness of its conceptualization.

All this having been said, it still remains true that Weber's impact upon German social thought during the inter-war period remained fragmentary and patchy. While many of his ideas and themes were widely discussed, few, if any, social scientists in Germany were prepared to follow directly in his footsteps.[18] It could be argued that this was partly due to the enormous breadth of Max Weber's approach to social reality, which could not easily be copied by anyone. It combined empirical analysis, theoretical conceptualization by means of ideal types and, later, pure types, often arranged like formulae in a systematic manner, with historical analysis, all of these approaches being informed and brought together by a particular notion of the universal-historical process which may well be called a substantive theory of history, albeit with the status of a hypothesis. It is otherworldly views which inaugurate social change of significant dimensions either through religious world-views or through value-beliefs which are established by charismatic individuals, be they prophets or leaders of whatever sort, though early on they are subjected to routinization and rationalization which eventually always gain the upper hand. However, Weber always steadfastly refused to state this theory in explicit terms inasmuch as this would lead straight into the realm of unsubstantiated value-judgements. Thus he succeeded in developing a system of social thought which focused upon the key problems of the modern age, that is to say the embattled position of the individual in the face of the seemingly almighty twin forces of bureaucratization and formal rationalization. He did so by interpreting the empirical data against the backcloth of universal history.

German sociology in the 1920s had been, for the most part, unwilling to accept this programme in its entirety. Instead it tended to emphasize model-building, or empirical social research, or explicit philosophical-historical theorizing. None of Weber's fellow social scientists succeeded in combining these approaches in an acceptable scholarly manner, let alone with the grandiose vision which had inspired Weber.

In addition, more general factors will also have to be taken into consideration. The intellectual climate in the 1920s was incompatible with most of what Max Weber had stood for. Undoubtedly Weber's ideas were firmly rooted in the German idealist tradition, much as those of his fellow social scientists in Germany. He had been influenced perhaps more thoroughly than others not only by Karl Marx but also by Friedrich Nietzsche. It is reported by Eduard Baumgarten that he once said to one of his students (presumably Baumgarten himself) that only those who had engaged themselves in a thorough study of the thought of these two thinkers could be considered capable of understanding the major problems of the age.[19] However, Weber's acceptance of Nietzsche had always been qualified. While he shared Nietzsche's fear that the individual might be overpowered by the social forces of the modern age, he strongly disagreed with his anti-democratic bias and his supreme disdain of the masses.[20] On the other hand Nietzsche's determined search for the ultimate, and his refusal to accept any halfway solutions, fully correlate with Weber's own philosophical convictions. In a way it might be said that Weber followed in the footsteps of Nietzsche's extreme intellectual elitism as far as it could be squared with the neo-Kantian approach, as formulated at the time by Rickert. Likewise he sympathized with Nietzsche's aristocratic individualism as far as it could be reconciled with his liberal notion of a social order which offered a maximum of opportunities for all individuals alike. None the less it should be kept in mind that Max Weber, unlike most of his contemporaries in Germany, also shared the essential elements of the western European intellectual tradition.

It should be borne in mind that Weber had a lifelong admiration for the political culture of the Anglo-Saxon countries. He attributed the success of the liberal sysem in Great Britain and the United States in part to the influence of Puritanism, whereas, conversely, the authoritarian features of German political culture could be traced back largely to the intellectual and religious heritage of Lutheranism. In his view, it was not least for this reason that there had never been a genuine breakthrough of liberalism in Imperial Germany. In particular, the intellectual example of John Stuart Mill certainly must be rated very highly for Weber's intellectual development. It may be said that Max Weber's thought represented a genuine symbiosis of the German and the western intellectual traditions. In this respect he stood in stark contrast to the great majority of German intellectuals of his day, perhaps with the notable exception of Ernst Troeltsch, whose endeavours in the early 1920s to bridge the gap between Western and German intellectual culture, however, proved singularly unsuccessful.

It is this orientation of Weber's sociological thought which accounts for its limited success in Weimar Germany, despite the fact that his work was in the back of everybody's mind and continued to be discussed a great deal. His influence did not prove strong enough to lead German sociology out of the rut of a predominantly idealist, spiritual and often organic-holistic approach to the study of society and culture.

Max Weber's theory of rationalization as the predominant feature of Western cultural development, in contrast to the development of the great cultures in the Middle and Far East, clearly spelled out the potential dangers for the liberal societies of the Western world in his own time. But he carefully abstained from condemning rationalization outright as a social force threatening the individualist culture of the West, as many of his fellow sociologists, including his own brother Alfred, were quick to do. In fact Max Weber left no doubt as to the ambivalent consequences of bureaucratization and formal rationalization, both positive and negative. Certainly bureaucratization and formal rationalization must be considered the twin forces which undermine indivdiual freedom in whatever sense of the word and eventually might bring about a petrified social order. But he refused to go any further. He did not want to have anything to do with the sort of emotive critique of modern industrial civilization represented by the work of Oswald Spengler or Stefan George.

Neither did he wish to get embroiled with the more common form of critique of modernity voiced by many of his colleagues from the vantage-point of an elitist intellectual culture in which the great personality plays an outstanding role. It was fashionable at the time to emphasize the contrast between the irrational life-sphere of the personality and industrial society, in such a way as to play into the hands of anti-modernist tendencies. Weber's own position on this count was rather more circumspect than those of many of his colleagues. He objected to the cult of 'personality', seen in radical juxtaposition to 'civilization', although he was fully aware of the secular dangers to man as an individual, as the only source of creative social action and imbued with a deep sense of personal responsibility. He refused to join in the fashion of condemning 'civilization' outright, and to indulge in a new intellectual romanticism. Instead he considered bureaucratization and formal rationalization as inevitable phenomena which modern man had to endure, unless he wished to opt out of modern society altogether, with all the consequences this involved. Rather, man is called upon to make the best of the situation in which he finds himself. While on one plane they put individual autonomy in jeopardy, on another plane bureaucratization and the rational techniques of the modern age provided new opportunities for creative (in other words, value-oriented) social action under the conditions of advanced industrial societies. There was, in his view, no easy way out. It was not possible simply to opt for either modern, formally rational culture or for the irrational cult of the personality and the cultivation of the individual life-sphere, as preached at the time by, among others, notably Stefan George and his disciples. One had to put up with the fact that modern life was dominated by the eternal struggle between conflicting value-principles, and one had to solve these value-conflicts by an adequate personal life-conduct rather than by looking for prophets or for a return to a traditional social order. Least of all did he favour convenient middle-of-the-road solutions. This plea for rationality and for accepting modern industrial culture and mass democracy separated Weber from the great majority of his fellow sociologists. For they were all, or almost all, influenced by the irrationalist tendencies of the current intellectual climate which played with anti-modernist ideas of various sorts.

This thesis may be illustrated in greater detail by referring to a few examples. The main stream of German sociology continued to be strongly influenced by Ferdinand Tönnies's famous distinction between *Gemeinschaft* and *Gesellschaft*. While *Gesellschaft* was the sphere of economic activity and political strife, *Gemeinschaft* was the sphere of personal values, religious and ideal factors, and, in political aspects, of the *people*. It was, in short, the dominant sphere of personal activity. This conceptualization idealized traditional forms of social organization and social interaction; at least implicitly it had anti-modernist implications. Neither Max Weber's typology of different forms of social action nor his theory of social groups would have anything in common with such an irrationalist conceptualization. Though he was the last to consider irrational or even emotional forms of motivation of social action as somehow negligible (and indeed he had developed his interpretative sociology in order to provide the methodological tools for correctly assessing non-rational forms of action in a rational manner), he refused to commend irrational types of social conduct. Neither did his methodological individualism allow social institutions to be interpreted in collectivistic terms, as, for instance, in Leopold von Wiese's work, or, at the other end of the political spectrum, by Ottmar Spann. In short, German systematic sociology in the 1920s followed a path of social analysis entirely different from that of Max Weber. It was influenced far more by traditional idealist, neo-romanticist or organic-holistic views than Max Weber would have tolerated.

An even stronger contrast of this sort developed in sociology of culture, as represented in the work of Franz Oppenheimer and Max Weber's brother Alfred. Both could not resist the temptation to present their sociological views in the form of substantive theories of history strongly critical of modern industrial civilization and mass culture. Oppenheimer ended up doing something which Max Weber had always refused to do, namely outlining a teleological model of the historical process terminating in the utopian vision of a free society of the future in many ways reminiscent of early nineteenth-century liberal views; he envisaged the eventual emergence of a new type of society of small proprietors within an economy devoid of big business; a decentralized political system would free all citizens from governmental oppression and state interference in social affairs.

In Alfred Weber's sociology we observe an even stronger fusion of liberal views with an irrationalist notion of culture. His cultural sociology had a strong anti-modernist bias. Originally Alfred and Max Weber had been very close in their views; both had been strong opponents of bureaucracy and authoritarian control in Wilhelmine Germany. Both had fought hard against Schmoller's conservative views and their predominant influence within the Verein für Sozialpolitik. Both had been associated with progressive liberal politics and had opposed extreme annexationist views during the war. But in the 1920s Alfred Weber significantly deviated from his brother's path; above all he became a defender of culture, defined in a predominantly rather irrationalist and traditionalist manner.[21] In doing so he had been partly under the influence of Bergson's vitalist philosophy as handed down to him via Bergson's German disciple Hans Driesch. Eventually Alfred Weber developed a cultural sociology which came close to a sort of substantive theory of history. He defined 'civilization' and 'culture' as antinomies; while civilization stood for the material sphere of human activity dominated by the powerful forces of technological change and material progress, culture stood for man's inner values, for the sphere of creative spontaneity, dominated by irrational motives which Alfred Weber summed up in the notion *Lebensgefühl* (life experience). Culture develops within specific *Geschichtskörper* (historical entities), that is to say particular socio-historical constellations which allow a certain degree of secluded development of individual styles, emotions and feelings which then may find expression in intellectual or aesthetic artefacts. Civilization, on the other hand, is subjected to the iron laws of the market-place and of material necessities; here there is no room for spontaneity.[22]

This sort of conceptualization was in direct conflict with fundamental notions of Max Weber's sociology. For the latter had carefully avoided opening up such a divide between rationality and the personal life-sphere, between civilization and culture, which, with hindsight, appears to be very much part of a specific German heritage. In fact, a good deal of German sociological thought, in so far as it concerned itself with macro-sociological issues, drifted more and more in this direction, namely a neo-romanticist critique of modernity and industrial society which originated in a cluster of motives partly idealist, partly neo-romanticist and partly anti-capitalist.

This is true also of Hans Freyer. Freyer seems to have grasped the gist of Max Weber's intellectual position more correctly than any of his colleagues. In his influential book *Soziologie als Wirklichkeitswissenschaft* published in 1930 Freyer explicitly acknowledged as being correct what he called 'the fundamental tendency' of Weber's sociological system. This system, he argued, was 'the greatest and, among the modern academic [sociological] systems, the *only* example of a sociology which aimed at system-building, but at the same time at ascertaining present-day reality, including its historical premises and future-oriented tendencies: in short, a concrete sociology.'[23] But Hans Freyer chose to follow a different path which deviated from Max Weber's position, even though nominally his own sociological work was meant to implement the programme of sociology as a *Wirklichkeitswissenschaft* (science of reality) in the tradition of Weber: a sociology of present-day society, seen in a historical perspective. Quite deliberately Freyer sacrificed what he called the formalistic aspects of Weber's sociology, notably the refusal to opt directly for one form of social organization rather than others. It goes without saying that in Max Weber's opinion this would have been a straight violation of the principle that the social scientist has to abstain from value-judgements. Instead, Freyer opted for a sociological position which sought to extrapolate objective trends from social reality. Thus he came to predict the eventual rise of a new authoritarian social order which would supplant class society and its constituent liberal elements once and for all. About the ideological nature of such an undertaking he was quite unequivocal: 'with such a thesis sociology establishes itself as a thoroughly antiliberal undertaking, as an intellectual position quite opposite to the ideology of bourgeois society.'[24] In this context Freyer addressed himself directly to Max Weber. He pointed out that Max Weber had shared the same theme and approach as Marx, but instead of drawing the obvious conclusions about the future of the bourgeois order – namely that modern class society ought to be rejected and replaced with a new social order guaranteed by a strong state – he had taken refuge in a formalistic casuistry.

It is not difficult to see why Hans Freyer eventually became an adherent of National Socialism, even though he remained a radical conservative at heart.[25] Indeed, as has been shown by Jerry Z. Muller in a most interesting study,[26] he soon found himself outflanked by far more radical tendencies. In 1934 Freyer had been elected *Führer* of the Deutsche Gesellschaft für Soziologie on the assumption that it might be possible for him to secure its survival with not too much sacrifice of scholarly standards. However, Freyer's relationship with official National Socialist academic policies turned out to be rather cool. He was not prepared to be instrumental in the implementation of National Socialist principles in sociology. Eventually he ended up in a position of semi-isolation.

All the same, Freyer's intellectual development in these years provides a significant insight into the development of German social thought during the period of National Socialist rule. In the intellectual climate prevailing in the late 1920s and early 1930s Max Weber's ideas were considered no longer satisfactory, precisely because they did not allow compromises between scholarship and political beliefs such as were considered imperative by Freyer and others. Besides, Freyer's qualification of Weber's sociology as typically liberal and bourgeois corresponded with views widely held in other quarters. In 1932 Christoph Steding published a doctoral thesis on *Politik und Wissenschaft bei Max Weber* in which he launched a vitriolic attack upon Weber as the last great representative of the age of bourgeois-liberal culture which by now had outlived itself and was about to be replaced by a new social order which, though not explicitly described, was clearly fascist in character.[27] According to Steding, the contradictions in Weber's own intellectual position and the perennial crises in his personal life had to be considered as symbolic representations of the fundamental contradictions of the 'liberalistic' (rather than 'liberal') ideology for which he had stood in politics and scholarship alike. Shortly afterwards Steding qualified as one of the hopeful young acolytes of Alfred Rosenberg; his book *Das Reich und die Krankheit der europäischen Kultur* which appeared only two years later pleaded for a National Socialist hegemony over Europe as the first step towards the creation of a new nationalist and organic European culture under Teutonic leadership which would conform to the principles of social organization predominant in the Middle Ages, though now at an infinitely higher level of historical development. As I have shown elsewhere, Weber's notion of charismatic domination and the radical formalization of parliamentary democracy in his political sociology had provided intellectual stepping-stones for the emergence of non-democratic views among the German intelligentsia. But in substance he had nothing in common with irrational political creeds like Steding's. His liberal convictions and his steadfast adherence to the principle of rationality made his sociology unacceptable in the intellectual climate prevailing under National Socialism.

Contrary to a widely held view, the National Socialist takeover did not lead to a sudden halt of sociological research. Given the fact that sociology had commonly been held to be closely associated to Marxist thought, its status as an independent discipline appeared now to be threatened; however, by redefining its subject-matter in terms acceptable to the new regime and occasionally by taking shelter under the roof of other disciplines – like, in Leipzig, universal history in the tradition of Lamprecht – it managed to survive.[28] As more recent research has shown, as a scholarly discipline sociology actually thrived under National Socialism as long as it conducted empirical research believed to be useful to the new regime.[29] In a way, Freyer's programme for creating a 'German sociology' proved rather successful, though under somewhat different auspices than he would have liked to see. Under the umbrella of the new 'German sociology' there gathered a considerable number of scholars from neighbouring disciplines like *Volkskunde*, ethnology, history, public law and political science conducting research on topics related to National Socialist ideology. They focused on *Volkstum* ('folkdom'), rather than upon bourgeois society, something which came to be considered as a typical shortcoming of sociology during the Weimar period. This helped to pull sociology close to the National Socialist camp and in some respects to make it a willing servant of the regime.[30]

On the other hand serious sociological research on fundamental issues was severely hampered. Macro-sociological theory, unless it subscribed to National Socialist ideology, all but disappeared. Muller arrives at the conclusion: 'Whereas in the National Socialist state "social technology" and "social-scientific handicrafts" greatly expanded, the theoretical social sciences stagnated.'[31] This was aggravated by the fact that a considerable number of scholars were forced to leave the country, notably (but not only) those of Jewish origin. Accordingly, with a few exceptions, serious sociological scholarship of the sort that Max Weber had initiated did not find a place in the Third Reich.

Weber's liberal convictions and the steadfast adherence to the principle of rationality made his sociology unacceptable in the intellectual climate prevailing under National Socialism. Therefore it will come as no surprise that during the period of National Socialism the intellectual heritage of Max Weber was largely abandoned; at best it survived in a fragmented and distorted form. A case in question was Alfred Müller-Armack's adaptation of Max Weber's thesis on 'Protestantism and the origins of capitalism'. Müller-Armack reinterpreted Weber's argument in an altogether idealistic manner, in order to enlist it as support for his own theory, according to which economic history is determined by a sequence of *Wirtschaftsstile* ('economic styles') which, in turn, are dependent upon secular changes in the prevailing spiritual climate. Thus he concluded that the rise of capitalism was due to 'the intellectual revolution of the sixteenth century' marked by a totally new religious attitude. Although he presented his own findings throughout as being supported by the conclusions of *The Protestant Ethic and the Spirit of Capitalism*, he was careful to dissociate himself from Weber's economic liberalism, as this was not fashionable at the time; he argued that National Socialism had found the necessary means to restrain the destructive dynamics of capitalism.[32]

Indeed, National Socialism claimed that it had replaced bourgeois society and its class divisions once and for all. Seen in this perspective all traditional sociology which had focused upon bourgeois society was completely outdated. In 1935 Hans Freyer found it necessary to defend bourgeois sociology of the nineteenth and early twentieth centuries against wholesale condemnation, even though he shared the view that the National Socialist revolution had in principle superseded bourgeois society.[33] He pointed in particular to the continuing importance of the work of Ferdinand Tönnies, and likewise that of Max Weber.[34] But this was of little avail. German sociology came to be preoccupied with the themes of German 'folkdom' and *Gemeinschaft*, while interest in Weber's work almost disappeared.

Instead Weber's sociological thought found a new home abroad, notably in the United States. Understandably, Raymond Aron's attempts to familiarize French scholarship with German social thought and German philosophies of history did not receive a great deal of response during the 1930s. The situation in Italy was somewhat better; Carlo Antoni's book *From Historicism to Sociology* was the first full acount of Weber's achievements in the Italian language.

However, as early as the 1920s Weber's work had received considerable general attention, though this had been restricted more or less to his *Essays on Puritanism and the Origins of Capitalism*. His famous thesis on the origins of capitalism was taken up everywhere, in Great Britain, in France,[35] in Italy, in the United States and even in Japan. On the whole, however, the response was a mixed and qualified one. R. H. Tawney discussed at considerable length Weber's thesis that Puritanism had been one of the roots of modern capitalism, arriving at the rather qualified conclusion that there had been a link between Puritanism and the rise of capitalism but that it was not a causal but rather a circumstantial one.[36] In 1925 Maurice Halbwachs directed the attention of French scholarship to Weber's interesting thesis about a direct relationship between religious attitudes and the development of capitalism.[37] Two years later Henri Sée reported on Weber's and Sombart's conflicting interpretations in a rather sceptical vein.[38] On the whole Weber's views found full approval nowhere, but his analytical power and his remarkable gift for describing complex historical processes in extraordinarily precise ideal-typical form met with universal respect. But beyond this aspect of Weber little was known of his work, except perhaps his studies on ancient history and on the ancient and medieval city, though only among the specialists in this particular field.

This situation changed in the 1930s, for a number of reasons. In the first place it should be borne in mind that Weber's ideas were brought to Great Britain and the United States by many social scientists who had left Germany for political reasons. The most faithful, though not necessarily most influential, was Paul Honigsheim, perhaps the most impressive was Joseph Schumpeter and the most original Alfred Schutz. Schutz later developed a social philosophy which may be described as a fusion of Husserl and Max Weber, a phenomenology with strong Weberian elements which subsequently was to prove highly influential in the Anglo-Saxon world.

A special position must be allotted in this context to Karl Mannheim. Perhaps more than most other German sociologists Mannheim was under the spell of Weberian thought which continued to be influential in Heidelberg even after Weber's premature death in 1920. Mannheim planned to publish a major study of Max Weber, and Weber's publisher Paul Siebeck had already entered into an agreement with him about it; it was originally to be entitled 'Wissenschaftssoziologische Analysen zur gegenwärtigen Denklage: Drei Essays über M. Weber, Troeltsch, und Scheler' ('Sociological analyses of the present state of thought: three essays on M. Weber, Troeltsch and Scheler').[39] Although Karl Mannheim was strongly influenced by Georg Lukács and continued to be an important member of the latter's *Sonntagskreis* (a regular debating club),[40] his own sociological thought was perhaps more strongly influenced by Weber than so far has been realized. His sociology of knowledge may be seen as a radical continuation of Weber's notion of *Wertbeziehung* (value-relationship) which had already implied that all social-scientific knowledge is oriented by specific value-attitudes which themselves are not subject to scientific verification but are a matter of the individual's subjective choice.[41] His studies on conservatism continue in Weber's tradition inasmuch as they are a fine example of historical sociology. But by 1933 Mannheim was in deep despair, since his great hope that a core of liberal social thinkers might have given the course of German history a different turn had proved to be in vain.[42] His book *Man and Society in an Age of Reconstruction*, first published in 1940,[43] in many ways builds upon Weberian foundations. In particular it takes up Weber's theme of formal rationality versus substantive rationality (he calls it 'functional' versus 'substantive' rationality)[44] and its consequences for the destiny of man in the age of mass society. Mannheim's intellectual indebtedness to Max Weber still awaits a proper scholarly assessment. It would appear that he helped to spread Weberian themes and Weberian approaches to the study of social reality particularly in the English academic community, although in a rather muted and indirect manner.[45]

However, the man who did the most to make Weber known as a great sociologist outside Germany was Talcott Parsons, who during his student years in Heidelberg in the 1920s had come into close contact with the Weberian tradition, though not with Weber himself, who had already died in June 1920. In his important work *The Structure of Social Action*, first published in 1937, Parsons presented Weber and his work in full to the American public for the first time, in conjunction with studies on Durkheim and Pareto. He did this, however, in the context of his own sociological approach, namely the development of a general sociological theory of social action which subsequently came to be known as structural functionalism. To some degree Weber's casuistry of different ideal or (rather) pure types of social action was used by Parsons as a launching-pad for his own theory. In a notable contrast to the trends in contemporary German sociology, which had turned away from Max Weber because his interpretative sociology had barred all substantive philosophizing about history, Parsons was attracted by its formalist character. In his own presentation of Weber's sociology Parsons emphasized above all the theoretical aspects of his work.[46] He paid particular attention to the casuistry of ideal types in the last part of *Economy and Society*, without fully ascertaining, however, that the systems of ideal types developed here were meant to be applied to concrete historical processes and developments in a medium- or even long-term perspective, and not just as elements of an essentially static social system. The historical and, as it were, developmental dimensions of Max Weber's thought were largely left aside, while the theoretical and empirical aspects were strongly emphasized.

The consequences of this interpretation of Weber, which marked a new stage of its reception in modern social thought, were far-reaching indeed. For more than a generation American social thought considered Weber's sociology primarily as an outstanding example of theoretical sociology.

Edward Shils's publication of an English edition of Weber's methodological essays in 1949, surprisingly, did little to correct this onesided view. Indeed, Shils himself assumed that Weber's efforts were aimed at developing a 'general theory', although this had been only partly achieved, in the first two chapters of *Economy and Society*.[47] This assumption, however, was based upon false premises, at any rate if Weber's methodological essays are taken as a point of reference. Weber had had something different in mind, namely the meaningful reconstruction of particular segments of social reality in the process of time, as seen in the light of particular cultural values, and not the development of a general social theory capable of more or less universal application. Likewise the historical dimension which was a built-in feature of Weber's conceptualizations tended to be largely overlooked. It was not realized for a long time that Weber's ideal-typical models about, say, bureaucracy, social stratification or class structure can be used in a meaningful manner only if they are applied to social systems subjected to significant change over time. Bureaucracy was, in Weber's view, not just a particular type of social institution; it was a form of institutionalization of human action which was likely to induce significant social change. While it provided a degree of efficiency for social action almost unknown in traditional societies, it had a far-reaching impact upon the life-conduct of the individual, with momentous long-term consequences for the cultural system.

To put it another way, in American sociology Weber's ideal-typical conceptualizations had all too often been taken in isolation from their original context and considered as descriptive models of empirical reality, whereas Weber had designed them as instruments for a meaningful interpretation of social reality from the vantage-point of specific cultural values. However, even in this distorted version Weber's ideal types proved most fruitful in encouraging sociological inquiry, as is witnessed, *inter alia*, by the development of organized sociology in the United States in the 1950s and 1960s.[48] The distortions in Max Weber's image, as it developed in the United States, were to some degree aggravated by the fact that satisfactory translations of his major works were slow to appear. Only in 1959 had Günther Roth eventually managed to publish *Economy and Society* in one piece in a good translation, but even then a variety of fragmentary translations, sometimes of rather poor quality, stood in the way of a proper understanding of his work.[49] Even now the English translation of key terms in Max Weber's sociology – such as '*authority*' for *Herrschaft* – results in massive distortions of the original meaning.

It would appear that Talcott Parsons's English edition of *The Protestant Ethic and the Spirit of Capitalism* in 1938 provided a stimulus for intensive research into Max Weber's thought in Japan. Japanese interest in his work went back as far as 1905, but it was only after 1945 that a spectacular renaissance of interest in Max Weber set in which was of an entirely different order. Weber's thought helped the Japanese to bridge the glaring gap between a feudalist past and a modernist future; it helped Japanese society to come to terms with post-1945 conditions. Weber was considered a thinker who could help the Japanese people to escape from the *Zaubergarten* (enchanted garden) of magic beliefs which so far had been dominant in Japanese thinking. However, right from the start both Weber and Marx were considered to be representatives of modernity and a rational social order, not, as in the West, as opposites. Moreover, in Japan the historical dimension of Weber's sociology was considered particularly useful, as it proved helpful in the rational reassessment of the Japanese past, in contrast to a present which was dominated by Western industrialism and the influx of Western values. Thus his analyses of patrimonial and patriarchal social structures were considered particularly helpful, whereas in the United States it was the theory of bureaucracy which attracted greatest interest.[50]

In a way the gradual decline of Talcott Parsons's 'structural functionalism' as the dominant sociological school in the United States and the rise of empirical social research in the 1950s and 1960s to hegemonic status intensified this frag-mented and, in certain respects, distorted image of Weber's sociology. But this is only a part of the story. Gradually his work became much better known, and interest in his work widened in scope. This was the case in particular for the sociology of world religions which was now considered to be a central theme of Weber's work, while previously attention had been focused almost exclusively upon the *Protestant Ethic*. But again most attention was given to the theoretical aspects, whereas it tended to be overlooked that the findings about the inter-relationship between religious attitudes, specific forms of social conduct and economic activity were embedded in ideal-typical reconstructions of particular segments of universal history; often this was considered merely incidental. However, Reinhard Bendix gradually did make Weber's achievements in historical sociology more widely known; indeed, he sought to bridge the gap between the predominant Parsonian theoretical interest in Weber and his universal-historical studies.[51] Likewise Benjamin Nelson turned to Weberian concept formation in his *Idea of Usury*.[52]

In addition, there developed a considerable interest in Max Weber's political sociology and in his role in contemporary German politics. In their collection of essays *From Max Weber: Essays in Sociology* H. H. Gerth and C. Wright Mills published Weber's most important political writings together with a masterly, sympathetic biographical account of his life and work.[53] Other scholars who had found new teaching positions in the United States did their best to make Weber's work better known, such as Paul Honigsheim and Karl Löwenstein. In his influential book *Consciousness and Society: The Reorientation of European Social Thought 1890-1930* H. Stuart Hughes described Max Weber along with Sigmund Freud as one of the outstanding thinkers on the eve of the age of modernity who revitalized the great traditions of the Enlightenment by demolishing the bastions of a degenerate positivism and a formalized idealism, which had become empty formulas, thereby opening up new ways of perceiving historical reality without prejudice and illusions, and free of the shallow belief in progress that had dominated European social thought in the nineteenth century.[54]

The upsurge of interest in Max Weber in the West can be explained in part also in political terms. As is well known, Weber always rejected any attempt at a substantive reconstruction of history. This was appropriate at a time when all 'holistic' reconstructions of history, as was forcefully argued by Karl Popper in *The Poverty of Historicism*, had fallen into disrepute, as they were suspected of leading potentially to totalitarianism. Weber's sociology was fundamentally individualistic, and, in spite of his strong leanings towards nationalism, it was broadly in line with liberal thought. Neo-liberalism, the dominant political creed of the day, pleaded for a return to the market economy and a social order built upon individual initiative, while governmental interference should be restricted to an absolute minimum. The examples of past and present forms of totalitarian government gave credence to a strictly individualist reconstruction of Western societies, in line with Tocqueville rather than Rousseau, who was often considered a precursor of totalitarian rather than liberal democracy. Max Weber's social thought appeared to be an ideal expression of these criteria for a free world. Accordingly, Weber's highly effective critique of bureaucratic government and state omnipotence was received quite favourably. Furthermore, he offered, or at least it so appeared, a consistent and convincing alternative to socialism which in the era of the Cold War was seen to produce ever more oppressive governmental bureaucracies and human misery. Indeed, Weber's critique of all centrally directed economies provided telling arguments against Marxism and its current Leninist varieties with their inherent tendency to subject the peoples within their sway to bureaucratic control, in stark contrast to its ideological message, which promised the liberation of the masses from capitalist suppression and human alienation.

In this intellectual climate there developed a tendency to present Weber's social theory in a harmonious way, by playing down the contradictions and antinomies in his thought. Reinhard Bendix's *Max Weber: An Intellectual Portrait* (first published in 1960) is a good example of this trend.[55] It was a competent presentation of Weber's intellectual achievements, covering the whole range of his scholarly and also his political writings. But it tended to emphasize the empirical side of his work, while the underlying philosophical assumptions, which were not always in line with present-day views, were dealt with only per-functorily.[56] The Nietzschean element in Weber, which was not in fashion at the time, was conveniently left out. Nor was the extreme radicality of many of his political opinions given adequate expression, particularly with regard to con-temporary German power politics. All in all Max Weber was presented here as a sensible man who was almost always taking the 'middle road' instead of as the radical thinker who loathed all compromise solutions and who always sought to push intellectual issues to their utmost limits rather than settle for sensible half-way solutions.

Even though the American reception of Max Weber's work had in many ways been onesided, incomplete and, in certain respects, rather distorted, it did not fail in addition to leave its mark upon the development of sociological thought in Europe, notably in the Federal Republic of Germany. It is often said, with a great deal of justification, that the revival of interest in Max Weber in the Federal Republic was due, above all, to American influence. Seen in this per-spective the *Deutscher Soziologentag* at Heidelberg in 1964, which was devoted to the commemoration of the 100th anniversary of Weber's birth, can be con-sidered an important encounter of American and German scholarship on Max Weber. It signified a revitalized interest in the Federal Republic in Max Weber's work and a willingness to take up the running where American scholarship had left off. However, things were not as simple as that.

In the first decade after 1945 German interest in Max Weber had actually been rather limited. While he was the subject of a number of essays in a few learned as well as popular journals, research into his work was slow to recom-mence. In the first decade after 1945 German sociological research on Max Weber could in no way match the large number of publications by American scholars. It is a commonplace that after 1945 the influence of American social science on German sociology was paramount. However, it must be realized that in 1945 there was in fact no straightforward break with the past in sociology, just as in many other academic disciplines, and that American, and indeed Western, influence made itself felt only after a considerable delay. In the first decade after 1945 West German sociology continued to be dominated by the grand old men of the 1920s and 1930s, notably Hans Freyer, Alfred Weber and Leopold von Wiese, none of whom had any strong interest in revitalizing the study of Max Weber, even though their own work contained quite a few elements which originated in his work. Only gradually did a new generation take over, among whom René König soon rose to prominence. Though himself rather more a representative of historical sociology, König worked hard to see American sociological methods adopted in the Federal Republic of Germany. However, those who took their guidance from American empirical social science were not particularly interested in Max Weber.

In fact it was primarily philosophers, political scientists and historians who turned to Max Weber as a great social thinker in the tradition of Niccolò Machiavelli and Alexis de Tocqueville. However, this was a slow and cumbersome process. In 1946 Karl Jaspers republished his short essay on Max Weber (written in 1932) in which he had blamed the German nation for not having given this great man a chance. But for the first time being the book apparently did not have the resounding success which Jaspers had hoped for. In 1950 Eduard Baumgarten published an essay with the impressive title 'Die Bedeutung Max Webers für die Gegenwart' in *Die Sammlung*, which was an influential journal at the time. It focused on Weber's lifelong search for a meaningful life-conduct in the modern, 'disenchanted' world. This should have appealed to his contemporaries, given the intellectual climate in the Federal Republic of Germany in the early 1950s. Max Weber was rediscovered as one of the few great figures who had correctly indicated the political path which the Germans ought to have followed in order to avoid the catastrophe of 1945. However, it is rather significant that it was not his substantive political or sociological views but rather the theory of abstention from value-judgements which Baumgarten considered to be of greatest relevance to the intellectual situation of the early 1950s, which was characterized above all by general disillusionment and disorientation. Baumgarten put it as follows: to learn from Max Weber meant in the given situation above all 'to understand at least in rudimentary terms what in fact happened to us before 1933, and between 1933 and today, and also that these events still determine our lives, however indirectly.'[57]

It was the philosophical aspects of Weber's work which were initially considered of primary importance, rather his sociological theories or his political views. Indeed, in their philosophical aspects one can observe an almost unbroken continuity of Weber studies from the early 1930s onward. Dieter Henrich's analysis of *Max Webers Wissenschaftslehre*, published in 1952, in fact followed in the tracks of the studies by Bienfait, Pfister and von Schelting, and bore testimony to the strong influence of the hermeneutical epistemology of Hans-Georg Gadamer. It focused on the notion of 'understanding' and the interpretative analysis of human or, to put it more precisely, individual action in Weber's work. It stressed especially that, according to Weber, social analysis is always oriented towards particular cultural values. Henrich conceded that there is to be found in Weber a theory of 'formal history'. This might be considered an equivalent to Parsons's structural-functionalist interpretation, but in fact Henrich meant, if anything, the exact opposite: 'formal history' is, according to Henrich, defined by 'a sequence of value-interpretations'.[58] We need not discuss here in detail whether Henrich's interpretation can be considered correct or not. Yet it definitely located Max Weber in the context of the cultural sciences rather than seeing in him a pioneer of modern social science. To be sure, this interpretation was considerably removed from the Parsonian interpretation of Weber prevalent in the United States at the time. It also had little in common with the opinions on Weber then prevailing among German sociologists.

By contrast, considerable and growing interest in Max Weber was developing among historians and political scientists. The historians discovered in Max Weber a sociologist who paved the way for a closer co-operation between history and the social sciences, which would not require history to abandon altogether its methodological traditions and notably its reliance upon the techniques of understanding and empathy. On the basis of Weber's methodology, the study of individual phenomena and theoretical analysis could be pursued alongside one another. Moreover, Weber's ideal types proved to be immensely useful to the historian's work, as Theodor Schieder in particular was quick to realize and to preach to his fellow historians.[59] Weber's methodology seemed to supply the conceptual tools for a modern form of typological history which followed in Jacob Burckhardt's footsteps while avoiding his logical imprecision and his often too unconnected methods of reasoning. Indeed, as Stuart Hughes aptly remarked, Weber represented a point of conjuncture between history and the social sciences at a moment when the latter were turning a blind eye to the historical dimension of social change. In the 1950s and 1960s, largely under the influence of Max Weber, German historiography slowly lowered its defences in relation to the social sciences. It was above all Theodor Schieder, but also Werner Conze, who led the way towards a new social history working with ideal-typical concepts. In this uphill struggle for a methodological reorientation of German historiography the intellectual weaponry was largely derived from Weber.

We may conclude that in the 1950s it was primarily Max Weber's methodology and his philosophical views which were at the centre of the revival of interest in his work. The sociological profession was somewhat slow to follow, and it was largely the influence of American sociology which helped to rekindle interest in Weber among social scientists in Germany. However, here also issues of methodology were paramount. In a masterly work *Die Genesis der Methodologie Max Webers* Friedrich Tenbruck in a way reclaimed Max Weber for the social sciences, given the fact that Henrich had viewed him primarily as a representative of the 'cultural sciences' (*Kulturwissenschaften*).

Tenbruck succeeded in demonstrating that the prime concern of Weber's methodological essays had been to find a new direction for the social sciences which would lead beyond Schmoller and Menger and which would not involve opting for either school of social inquiry, the historicist in the former case and the theoretical in the latter. Even so Tenbruck's final conclusion was entirely negative: 'As a general theory Max Weber's methodology had lost all its significance for us today. We cannot build upon its premises, concepts, postulates and conclusions any more, unless we are prepared to sacrifice our own understanding of sociological research, of sociological theory, or our own notion of the scientific objectives of sociology.'[60] Tenbruck's conclusion was that the methodological essays had been important for Weber only inasmuch as they had helped him find his way to empirical sociological research. By 1906 Weber was, or at least intended to become, an empirical sociologist, and not a 'cultural scientist'. These findings were certainly in line with the trends in German and indeed international sociology during the 1950s and 1960s. The social sciences were about to move away from Weber's macro-sociology and to embark upon empirical social research rather than upon general theorizing.

While empirical social research was definitely on the advance, partly owing to the strong influences from the United States, the intellectual scene in the Federal Republic was dominated by the controversy between logical positivism on the one hand, and the Frankfurt School on the other. The Frankfurt School fought a sort of rearguard battle against the rising tide of empirical social science which demanded that scholars should concentrate upon augmenting instrumental knowledge rather than conducting ideological battles. On the whole, empirical social research won the day, although the defence of grand theory conducted by Jürgen Habermas attracted considerable support from neighbouring disciplines. In this debate Weber's sociology remained on the sidelines. It was used by both sides primarily as ammunition for their own cause, and not so much for its own sake. In view of this it is not surprising to see that it was Max Weber's theory of abstention from value-judgements (though understood in a neo-positivist manner) which was given prominent attention and not his substantive sociological writings.[61]

At the Weber Congress in Heidelberg in 1964 the postulate of abstention from value-judgements was hailed as Weber's greatest achievement, as opposed to his sociological theories or his empirical work. Talcott Parsons expressed disappointment at the fact that none of the speakers in the debate on his paper on 'Value-freedom and objectivity' had related this postulate to Weber's substantive sociology.[62] This was a correct reflection of the state of affairs at the time. Weber's substantive theories, and their roots in a particular world-view, were less in demand than his methodology and his contributions to specific areas of empirical research. The observation that Weber's sociological and

political thought had been influenced by political value-options of a controversial nature, like his explicit identification with the German nation-state, not
surprisingly under such conditions, was received with a great deal of
misgiving.[63]

In some degree this was due to the fact that sociologists and political
scientists had followed different patterns of evaluation in their reading of
Weber. The social scientists welcomed Weber's sociological work precisely
because it adhered strictly to the principle of abstention from value-judgements. Political science, on the other hand, was strongly influenced by a revival
of natural law; for this reason many political scientists tended to take the
opposite view. They treated the largely formalistic character of Weber's theory
of politics with suspicion. This is reflected in the rather cool reception of
Weber's political ideas by contemporary political science.

From the very start Max Weber's political writings had received considerable attention. German democracy was short of father figures, and Max Weber
qualified as one of them. After all, he had been among the few determined
liberals who had already publicly advocated the introduction of parliamentary
government in Germany before the First World War, and who had criticized
the authoritarian features of German politics in his own time in the strongest
terms conceivable; obviously history had proved him right on this point.
However, for the time being little substantive research into his political
thought was actually undertaken. It would appear that there was some hesi-
tancy in doing so, inasmuch as Weber's often rather extreme political views
did sometimes cause irritation. In 1957 Arnold Bergstraesser published an
important essay on Max Weber's inaugural lecture at Freiburg. Here he voiced
his disagreement with the ambivalence of some of Weber's key positions
rather strongly. Although he was full of praise for Weber's intellectual genius,
he cautioned his readers with regard to a number of features in his political
and philosophical thought. Bergstraesser took exception in particular to
Weber's notion that the eternal struggle between different values cannot be
decided in any way whatsoever by scientific means. This did not seem acceptable at a time when a revival of fundamentalist thinking, notably in terms of
natural law, was taking place in the Federal Republic. Neither was
Bergstraesser particularly happy with Weber's concept of charismatic leadership. Above all, however, he objected to the formalistic character of Weber's
theory of government, which argued mainly in exclusively instrumental-
rational terms, without reference to the fundamental values on which parliamentary democracy is built: 'In his political sociology we do not find a normative orientation which may help us to resist the dehumanization of politics
through which we have lived and which we still experience around us; indeed,

we *cannot* find it there, for the notion of scholarship upon which it is built is value-neutral; in fact, it is derived from an agnostic epistemology.'[64] Wilhelm Hennis attacked Max Weber even more harshly in his essay 'Zum Problem der deutschen Staatsanschauung' for his extreme subjectivism and for the utter hollowness of his idea of the state. According to Hennis, his purely techno-cratic conception of the state completely omitted a vital dimension, namely any substantive notion of politics without which no sort of public order can thrive.[65] That is to say, neither those who argued that modern constitutional democracy derives its legitimacy and its ethos from fundamental ethical principles nor those who looked for a neo-Aristotelian model of modern politics were prepared to accept Max Weber's theory of government.

In part this can be accounted for by the prevailing belief that a democracy can survive only if it is built upon a set of value-principles unquestionably accepted by all the citizens. In the 1950s it was the common opinion that the Weimar Republic had collapsed especially because it had practised a policy of value-neutrality even towards its determined enemies. Carl Schmitt's rather cynical theory of parliamentary government and his plea for a system of presi-dential rule which could do without the outdated mechanism of parliamentary control was well known, and it was considered an ugly example of how things went wrong. Indeed, Johannes Winckelmann, who devoted his life to bringing about a revival of interest in Max Weber, found it necessary to defend Weber against the charge that his theory of democratic government was wholly technocratic and devoid of all substantive foundation in moral terms. His first major book *Legitimität und Legalität in Max Webers Herrschaftssoziologie*,[66] followed by a series of smaller essays and, later, by new editions of Weber's writings, sought to show that Weber's theory of democratic government, though it had been defined by him as a sub-type of formal legal domination, did in fact contain 'immanente Legitimitätsschranken', that is to say inherent barriers to a merely formal-legal interpretation of constitutional government which would consider anything correctly enacted according to the usual procedures as legitimate. In other words, Winckelmann tried to prove once and for all that Max Weber and Carl Schmitt had nothing in common, and that there was no justification at all for attacking Weber's notion of constitutional government as merely technocratic and value-neutral. In fact Winckelmann's conclusion amounted to a well-intended reinterpretation of Weber in the light of the views prevailing in the Federal Republic at the time; in substance, however, it was simply false.[67]

In fact the view which considered that Weber had argued the case for democracy in far too technocratic terms was hard to dispel. Even so, interest in his political theory was gradually picking up. In 1958 Winckelmann succeeded in getting Theodor Heuss, then President of the Federal Republic, to write an introduction to a new edition of the *Gesammelte Politische Schriften*, which underlined the importance of Weber's political views and political theory for present-day Germany, even though Heuss was careful to point out that Weber had died long before the rise to power of charismatic figures who did their utmost to destroy parliamentary democracy, rather than to operate within its constraints and make it successful.[68]

On the whole, however, Weber was seen as one of the precursors of German democracy, and one of those who had always pleaded for a sensible, modest foreign policy which did not tread on everybody's toes at the same time. This view was rudely shaken with the publication of the present author's book *Max Weber und die deutsche Politik, 1890–1920* in 1959.[69] It became apparent that Weber's political views had not in fact been a blueprint for liberal and democratic views, as had been commonly assumed. Nor had his views on foreign policy been all that sensible, modest or realistic. On the contrary, it emerged that Weber had been an ardent nationalist, and that at any rate in his earlier career he had pleaded in almost violent language for a hard-headed policy of imperialist expansionism. Even worse, his concept of charismatic leadership appeared to be disturbingly close to fascist notions of plebiscitarian leadership. Nor did his theory of 'leader democracy' appear foolproof, since it lent itself all too readily to an authoritarian reinterpretation (Carl Schmitt and Roberto Michels had both taken this course and had ended up by lending support to National Socialism and Italian fascism respectively).

The book caused a major upheaval; a considerable number of academics at once criticized it in rather vitriolic terms, among them notably Karl Löwenstein, Reinhart Bendix and Paul Honigsheim. Indeed, it motivated Löwenstein to put forward his own views on Weber in a series of essays. The ensuing debate was passionate and at times extremely acrimonious. Not surprisingly, it focused on the issue of whether, and in what sense, Max Weber's views on charismatic leadership had contributed to making the German people ready to fall prey to Hitler's charismatic appeal over and above parliament, and not so much on the substantive findings of the book. Nobody paid any attention to the fact that as early as 1944 Jacob Peter Mayer had published a far more critical book on Max Weber; he had been portrayed by Mayer as 'the Machiavelli of the age of steel'.[70]

Things came to a head at the 15th German Sociological Congress held at Heidelberg in 1964 to commemorate the centenary of Max Weber's birth. One of the major themes with which the conference concerned itself was Max Weber as a political thinker and his role in Wilhelmine politics. It was at last recognized that the older view of Weber as a genuine champion of democratic reform could no longer be maintained unreservedly. A thorough reassessment had become necessary. Certain aspects of Weber's sociology of domination had caused a few qualms among political scientists for some time previously. It was, notably, the theory of charismatic leadership which had always caused considerable uneasiness among political theorists like Karl Joachim Friedrich or Karl Löwenstein, but this had been seen as an isolated aberration from the right path and not as a structural flaw in Weber's theory of democratic government. More controversial was the question whether Carl Schmitt's theory of decisionism had to be seen as a direct consequence of Weber's formalistic theory of democracy. Furthermore, Weber's role as a German nationalist and a believer in power politics was now also made the subject of a critical reassessment.

At the Heidelberg Congress Raymond Aron was asked to give an authoritative judgement on this issue, presumably in order to refute once and for all the theses put forward in my book. However, Raymond Aron chose to act as a sort of arbiter rather than as a judge who was to pass a final verdict. In his paper on 'Max Weber and power politics' presented on this occasion Aron pointed out that the dispute was perhaps more about recent German history than about Max Weber himself, whose nationalist views could not be seriously questioned.[71] Instead he chose to point out the different strands in Weber's thinking, or *Weltanschauung*, notably its Darwinian, its Nietzschean, its economic and its Marxian components. Jürgen Habermas, on the other hand, emphasized, to the dismay of the more orthodox of the Weber experts, that Carl Schmitt's decisionism as well as his theory of plebiscitarian rule must indeed be seen as radical consequences following on from Weberian premises, even though Weber himself clearly had not intended ever to go that far.[72] In the end the issue of whether Weber's value-agnosticism coupled with his strong nationalist views and his acceptance of power politics had a negative impact on the political developments in the Weimar Republic remained undecided.

However, this debate was overshadowed by an even more controversial one which had been initiated by Herbert Marcuse. Marcuse had argued that Weber, by assigning to capitalism a maximum degree of formal rationality in comparison with other socio-economic formations, had in fact assigned to it a higher form of rationality, thereby making capitalism appear as the embodiment of reason. Marcuse protested vehemently at this apology for capitalism presented in the guise of allegedly value-free scholarship.[73] This was tantamount to a frontal attack on the dominant methodological traditions of American sociology and, indeed, on its whole conception of itself. Furthermore, Marcuse's line of reasoning anticipated a tendency of thought which was to appear a little later on a broader scale, namely the fundamentalist critique of 'bourgeois' sociology by the New Left. Understandably this led to passionate protests, notably from American scholars. Emotions were high, and revealed the ideological concern which motivated the defence of Max Weber against the critique voiced by the left, be it radical-liberal or Marxist.

The Heidelberg Congress marked a high point of scholarly and public interest in Max Weber. However, this deserves to be qualified somewhat. For Weber had been rediscovered above all as an empirical social scientist, whereas his universal-historical conceptualizations had been given little attention, with the exception, perhaps, of the *Sociology of Religion* (which was also seen primarily as pioneering empirical research). Above all, he was regarded as one of those thinkers who paved the way for value-free social research. Ernst Topitsch hailed Max Weber for having freed 'himself from traditions which for thousands of years have presented the world to men as if it were a value-rational order of things. . . . He was able to dismantle these patterns of thought without replacing them by other forms of evaluative interpretation of the universe.'[74] This statement reflected the great hope of logical positivism that it would be possible to reach an entirely new level of knowledge about social processes by means of value-free empirical social investigation strictly in line with the principles of instrumental rationality. Similarly, Daniel Bell had argued that with the arrival of empirical social science the classical holistic ideologies were finished once and for all. The age of ideology was about to become a phenomenon of the past.

This optimistic assumption was proved wrong by events within only a few years' time. Instead, the late 1960s brought momentous changes in the general political climate of the West. The student movement put a sudden end to the hopes of many social scientists that a new age free of ideologies was about to begin. Rather, the students voiced the widespread dissatisfaction among young people with the complacency and materialism of the older generation, and above all at the complete absence of moral issues worth striving for. A wave of romantic neo-Marxism swept the West and for a while also strongly influenced academic sociology. Structural functionalism and empirical social research both came under fire, for allegedly merely perpetuating the status quo. Max Weber's sociology did not escape this general offensive against traditional 'bourgeois sociology' which was accused of being inherently conservative. However, the enthusiasm for neo-Marxism soon blew over, as it turned out to be even less satisfactory in view of the new problems with which the industrial societies of the West were confronted in the early 1970s. The economic recession and the breakdown of neo-Keynesian strategies for providing simultaneous economic growth and full employment indicated that the social sciences were unlikely to provide governments with the instrumental knowledge to enable them to steer clear of any major crises and to avoid major social conflicts. The growing scepticism regarding technocratic solutions to the pressing problems of the day gave rise to a renewed interest in sociological theories capable of taking the whole of past history into account and providing practical orientation rather than merely instrumental knowledge.

It is this new intellectual climate which explains why by the 1970s there was a sudden revival in Max Weber studies. Interest in his work now revived not because he had been the pioneer of value-free social research but conversely because his sociology would appear to provide a general orientation while empirical social science had been unable to deliver the goods.

It is therefore no mere coincidence that it was only after the failure of the so-called student movement and the crisis of the philosophy of social engineering, which had derived much of its inspiration from the empirical social sciences, that interest in Max Weber was on the upturn again. It soon gathered momentum, as is signified by the steadily growing number of studies published since the early 1970s. Wolfgang Schluchter's *Aspekte bürokratischer Herrschaft* (first published in 1972), which used Weber's categories for a reconstruction of the history of social thought about the emergent industrial system, alerted sociologists and historians alike to the significance of Weber's theory of bureaucracy in understanding modern industrial society against the background of history.[75] S. N. Eisenstadt's studies of civilization, which carry the tradition of Max Weber's universal-historical analysis into new regions, belong in a similar category.[76] The following decade saw a rich and constantly widening stream of work on Max Weber, which focused particularly on the theme of rationalization and its social, economic and religious roots.

The renewed demand for macro-sociological theory which could provide not only instrumental knowledge but also information about different value-options and about the significance of the development of modern industrial society provided the stimulus for a universal revival of Weber studies. Moreover, it became clear that the neo-positivist recognition of Max Weber as a pioneer of value-free social science was partly based on a misunderstanding. It goes without saying that he had conducted a lifelong campaign against value-judgements in the social sciences. He always objected to any sort of research which propagated ideologies wrapped in a scholarly disguise. However, he certainly did not share the view that scholarship ought to restrict its endeavours to the search for instrumental knowledge – or, as he put it, *Herrschaftswissen*. Its prime duty is to give orientation to the individual by providing rational, scientifically controlled information about possible lines of action and the different value-decisions involved in such actions at any given moment in time. This implies that sociology must above all establish the significance of social processes in the light of cultural values. For this very reason Weber always considered the historical dimension to be an essential part of sociological inquiry. It is the great strength of his sociology that it poses its questions against the back-cloth of universal history. Through ideal-typical reconstructions of particular segments of historical reality considered to be of significance for the future of mankind as we know it today, sociology seeks to enlighten us about alternative developmental paths and their respective consequences for human beings.

This circumstance explains why in recent years research on Max Weber has experienced an upsurge of unprecedented proportions, not only in the West, but also in the countries of the communist bloc. Its achievement in pinpointing the key issues of our modern world and in suggesting possible lines of inquiry regarding the fundamental problems of value is still unsurpassed. Moreover, his sociology appears to provide a good point of departure for macro-sociological research which seeks to provide practical orientation without supplying merely ideological answers. What is more, the social sciences have now rediscovered the importance of the historical dimension. As Ralf Dahrendorf pointed out recently, this also recommends Max Weber's sociological thought to modern social science, even though empirical research has now advanced far beyond him (which he himself has described as the natural course of things in the realm of scholarship).[77] This is another reason for the astounding worldwide renaissance of interest in Max Weber which we are witnessing today.

It would appear that, among others, the following avenues of inquiry in and beyond Max Weber scholarship are being pursued: research into his ideal-typical reconstruction of Western history and the process of rationalization;[78] research into the relationship between religious attitudes, social conduct and economic activities in both Western and non-Western cultures (a subject increasingly being discussed by scholars from non-Western countries); Weber's concept of social change and the dichotomy of value-oriented and instrumental social action (which is closely linked to the problem of formal and substantive rationality);[79] Weber's contribution to the study of history;[80] and his theory of politics and legitimacy, which attaches priority to the question of how individual freedom can survive in modern bureaucratic societies, whether capitalist or socialist. Besides these areas of inquiry, there is renewed interest in the philosophical and cultural background which conditioned Max Weber's social thought, a theme already treated by Karl Löwith and Siegfried Landshut in the early 1930s. Wilhelm Hennis recently argued with great fervour that in the final analysis Weber was concerned with one issue above all others, namely in what way the rise of specific types of human beings or the emergence of particular human lifestyles is conditioned by the selective mechanisms and social conditions which are typical of particular social institutions or social formations. Certainly this is a leitmotiv which strongly influenced Max

Weber's choice of approaches to the social investigation of reality; but one ought also to take into account the conclusions at which he arrived. They undoubtedly far transcend this question. They try to give concrete answers to the question how and under what political and social conditions in the course of history a personal life-conduct may prevail which allows for responsibility and creativity, in spite of the perennial working of institutional forces to the contrary that tend to stifle all individual initiative.

There will always be disagreement about the interpretation of Max Weber's ultimate objectives as a scholar, a citizen and a personality of great intellectual vigour. However, the absoute honesty with which he approached the problems of his own day will always gain our admiration, even if we no longer share all his views and his values.

Notes

CHAPTER 1   POLITICS AND SCHOLARSHIP

1 Karl Jaspers, *Max Weber: Politiker, Forscher, Philosopher* (Munich, 1958), p. 4.
2 See Reinhard Bendix and Günter Roth, *Scholarship and Partisanship: Essays on Max Weber* (Berkeley, 1971), pp. 55-6.
3 Cf. Peter Theiner, *Sozialer Liberalismus und deutsche Weltpolitik: Friedrich Nauman im Wilhelminischen Deutschland (1860-1919)* (Baden-Baden, 1983).
4 For the following comments on this point, see Mommsen, *Max Weber*, pp. 154-67; English edn, pp. 143-54.
5 On these and the following statements, see *MWG*, I/16, 'Introduction', pp. 3ff.
6 Extensive documentary evidence of Max Weber's electoral campaign work for the German Democratic Party (DDP) can be found in *MWG*, I/16, pp. 343ff.
7 Ibid., p. 273.
8 Quoted in ibid., p. 21, n. 53.
9 Cf. *GPS*, p. 532: 'professional politicians without a vocation, i.e. without the inner charismatic qualities that make a leader'.
10 *MWG*, I/15, p. 425.
11 Cf. *MWG*, I/16, p. 98.
12 *GPS*, p. 13.
13 Cf. *GASS*, pp. 400-1, 412, 413-14.
14 Cf. ibid., p. 400.
15 This argument appears again and again, especially in Max Weber's election speeches of 1918-19. Cf. *MWG*, I/16.
16 For a more detailed elaboration of this aspect of Max Weber's theory of democratic rule, see chapter 2 above.
17 On the relationship between Max Weber and Roberto Michels, see chapter 6 above.
18 *WuG*, p. 568; *EaS*, p. 985.

19 Cf. Mommsen, *Max Weber*, p. 363; English edn, p. 339. This aspect of my inter-
    pretation of Max Weber's position was given a critical reception by among others
    Gustav Schmidt in his book *Deutscher Historismus und der Übergang zur parlamen-
    tarischen Democratie: Untersuchungen zu den politischen Gedanken von Meinecke, Troeltsch,
    Max Weber*, in *NPL*, 21 (1976); and David Beetham, *Max Weber and the Theory of
    Modern Politics* (London, 1974). The sources give a clear message, however. A
    solution to the problem is not to be found in a harmonization of Max Weber's
    arguments, but, if at all, in the full representation of the antinomical structure of his
    theory of democratic rule.

20 *GPS*, p. 544.

21 Cf. Wolfgang Schluchter, *Wertfreiheit und Verantwortungsethik: Zum Verhältnis von
    Wissenschaft und Politik bei Max Weber* (Tübingen, 1971).

22 In a lecture to the Staatswissenschaftliche Vereinigung in Vienna on 25 October
    1917, about which we have only a report by the *Neue Freie Presse*, Weber appears to
    have subsumed parliamentary government under the type of value-rational legal
    rule; but he certainly abandoned this solution again very soon. Cf. *Neue Freie Presse*,
    no. 19102, 26 October 1917, p. 10.

23 *WuG*, p. 156; *EaS*, p. 268.

24 *GPS*, p. 544.

25 Wilhelm Hennis, 'Max Weber's "Liberalismus"', quoted from the manuscript
    version (p. 30). Cf. also Wilhelm Hennis, *Max Webers Fragestellung* (Tübingen, 1987),
    p. 52.

CHAPTER 2   THE ANTINOMICAL STRUCTURE OF MAX WEBER'S POLITICAL THOUGHT

1 Karl Jaspers, *Notizen zu Martin Heidegger*, ed. H. Sahner (Basle, 1977), p. 215.

2 Mommsen, *Max Weber*, pp. 13ff.; English edn, pp. 21ff.

3 Jürgen Kocka, 'Kontroversen über Max Weber', *NPL*, 21 (1976), pp. 282ff.; David
    Beetham, *Max Weber and the Theory of Modern Politics* (London, 1974); Anthony
    Giddens, *Politics and Sociology in the Thought of Max Weber* (London, 1972).

4 In contrast to older interpretations, Kocka ('Kontroversen') stresses the importance
    of 'enlightenment-rational' elements in Weber's thought and comes to the con-
    clusion that 'If one takes seriously Weber's orientation to such meta-values, it
    becomes impossible to accept the view that this support for a public sphere and civil
    maturity, for parliamentarism and democratization, were all instrumental means to
    the ends of the nation-state and of power-politics.' See also Giddens, *Politics*, p. 55;
    Beetham, *Max Weber*, pp. 113ff. Cf. also Gerhard Hufnagel, *Kritik als Beruf: Der
    kritische Gehalt im Werk Max Webers* (Frankfurt, 1971), pp. 102-3, who has chosen
    Weber 'the critic' as the focus of his presentation, arguing that 'the critic who wants
    to fight against the currents of his time still has to plunge into those currents.' These
    pragmatic interpretations tend, however, to overlook the true span of Weber's
    thought, reducing it to routine, everyday positions. As expedient as this may be, it
    does not correspond to Weber's own intentions.

5 *GPS*, p. 306.

6 *MWG*, I/15, p. 234.

7 Karl-Siegbert Rehberg, 'Rationales Handeln als grossbürgerliches Aktionsmodell: Thesen zu einigen handlungstheoretischen Implikationen der "Soziologischen Grundbegriffe" Max Webers', *KZSS*, 31 (1978), pp. 199–236; at p. 222.

8 I concur here with M. Rainer Lepsius, 'Max Weber in München', *Zeitschrift für Soziologie*, 6 (1977), p. 114, who, starting from the inconsistencies evident in Weber's political position, goes on to show that this phenomenon is related to the peculiar character of his sociological method: 'His comparative social research into different systems of domination led him to the view that, given the changing conditions of interests, there was no ideal order which could be institutionalized permanently, nor could one deduce a hierarchy of ultimate values.' The discussion of Weber's sociology 'fell all too easily into the temptation of isolating his value-judgements from the context of his comparative theory of institutions and of overlooking the antinomies between formal and substantive, instrumental and value rationality, which Weber always took such pains to elaborate.' It was precisely Weber's concern 'to dramatize these antinomies.' It is the purpose of this essay to elaborate on these antinomies in the political sphere. At any rate, what distinguishes my position from that of Lepsius is the view that the antinomical structure of his thought was not simply methodologically determined but that it actually seems to pervade his whole life. Cf. 'A liberal in despair', in Wolfgang J. Mommsen, *The Age of Bureaucracy: Perspectives on the Political Thought of Max Weber* (Oxford, 1974), pp. 95ff.

9 Eduard Baumgarten, *Max Weber: Werk und Person* (Tübingen, 1964), pp. 555–6. See also Robert Eden, *Political Leadership and Nihilism: A Study of Weber and Nietzsche* (Tampa, 1983); and Wolfgang J. Mommsen, *Max Weber: Gesellschaft, Politik und Geschichte* (Frankfurt, 1974), pp. 128ff.; and Eugène Fleischmann, 'De Weber à Nietzsche', *Archives européennes de sociologie*, 5 (1964).

10 Cf. letter to Roberto Michels, 4 August 1908, Fondazione Luigi Einaudi, Turin.

11 *GPS*, p. 176.

12 In Giddens, *Politics*, one already finds, almost counter to his intentions, a partial recognition of the antinomical position which emerges here.

13 See letter to Roberto Michels, 4 August 1908, Fondazione Luigi Einaudi, Turin.

14 Ibid.

15 Ibid.

16 Letter to Roberto Michels, 6 November 1907, Fondazione Luigi Einaudi, Turin: 'Political democratization is the only thing which may be achievable in the foreseeable future – and this is not at all insignificant.'

17 *WuG*, p. 156; *EaS*, p. 268.

18 *GPS*, p. 544.

19 *WuG*, p. 157; *EaS*, p. 269.

20 *GPS*, p. 333.

21 Wolfgang J. Mommsen, *Max Weber: Gesellschaft, Politik und Geschichte* (Frankfurt, 1974), pp. 88–9.

22 *GPS*, p. 544.

23 *GPS*, pp. 63–4.

24 *GPS*, p. 64.

25 For a more detailed analysis of this point, see Mommsen, *Max Weber: Gesellschaft, Politik und Geschichte*, pp. 123ff.

26 Bernhard Schäfers, 'Ein Rundschreiben Max Webers zur Sozialpolitik', *Soziale Welt* 18 (1967), pp. 261ff.; and Mommsen, *Max Weber*, pp. 126–7.

27 Max Weber, *The Protestant Ethic and the Spirit of Capitalism*, trans. Talcott Parsons, Introduction by Anthony Giddens (New York, 1958).

28 Mommsen, *Max Weber: Gesellschaft, Politik und Geschichte*, pp. 156–7.

29 *GARS*, I, p. 203; Weber, *Protestant Ethic*, p. 181.

30 *WuG*, p. 78; *EaS*, p. 173.

31 *WuG*, p. 77; *EaS*, p. 138.

32 In a typical accentuation of the antinomical character of the capitalist system, viewed from the perspective of a liberalism of humanistic slant, Weber (*WuG*, p. 78; *EaS*, p. 113) writes: 'The fact that the maximum of formal rationality in capital accounting is possible only where the workers are subjected to domination by entrepreneurs is a further specific element of substantive irrationality in the modern economic order.'

33 *MWG*, I/10, p. 269.

34 The famous question posed by Herbert Marcuse as to what extent Weber aimed at a justification of capitalism through the identification of capitalism with formal rationality is in fact grounded on this antinomy, which Weber himself explicitly stressed. See, for example, the debate at the 15th Conference of German Sociology held in 1965, in Otto Stammer (ed.), *Max Weber and Sociology Today* (Oxford, 1971), pp. 152–86.

35 *GPS*, p. 63.

36 *GPS*, p. 269.

37 Letter to Roberto Michels, 4 August 1908, Fondazione Luigi Einaudi, Turin, extensively quoted in chapter 6, pp. 96–7. See also Weber's basic acceptance of the principle of domination of man over man, even within a legitimate democratic system, in 'Politics as a vocation', in *GPS*, p. 507.

38 Cf. Wilfried Röhrich, *Robert Michels: Vom soziologisch-syndikalistischen zum faschistischen Credo* (Berlin, 1972), pp. 143–4.

39 Rehberg, 'Rationales Handeln', *KZSS*, 31 (1978), p. 216, comes to the somewhat overbearing conclusion that one is dealing here with 'the theory of a liberalism that has lost all emphasis as well as future orientation, constituting a sociological counterpart to the "subjectivistic", muddled political economy.' This certainly seems to go too far, since the strength of Weber's position rests precisely on its principled openness towards novel types of social development, for which different political strategies and models of action can be presented.

CHAPTER 4   CAPITALISM AND SOCIALISM

1 Albert Salomon, 'Max Weber', *Die Gesellschaft*, 3 (1926), p. 144, wrote: 'Thus, in the final analysis, it is not just methodological questions but "ideological" ones which separated Weber from socialism and caused him to derive the dialectics and ultimate goal of socialist society from the Marxist philosophy of history. One can, in order to highlight the paradox of this position, call him a bourgeois Marx.' Similarly, Ernst Topitsch, 'Max Webers Geschichtsauffassung', *Wissenschaft und Weltbild*, 3 (1950), p. 262.

2 *GPS*, p. 20.

3 Letter to Roberto Michels, 6 November 1907, Fondazione Luigi Einaudi, Turin.

4 In this regard, see the analysis by Karl Löwith, *Max Weber and Karl Marx*, ed. Tom Bottomore and William Outhwaite (London, 1982), pp. 19ff.

5 *MWG*, I/15, p. 616; Max Weber, 'Socialism', in Eldridge, p. 205.

6 Eduard Baumgarten, *Max Weber: Werk und Person* (Tübingen, 1964), pp. 554-5, n. 1.

7 For a detailed exposition of this point of view, see Wolfgang J. Mommsen, *The Age of Bureaucracy: Perspectives on the Political Sociology of Max Weber* (New York, 1974), pp. 103-7, and Mommsen, 'Universalgeschichtliches und politisches Denken bei Max Weber', *Historische Zeitschrift*, 201 (1965), pp. 597ff., reprinted in Mommsen, *Max Weber: Gesellschaft, Politik und Geschichte* (Frankfurt, 1974), pp. 129-43.

8 Note the meagre results of Günther Roth's efforts to put together the textual documentation for Weber's attitude towards Marx in 'Das historische Verhältnis der weberschen Soziologie zum Marxismus', *KZSS*, 20 (1968), pp. 429-47; also printed in Reinhard Bendix and Günter Roth, *Scholarship and Partisanship: Essays on Max Weber* (Berkeley, 1971), pp. 227-46. In addition, see Anthony Giddens, *Capitalism and Modern Social Theory: An Analysis of the Writings of Marx, Durkheim and Max Weber* (Cambridge, 1971), pp. 191ff., and Giddens, 'Marx, Weber and the development of capitalism', *Sociology*, 4 (1970), pp. 289-310.

9 See Mommsen, 'Universalgeschichtliches und politisches Denken', pp. 97-143.

10 For an ideal-typical interpretation of the economic view of history as seen by Max Weber, cf. Judith Janoska-Bendl, *Methodologische Aspekte des Idealtypus: Max Weber und die Soziologie der Geschichte* (Berlin, 1965), pp. 89-114.

11 Max Weber, *The Methodology of the Social Sciences*, trans. Edward A. Shils and Henry A. Finch (Glencoe, Ill., 1949), p. 68 (translation modified slightly).

12 This is according to Jürgen Kocka's interpretation, 'Karl Marx und Max Weber: ein methodologischer Vergleich', *Zeitschrift für die gesamte Staatswissenschaft*, 122 (1966), pp. 328-57; also in Hans-Ulrich Wehler (ed.), *Geschichte und Ökonomie* (Cologne, 1973), and in Jürgen Kocka, *Sozialgeschichte* (Göttingen, 1977). See also Richard Ashcraft, 'Marx and Weber on liberalism as bourgeois ideology', *Comparative Studies in Society and History*, 14 (1972), pp. 130-68.

13 Cf. Helmut Fleischer, *Marxismus und Geschichte* (Frankfurt, 1969), pp. 52–5.

14 See Erich Matthias, 'Kautsky und der Kautskyanismus: Die Funktion der Ideologie in der deutschen Sozialdemokratie vor dem ersten Weltkrieg', *Marxismusstudien*, 2 (1957), p. 151, and recently, in cautious defence of Kautsky, Hans-Joseph Steinberg, *Sozialismus und deutsche Sozialdemokratie: zur Ideologie der Partei vor dem I. Weltkrieg* (Bonn/Bad Godesberg, 1972), pp. 60–1.

15 See also, in greater depth, chapter 5, 'Joining the Underdogs?', pp. 75–86.

16 *MWG*, I/10, pp. 275–6.

17 *GASS*, p. 456.

18 Marianne Weber, *Max Weber: A Biography*, trans. Harry Zohn (New York, 1975), p. 604.

19 Thus, in Weber's second essay on the Protestant ethic (cf. *The Protestant Ethic and the Spirit of Capitalism*, trans. Talcott Parsons (New York, 1958), p. 183), he insisted it had not been his intention 'to substitute for a onesided materialistic an equally onesided spiritualistic causal interpretation of culture and history. Both are equally possible.' See also Max Weber, 'Kritische Bemerkungen zu den vorstehenden "Kritischen Beiträgen"' (article under review by Karl Fischer), in Johannes Winckelmann (ed.), *Die protestantische Ethik*, vol. II (Gütersloh, 1972), p. 28, and Weber, 'Bemerkungen zu der vorstehenden "Replik"' (also by Karl Fischer), in ibid., pp. 46–7. Here Weber protests expressly at the assumption that he had 'undertaken an idealistic construction of history' and states that he considers 'the question of the influence of economic processes upon religious movements' has by no means been resolved by his 'current observations regarding the way in which influence has moved in the *opposite* direction'. For a systematic discussion of this problem, which I have largely ignored here, see Norman Birnbaum, 'Conflicting interpretations of the rise of capitalism: Marx and Weber', *British Journal of Sociology*, 4 (1953), pp. 125–41.

20 Cf. Weber, *The Protestant Ethic*, p. 181: 'The Puritan wanted to work in a calling; we are forced to do so. For when asceticism was carried out of monastic cells into everyday life, and began to dominate worldly morality, it played its part in building the tremendous cosmos of the modern economic order. This order is now bound to the technical and economic conditions of machine production which today determine the lives of all the individuals who are born into the mechanism, and not only those directly concerned with economic acquisition, with irresistible force. Perhaps it will so determine them until the last ton of fossilized coal is burnt. In Baxter's view the care for external goods should only lie on the shoulders of the "saint like a light cloak, which can be thrown aside at any moment". But fate decreed that the cloak should become an iron cage. Since asceticism undertook to remodel the world and to work out its ideals in the world, material goods have gained an increasing and ultimately inexorable power over the lives of men as at no previous period in history.'

21 Cf. *GPS*, p. 63, and Mommsen, *Max Weber*, pp. 89–90; cf. also English edn, pp. 83–4.

22 Cf. *From Max Weber: Essays in Sociology*, ed. H. H. Gerth and C. Wright Mills (New York, 1946), p. 280.

23 Löwith, *Max Weber and Karl Marx*, esp. pp. 50–1.

24 Cf. *GPS*, p. 64: 'the much reviled "anarchy of production"', similarly p. 333. See also 'Der Sozialismus', *MWG*, I/15, pp. 613–14; Eldridge, p. 202.

25 The lecture on 'Socialism' (see note 5) should only be used with caution for Weber's understanding of Marx, since it is not free of tactical political considerations. In it, Weber sought to counteract the uncertain atmosphere regarding Austria-Hungary. Cf. *MWG*, I/15, pp. 597–8.

26 Ibid., pp. 613–14; Eldridge, pp. 202–3.

27 Ibid., p. 619; Eldridge, p. 207.

28 Cf. Mommsen, *Max Weber*, pp. 126–7; English edn, pp. 117–18.

29 Ibid., pp. 299–302; English edn, pp. 277–9.

30 *MWG*, I/15, p. 609; Eldridge, p. 199.

31 *WUG*, p. 79; *EaS*, p. 139.

32 *MWG*, I/15, p. 464; *EaS*, pp. 1401–2 (translation modified slightly).

33 *MWG*, I/15, pp. 465–6; *EaS*, p. 1403.

34 *MWG*, I/15, p. 621; Eldridge, p. 209.

35 *WuG*, p. 533; *EaS*, p. 930 (translation modified slightly).

36 For what follows, see *WuG*, pp. 177–8; *EaS*, pp. 302–3.

37 *WuG*, p. 178; *EaS*, p. 304.

38 *WuG*, p. 179; *EaS*, p. 305. There Max Weber refers directly to an unfinished passage in the third volume of *Capital*, and speculates that Marx became aware of this problem in the final years of his life and therefore wanted to extend his analysis.

39 *WuG*, p. 179; *EaS*, p. 305.

40 *MWG*, I/15, p. 615; Eldridge, p. 204.

41 In 1908 he pointed out to Roberto Michels that it was utopian to assume that it might be possible to overcome the 'domination of man over man' by whatever sort of socialist system. See letter to Roberto Michels of 4 August 1908. See also chapter 6, pp. 96–7.

42 Cf. Gerhard Hufnagel, *Kritik als Beruf: der kritische Gehalt im Werk Max Webers* (Frankfurt, Berlin and Vienna, 1971), pp. 148–54. When Hufnagel attributes the fact that Weber refused to develop an alternative prescription for ending 'alienation' 'to the caution of the scientist' and to 'the critic's tendency not to go beyond the negative activity of critical destruction' (p. 152), I am unable to follow him. It is not 'caution', nor is it mere critical negativity, but rather realistic insight into the conditions of industrial societies which made Weber come to the realization that there was no quick solution to the problems that Marx had raised. It led him to develop a range of strategies designed to make the best of a situation which was in and of itself irreversible.

43 'Only political democratization is perhaps achievable in the foreseeable future, and it is not so insignificant. I cannot prevent you from believing that there may indeed be more to it, but neither can I force myself to think so': letter to Roberto Michels of 6 November 1907. See also chapter 6, p. 97.

44 Cf. Weber's contribution to the discussion at the 1905 convention of the Verein für Sozialpolitik held in Mannheim, reprinted in *GASS*, pp. 396–7; see also Mommsen, *Max Weber*, pp. 125–7; English edn, pp. 116–19.

45 Weber referred to the state as 'the seat of political power which dominates national society'. See 'Die Lehrfreiheit der Universitäten', in *Münchner Hochschulnachrichten*, 19 (1909), trans. Edward Shils in 'The power of the state and the dignity of the academic calling in imperial Germany: the writings of Max Weber on university problems', *Minerva*, 11 (1973), pp. 18–23 (quotation on p. 20); see also *EaS*, pp. 975, 983–90.

46 'Industrialisierung und Kapitalismus in Werk Max Webers', *Kultur und Gesellschaft* (Frankfurt, 1965), vol. 2, pp. 125ff.; English version in Otto Stammer (ed.), *Max Weber and Sociology Today* (Oxford, 1971), pp. 133–51. Cf. Mommsen, *Max Weber: Gesellschaft, Politik und Geschichte*, pp. 41ff.

47 In the light of this, it is astonishing that Wolfgang Lefèvre has tried once again to seek the solution to the problems posed (in quite different ways) by Marx and Weber by completely doing away with state power. This is on a level of utopianism exceeding that already reached by Marx. See Wolfgang Lefèvre, *Zum historischen Charakter und zur historischen Funktion der Methode bürgerlicher Soziologie: Untersuchungen am Werk Webers* (Frankfurt, 1971), pp. 86–97.

48 *WuG*, pp. 59–60; *EaS*, pp. 109–10.

49 *WuG*, p. 87; *EaS*, p. 151.

50 Here I draw on Wolfgang Schluchter's brilliant analysis of Herbert Marcuse's critique of Max Weber, in *Aspekte bürokratischer Herrschaft: Studien zur Interpretation der fortschreitenden Industriegesellschaft* (Munich, 1972), pp. 257–68.

51 Cf. Schluchter's point (ibid., p. 267) that 'at the height of the inferno which he has set ablaze Marcuse does not so much' unmask 'Weber as truly understand him for the first time.'

52 *WuG*, p. 44; *EaS*, p. 84. See also *WuG*, p. 78; *EaS*, p. 138: 'The fact that the maximum of formal rationality in *capital accounting* is possible only where the workers are subjected to domination by entrepreneurs is a further specific element of *substantive* irrationality in the modern economic order.'

53 Letter to Roberto Michels of 4 August 1908; see also chapter 6, pp. 96–7.

54 *WuG*, p. 65; *EaS*, p. 118.

55 *WuG*, p. 60; *EaS*, p. 111.

56 *GPS*, p. 12.

57 Cf. the reports on Max Weber's speech to the Deutscher National-Ausschuss on 1 August 1916, *MWG*, I/15, pp. 656–90.

58 For further details, see chapter 6, pp. 85–6.

59 Cf. *MWG*, I/10, Introduction, p. 25.

60 Letter to Mina Tobler, 10 December 1919 (date not quite certain), A.E. II, 116, in the possession of Professor Eduard Baumgarten: 'during the summer I *hope* to find more pleasure in lecturing (government, socialism).' See also his letter to Lederer, 12 May 1920, Central Archives of the German Democratic Republic, Merseburg.

CHAPTER 5 JOINING THE UNDERDOGS?

1 Letter to Roberto Michels, 6 November 1907, Fondazione Luigi Einaudi, Turin; cf. Mommsen, *Max Weber*, p. 116, n. 84; English edn, p. 109, n. 84.
2 See chapter 4, 'Capitalism and Socialism'.
3 *GPS*, p. 22.
4 Ibid.
5 For a more detailed account of the relationship between Weber and Michels, see chapter 6, 'Roberto Michels and Max Weber'.
6 For the following analysis see Wolfgang J. Mommsen, 'Max Weber and Roberto Michels: an asymmetrical partnership', *Archives européennes de sociologie*, 22 (1981), pp. 100–16, and Mommsen, 'Roberto Michels and Max Weber' (chapter 6). See also W. Röhrich, *Robert Michels: Vom sozialistisch-syndikalistischen zum faschistischen Credo* (Berlin, 1972); D. Beetham, 'From socialism to fascism: the relation between theory and practice in the work of Robert Michels', *Political Studies*, 25 (1977), pp. 3–24, 161–81; and L. A. Scaff, 'Max Weber and Robert Michels', *American Journal of Sociology*, 96 (1981), pp. 1269ff. See also Günther Roth's short assessment of the attitudes of Weber and Michels to socialism, in R. Bendix and G. Roth, *Scholarship and Partisanship: Essays on Max Weber* (Berkeley, 1971), pp. 247–52.
7 Letter to Michels, 8 October 1906, Fondazione Luigi Einaudi, Turin; cf. Mommsen, *Max Weber*, p. 115; English edn, p. 108.
8 Letter to Michels, 12 May 1909, Fondazione Luigi Einaudi, Turin; cf. Mommsen, *Max Weber*, p. 118, n. 91; English edn, p. 110.
9 'Zur Lage der bürgerlichen Demokratie in Russland', *AfSSP*, 22, 'Beilage', pp. 120–1; *MWG*, I/10, pp. 271–2.
10 Ibid., p. 256; here quoted from Weber, *Selections in Translation*, ed. W. G. Runciman (Cambridge UP, 1976), pp. 276–7.
11 Cf. above, n. 7.
12 See chapter 6.
13 For a more detailed account, see Mommsen, *Max Weber*, pp. 125–7; English edn, pp. 118–20.
14 Ibid., and also B. Schäfers, 'Ein Rundschreiben Max Webers zur Sozialpolitik', *Soziale Welt*, 18 (1967), pp. 261–72.
15 'Das Preussische Wahlrecht', in *MWG*, I/15, pp. 222–35.
16 Ibid., pp. 720–7.
17 Cf. Mommsen, *Max Weber*, p. 274; English edn, p. 254.
18 'Das neue Deutschland', speech of 4 December 1918 in Frankfurt, in *MWG*, I/16, pp. 207–13.
19 Ibid., p. 312.
20 Ibid. See also Weber's notes for a political speech, early in 1919, which confirm the report in the *Frankfurter Zeitung*: 'Why not be a socialist? In order not to shield charlatanism, not [to join] in *grave-digging*': Arbeitstelle und Archiv des Max Weber

Ausgabe bei der Kommission für Sozial- und Wirtschaftsgeschichte der Bayerischen Akademie der Wissenschaften, Munich, Baumgarten MS collection; reprinted in Mommsen, *Max Weber*, appendix VI.

21 *GPS*, pp. 458 ff.; cf. Mommsen, *Max Weber*, pp. 320–1, 325–6.

22 Letter to Karl Petersen, 14 April 1920, Petersen collection no. 53, in the possession of Dr Edgar Petersen, Hamburg; first published, but with numerous misreadings distorting its meaning, by Bruce F. Frye, 'A letter from Max Weber', *Journal of Modern History*, 39 (1967), pp. 122–4. For a corrected text, see Mommsen, *Max Weber*, p. 333, n. 105.

23 As early as 1909 the idea of eventually joining the Social Democratic Party occurred to Weber as a theoretical possibility, because he thought that effective support for the interests of the proletariat would be possible only if he unreservedly identified with the Social Democrats. At that time he wrote to Tönnies: 'But I could not honestly subscribe to the credo of Social Democracy, and that prevented me from joining – even if I did not "serve other gods" as well – although it is after all every bit as much lip-service as the Apostles' Creed.' Cf. Mommsen, *Max Weber*, p. 137, n. 152; English edn, p. 128. See also *GPS*, p. 485, and Weber's analogous statement in the *Wiesbadener Zeitung*, evening edition of 6 December 1918 (cf. Mommsen, *Max Weber*, p. 316; English edn, p. 294), and finally the letter of 14 April 1920 to Petersen: 'I cannot become a "majority socialist" [*Mehrheitssozialist*] because this party *must* make the same compromises concerning socialism (against the convictions of its scientifically trained members)' (see note 22). According to this, he might otherwise have joined the party.

CHAPTER 6   ROBERTO MICHELS AND MAX WEBER

1 D. Beetham, 'Michels and his critics', *Archives européennes de sociologie*, 22 (1981), pp. 81–99.

2 The ideas developed here bear closely on the argument of my earlier article, 'Max Weber and Roberto Michels: an asymmetrical partnership', *Archives européennes de sociologie*, 22 (1981), pp. 100–16. See also W. Röhrich, *Robert Michels: Vom sozialistisch-syndikalistischen zum faschistischen Credo* (Berlin, 1972), and his concise essay on Robert Michels in D. Käsler (ed.), *Klassiker des soziologischen Denkens*, vol. 2 (Munich, 1978), pp. 226–53; A. Mitzman, *Sociology and Estrangement: Three Sociologists of Imperial Germany* (New York, 1973), pp. 267–344. For a trenchant critique of the interpretations of both Röhrich and Mitzman, see D. Beetham, 'From socialism to fascism: the relation between theory and practice in the work of Robert Michels', *Political Studies*, 25 (1977), pp. 3–24, 161–81; see also F. Pfetsch, 'Robert Michels als Elitentheoretiker', *Politische Vierteljahresschrift*, 7 (1966), pp. 208–27, and, on the relationship between Weber and Michels, W. J. Mommsen, *Max Weber*, pp. 115–19; English edn, pp. 107–12, and the article by L. A. Scaff, 'Max Weber and Robert Michels', *American Journal of Sociology*, 86 (1981), pp. 1269 ff.

3 Max Weber to Roberto Michels, 1 January 1906, Fondazione Luigi Einaudi, Turin. The article is R. Michels, 'Die deutsche Sozialdemokratie', *AfSSP*, 23 (1906), pp. 471-556.

4 R. Michels, 'Proletariat und Bourgeoisie in der sozialistischen Bewegung Italien', *AfSSP*, 21 (1905), pp. 347-416, and 22 (1906), pp. 80-125, 424-66, 664-720.

5 R. Michels, 'Max Weber', *Nuova Antologia*, 16 December 1920, p. 7.

6 Mommsen, 'Max Weber and Roberto Michels', pp. 100-1.

7 Röhrich, *Robert Michels*, p. 14.

8 Max Weber, 'Die sogenannte "Lehrfreiheit" an den deutschen Universitäten', *Frankfurter Zeitung*, 20 September 1908, 3rd morning edn. Cf. Mommsen, *Max Weber*, pp. 119-20; English edn, pp. 112-13.

9 Max Weber to Roberto Michels, 21 October 1915, copy in Max Weber papers, Central Archive of the German Democratic Republic Meiseburg, Rep. 52. See also Mommsen, 'Max Weber and Roberto Michels', p. 102.

10 Max Weber to Roberto Michels, 19 August 1909, Fondazione Luigi Einaudi, Turin.

11 Michels, 'Die deutsche Sozialdemokratie', p. 555.

12 Max Weber to Roberto Michels, 8 October 1906, Fondazione Luigi Einaudi, Turin; see Mommsen, *Max Weber*, p. 115; English edn, p. 108.

13 See Max Weber, 'Zur Lage der bürgerlichen Demokratie in Russland', *AfSSP*, 22 (1906), pp. 120-1; *MWG*, I/10, p. 272.

14 R. Michels, 'Die deutsche Sozialdemokratie im internationalen Verbande', *AfSSP*, 25 (1907), pp. 148-231.

15 Ibid., p. 179.

16 Ibid., pp. 219-20.

17 *GASS*, p. 410.

18 Max Weber to Roberto Michels, 6 November 1907, Fondazione Luigi Einaudi, Turin. Michels was in fact later to describe the party in similar terms. See his *Zur Soziologie des Parteiwesens in der modernen Demokratie: Untersuchungen über die oligarchischen Tendenzen des Gruppenlebens* (Leipzig, 1911), p. 293, n. 2. An English translation of this work (from the Italian) was published under the title *Political Parties: A Sociological Study of the Oligarchical Tendencies of Modern Democracy* (London, 1915).

19 Max Weber to Roberto Michels, 19 August 1908, Fondazione Luigi Einaudi, Turin; see Mommsen, *Max Weber*, p. 115, n. 80; English edn, p. 108.

20 R. Michels, 'Die oligarchischen Tendenzen der Gesellschaft: Ein Beitrag zum Problem der Demokratie', *AfSSP*, 27 (1908), pp. 73-135.

21 Ibid., pp. 77-8, 118ff.

22 Max Weber to Roberto Michels, 4 August 1908, Fondazione Luigi Einaudi, Turin; see Mommsen, *Max Weber*, pp. 111-12; English edn, pp. 104-5.

23 Michels, *Zur Soziologie* (see note 18 above).

24 The 2nd edn was published by Kröner in Leipzig in 1925. A reprint was published in Stuttgart in 1957, with an introduction by Werner Conze.

25 Michels, *Zur Soziologie*, 1st edn, p. 349. In the more emphatic formulation in the 2nd

edn (p. 340), anarchy is said not to have 'succeeded in realizing its theory in any practically applicable form'.

26 Ibid. (1st edn), pp. 387ff.

27 Ibid., p. 391; see also 2nd edn, p. 377.

28 Ibid.

29 See the undated letter from Weber, written some time in 1911, in which he thanks Michels for the dedication and lists a whole series of points of criticism, Fondazione Luigi Einaudi, Turin. It is worth noting that the same letter is explicitly mentioned in Michels's Preface to the second edition: 'For the first time the opportunity now presents itself to give this detailed letter, containing a critique which is both positive and negative, the attention it deserves'; ibid., p. xxviii.

30 *MWG*, I/15, p. 483.

31 Cf. Mommsen, *Max Weber*, pp. 363–70; English edn, pp. 339–46, and W. J. Mommsen, *The Age of Bureaucracy: Perspectives on the Political Sociology of Max Weber* (Oxford, 1974), pp. 89–94.

32 See note 19 above.

33 This formulation does not, however, appear until the 2nd edn of Michels, *Zur Soziologie* (p. 130).

34 *WuG*, pp. 531–40. In Weber's 'Parlament und Regierung im neugeordneten Deutschland' (*MWG*, I/15, especially pp. 454–64) of 1917, his position on the sociology of parties appears in fully developed form; it stands in direct contrast to the hypotheses developed by Michels, despite the fact that the contents of their analyses are, to a large extent, the same. It was not until 1919–20 that Weber set his study of political parties within the framework of a 'typology of forms of domination' (*WuG*, pp. 167ff.).

35 *GPS*, p. 532.

36 See *WuG*, pp. 155–7, and the comments in Mommsen, *Max Weber*, pp. 427–9; English edn, pp. 401–4; also Mommsen, *The Age of Bureaucracy*, pp. 90–4.

37 See Röhrich, *Robert Michels*, pp. 143ff., and Beetham, 'From socialism to fascism', pp. 175–7.

38 *WuG*, p. 156.

39 See Mommsen, *Max Weber*, pp. 407–15; English edn, pp. 381–9.

40 R. Michels, 'Grundsätzliches zum Problem der Demokratie', *Zeitschrift für Politik*, 17 (1927), pp. 291–2.

41 Michels, 'Authority', in *Encyclopaedia of the Social Sciences*, vol. 2 (New York, 1939), p. 319, quoted from Röhrich, *Robert Michels*, p. 164.

42 Ibid., p. 160.

43 Michels, 'Grundsätzliches zum Problem der Demokratie', p. 295.

44 R. Michels, 'Der Homo Oeconomicus und die Kooperation', *AfSSP*, 29 (1909), pp. 59–83 (quotation from p. 79).

45 Ibid., p. 66.

46 Ibid., p. 68.

47 Ibid., p. 65.

48 Max Weber to Roberto Michels, 19 August 1909, Fondazione Luigi Einaudi, Turin.

49 R. Michels, 'August Bebel', *AfSSP*, 37 (1913), pp. 671–700.

50 See Röhrich, *Robert Michels*, pp. 55ff.

51 Michels, 'August Bebel', p. 697.

CHAPTER 7   MAX WEBER ON BUREAUCRACY AND BUREAUCRATIZATION

1 Max Weber, *The Protestant Ethic and the Spirit of Capitalism*, 2nd edn (London, 1976), p. 181.

2 W. G. Runciman, *A Critique of Max Weber's Philosophy of Social Science* (Cambridge, 1972), p. 5.

3 W. J. Mommsen, *The Age of Bureaucracy: Perspectives on the Political Sociology of Max Weber* (Oxford, 1974), pp. 20–1.

4 *WuG*, p. 128; *EaS*, p. 223.

5 *WuG*, p. 561; *EaS*, p. 973.

6 *MWG*, I/15, p. 464.

7 *MWG*, I/15, p. 465.

CHAPTER 8   IDEAL TYPE AND PURE TYPE

1 A representative example is Theodor Schieder, 'Der Typus der Geschichtswissenschaft', *Staat und Gesellschaft im Wandel unserer Zeit* (Munich, 1958), pp. 176ff.

2 H. Stuart Hughes, 'The historian and the social scientist', *American Historical Review*, 66 (1961), pp. 20ff.

3 Jürgen Streisand, *Studien über die deutsche Geschichtswissenschaft*, vol. II: *Die bürgerliche deutsche Geschichtsschreibung von der Reichseinigung bis zur Befreiung Deutscholands vom Faschismus* (Berlin, 1965), pp. 179ff.

4 *WL*, p. 204.

5 See chapter 2.

6 On this see Wolfgang J. Mommsen, '"Towards the iron cage of future serfdom"? On the methodological status of Max Weber's ideal-typical concept of bureaucratization', *Transactions of the Royal Historical Society*, 5th series, 30 (London, 1980), pp. 131ff.

7 *WL*, p. 202.

8 Bernhard Pfister, *Die Entwicklung zum Idealtypus: Eine methodologische Untersuchung über das Verhältnis von Theorie und Geschichte bei Menger, Schmoller und Max Weber* (Tübingen, 1928); Judith Janoska-Bendl, *Methodologische Aspekte des Idealtypus: Max Weber und die Soziologie der Geschichte* (Berlin, 1965).

9 See Mommsen, *Max Weber: Gesellschaft, Politik und Geschichte*, pp. 224–5.

10 *WL*, p. 204.

11 See Wolfgang J. Mommsen, 'Persönliche Lebensführung und gesellschaftlicher Wandel: Versuch einer Rekonstruktion des Begriffs der Geschichte bei Max

Weber', in P. Alter, T. Nipperdey and W. J. Mommsen (eds), *Geschichte und politisches Handeln: Studien zu Europäischen Denkern der Neuzeit* (Stuttgart, 1985), pp. 261–81. An English version, 'Personal conduct and societal change', appeared in Sam Whimster and Scott Lash (eds), *Max Weber: Rationality and Modernity* (London, 1987), pp. 35–51.

12 *WL*, pp. 427–74.

13 *WuG*, pp. 1–119; *EaS*, pp. 3–211.

14 See *WL*, pp. 437ff.

15 Ibid., p. 438, n. 1.

16 See 'Einleitung in die Wirtschaftsethik der Weltreligionen', *GARS*, I, p. 265. At the beginning of the 'Zwischenbetrachtung', ibid., p. 537, Weber explains his research strategy even more clearly: to isolate 'durch zweckmässig rational konstruierte Typen die innerlich "konsequentesten" Formen eines aus fest gegebenen Voraussetzungen ableitbaren praktischen Verhaltens'. In this context he points out (ibid., p. 544) that it is necessary to distinguish between formal and substantive rationality, and to note that they can come into conflict with each other. See also, on the inevitable conflict between formal rationality and substantive rationality in modern capitalism, *WuG*, pp. 44ff., esp. pp. 78ff.; *EaS*, pp. 85ff., esp. pp. 138–9. On this subject see also Roger Brubaker, *The Limits of Rationality: An Essay on the Social and Moral Thought of Max Weber* (London, 1984), pp. 35ff.

17 *WL*, p. 438.

18 *WuG*, pp. 3–4; *EaS*, pp. 3–4.

19 For a good example, see 'Parlament und Regierung im neugeordneten Deutschland', in *MWG*, I/15, p. 487: 'Es ist . . . nicht Sache des Beamten, nach seinen eigenen Überzeugungen mitkämpfend in den politischen Streit zu treten und, in diesem Sinn, "Politik zu treiben", die immer Kampf ist. . . . Politiker müssen der Beamtenherrschaft das Gegengewicht geben.'

20 *WuG*, p. 61; *EaS*, pp. 112–13.

21 See *WuG*, pp. 59ff; *EaS*, pp. 109ff.

22 See chapter 2 for a more detailed elaboration of this point.

23 *WL*, p. 266.

CHAPTER 9   RATIONALIZATION AND MYTH IN WEBER'S THOUGHT

1 *WL*, p. 552.

2 Günter Dux, 'Religion, Geschichte und sozialer Wandel in Max Weber's Religionssoziologie', in C. Seyfarth and W. M. Sprondel (eds), *Seminar: Religion und gesellschaftliche Entwicklung. Studien zur Protestantismus-Kapitalismus-These Max Webers* (Frankfurt, 1973), p. 328.

3 *WL*, p. 154.

4 Letter to Dr Gross of 13 September 1907, in private collection; reproduced in part in E. Baumgarten, *Max Weber: Werk und Person* (Tübingen, 1964), p. 647.

5 According to a manuscript bequeathed to Georg Kaiser reproduced in ibid., p. 646.

6 Cf. especially *WuG*, pp. 247-9; *EaS*, pp. 402-4.

7 *WuG*, p. 247; *EaS*, p. 402.

8 *WL*, p. 613.

9 Ibid., pp. 604-5.

10 *GARS*, I, p. 94. F. Tenbruck was first to point out that in the new edition of the essays on the Protestant ethic this passage had been added by Weber and thus must be attributed to the last phase of his work.

11 Letter to Adolf von Harnack of 2 May 1906, Max Weber papers, Central Archives of the German Democratic Republic, Merseburg; quoted in Mommsen, *Max Weber*, p. 100; English edn, p. 94.

12 Cf. the account of this in *Lebensbild*, pp. 469-70.

13 Cf. the letter from Max Weber to P. von Klenau of 26 November 1910, quoted in ibid., p. 467.

14 Cf. W. J. Mommsen, 'Max Weber and Roberto Michels: an assymetrical partnership', *Archives européennes de sociologie*, 22 (1981), pp. 110-16, with futher references.

15 Letter to Roberto Michels of 12 May 1909, Michels Papers, Fondatione Luigi Einaudi, Turin.

16 *MWG*, I/15, pp. 462, 660. See also Mommsen, *Max Weber*, pp. 257-8; English edn, p. 238.

17 Cf. among others Eugen Diederichs, *Politik des Geistes* (Jena, 1920).

18 For Weber's role at the Lauenstein conferences, see *MWG*, I/15, pp. 701-8.

19 For the dating of and the background to the writing of the address 'Science as a vocation', see Mommsen, *Max Weber*, p. 289, n. 292; English edn, pp. 268-9, and the definitive account in Wolfgang Schluchter, *Rationalismus der Weltbeherrschung: Studien zu Max Weber* (Frankfurt, 1980), pp. 236-40.

20 *WL*, p. 598.

21 Erich von Kahler, *Der Beruf der Wissenschaft* (Berlin, 1920).

22 *WL*, p. 594.

23 Cf. the complete text of this passage, *WL*, p. 564: 'It is like in the old world, still not disenchanted of its gods and demons, only in another sense. As Hellenic man at times sacrificed to Aphrodite and at other times to Apollo, and above all as everybody sacrificed to the gods of his city, so do we to this day, only such behaviour is disenchanted and denuded of its mythical but inwardly genuine plasticity. Fate, but certainly not "science", holds sway over these gods and their struggles.'

24 *WL* p. 565.

25 For the recent debate about Weber's views on universal history, see chapter 10.

26 See Wolfgang J. Mommsen, 'Neue Max-Weber-Literatur', *Historische Zeitschrift*, 211 (1969), pp. 616-30, and *Max Weber: Gesellschaft, Politik und Geschichte* (Frankfurt, 1974), pp. 259-60, n. 109. It is to the credit of Friedrich Tenbruck that the significance of this issue has at last been recognized. See Friedrich H. Tenbruck, 'Das Werk Max Webers', *KZSS*, 27 (1975), pp. 663-702.

27 On the antinomical structure of the ideal-typical method in Weber's work, cf. chapter 2.

28　WuG, p. 726; EaS, p. 1209.

29　WuG, p. 142; EaS, p. 245.

30　GARS, I, p. 564.

31　Cf. 'Zwischenbetrachtung', GARS, I, pp. 570ff.

32　WL, p. 547.

CHAPTER 10　THE TWO DIMENSIONS OF SOCIAL CHANGE IN MAX WEBER'S
SOCIOLOGICAL THEORY

1　See Wolfgang J. Mommsen, *The Age of Bureaucracy: Perspectives on the Political Sociology of Max Weber* (Oxford, 1974), pp. 52–3.

2　Cf. Wolfgang J. Mommsen, *Max Weber: Kultur, Gesellschaft und Geschichte* (Frankfurt, 1974), pp. 99–103.

3　Cf. Wolfgang Schluchter, *Die Entwicklung des okzidentalen Rationalismus: Eine Analyse von Max Webers Gesellschaftsgeschichte* (Tübingen, 1975), p. 158. See also Wolfgang Schluchter, 'Max Webers Gesellschaftsgeschichte', *KZSS*, 31 (1979), pp. 318–27; Günther Roth and Wolfgang Schluchter, *Max Weber's Vision of History: Ethics and Methods* (Berkeley, 1979); Wolfgang Schluchter, *Rationalismus der Weltbeherrschung: Studien zu Max Weber* (Frankfurt, 1980).

4　GARS, I, p. 252; see also Schluchter, *Die Entwicklung des okzidentalen Rationalismus*, pp. 39–40.

5　Cf. ibid., pp. 12–13.

6　Friedrich Tenbruck, 'Das Werk Max Webers', *KZSS*, 27 (1975), pp. 663ff.; Tenbruck, 'Wie gut kennen wir Max Weber?', *Zeitschrift für die gesamte Staatswissenschaft*, 191 (1975), pp. 719ff.

7　Tenbruck, 'Das Werk Max Webers', p. 689.

8　Wilhelm Hennis, 'Max Webers Fragestellung', *Zeitschrift für Politik*, 29 (1982), pp. 241ff.; Hennis, 'Max Webers Thema', *Zeitschrift für Politik*, 31 (1984), pp. 11–52. See also Wilhelm Hennis, *Max Webers Fragestellung: Studien zur Biographie des Werks* (Tübingen, 1987).

9　In the proofs of the last version of *The Protestant Ethic and the Spirit of Capitalism* which was to be published as part of the *Collected Essays on the Sociology of Religion* Weber inserted the word 'modern' before 'Capitalism', but struck it out again presumably so as not to be charged with having made major revisions of his thesis under the pressure of contemporary criticism.

10　Cf. Max Weber, *Die Protestantische Ethik*, vol. II: *Kritiken und Antikritiken*, ed. Johannes Winckelmann (Hamburg, 1972), in particular pp. 27–31 and 303–5.

11　GARS, II, p. 131.

12　See GARS, I, p. 252, and the earlier version in which the passage just quoted is still lacking, in *AfSSP*, 41 (1916), p. 15.

13　WuG, p. 15; EaS, p. 30.

14　WuG, p. 658; EaS, p. 1117.

15　GARS, I.

16 Cf. Eva Karádi, 'Ernst Bloch and Georg Lukács in Max Weber's Heidelberg', in Wolfgang J. Mommsen and Jürgen Osterhammel (eds), *Max Weber and his Contemporaries* (London, 1987), pp. 505-7.

17 *GARS*, II, p. 365.

18 See G. Abramowski, *Des Geschichtsbild Max Webers: Universalgeschichte am Leitfaden des universalen Rationalisierungsprozesses* (Stuttgart, 1966).

19 Cf. Tenbruck, 'Das Werk Max Webers', p. 670; see also ibid., p. 687.

20 Cf. Schluchter, *Die Entwicklung des okzidentalen Rationalismus*, p. 12.

21 See *WL*, pp. 291ff.

22 See Mommsen, *Max Weber: Gesellschaft, Politik und Geschichte*, p. 212.

23 See Günther Roth, 'Politische Herrschaft und persönliche Freiheit', *Heidelberger Max Weber-Vorlesungen 1983* (Frankfurt, 1987), pp. 285ff.

24 Cf. *GARS*, II, p. 365.

25 *GARS*, I, pp. 1-2.

26 Cf. Schluchter, *Die Entwicklung des okzidentalen Rationalismus*, pp. 12-13.

27 See *GARS*, I, p. 2.

28 Ibid.

29 Cf. Wolfgang Schluchter, 'Max Webers Religionssoziologie', *KZSS*, 36 (1984), p. 361.

30 Cf. *GARS*, I, p. 259.

31 *GARS*, I, p. 12.

32 *GARS*, I, p. 62.

33 *GARS*, I, p. 62.

34 *GARS*, I, p. 35, n. 1. Weber had been encouraged to add this rejoinder by the critique of Lujo Brentano.

35 Cf. *RS*, p. 261. It is doubtful whether this heading (like others which had been inserted into the manuscript on separate sheets before publication) dates from 1911-13. It had probably been inserted only in 1919 when the manuscript was sent to the printers.

36 Ibid., p. 346.

37 Ibid., pp. 346-7; quoted from *EaS*, p. 895.

38 *WuG*, p. 59; *EaS*, p. 108 (translation amended by the author).

39 *WuG*, p. 129; *EaS*, p. 225.

40 Cf. *WuG*, p. 129; *EaS*, p. 225.

CHAPTER 11   MAX WEBER IN MODERN SOCIAL THOUGHT

1 Raymond Aron, *La Sociologie allemande contemporaine* (Paris, 1935); quoted from the German edition *Die deutsche Soziologie der Gegenwart* (Stuttgart, 1953), p. 92.

2 The account of publications on Max Weber prepared by Constans Seyfarth and Gerd Schmidt, *Max Weber, Bibliographie: Eine Dokumentation der Sekundärliteratur* (Stuttgart, 1977), was of invaluable help in preparing this study.

3 Hereafter reference is made to the new edition of *Die Zerstörung der Vernunft*, George Lukács, *Werke*, vol. 9 (Darmstadt, 1974).

4 See, in particular, M. Rainer Lepsius, 'Die Soziologie der Zwischenkriegszeit: Entwicklungstendenzen und Beurteilungskriterien', in *Soziologie in Deutschland und Österreich* (Opladen, 1981), pp. 6ff., and the essays and studies collected in this volume; C. Klingemann, 'Vergangenheitsbewältigung oder Geschichtsschreibung? Unerwünschte Traditionsbestände deutscher Soziologie zwischen 1933 und 1945', in S. Papke (ed.), *Ordnung und Theorie: Beiträge zur Geschichte der Soziologie in Deutschland* (Darmstadt, 1986); Dirk Käsler, *Die frühe deutsche Soziologie in ihren Enstehungsmilieus* (Opladen, 1984).

5 See in particular Ottheim Rammstedt, *Deutsche Soziologie 1933-1945: Die Normalität einer Anpassung* (Frankfurt, 1986). However, Rammstedt's study does not pay sufficient attention to the fact that numerous scholars from other fields decided to call themselves sociologists although this was often hardly justified when their actual work is taken into account.

6 Aron, *La Sociologie allemande contemporaine*, 2nd edn (Paris, 1950); German edition *Die deutsche Soziologie der Gegenwart: Eine Einführung* (Stuttgart, 1953).

7 Cf. Helmut Fogt, 'Max Weber und die deutsche Soziologie der Weimarer Republik: Aussenseiter oder Gründervater?', in Lepsius (ed.), *Soziologie in Deutschland und Österreich*, pp. 248ff.

8 Lepsius, 'Die Soziologie der Zwischenkriegszeit', p. 10.

9 Here reference is made to the 2nd edn (Munich, 1958), p. 88.

10 Cf. Dirk Käsler, *Soziologische Abenteuer: Earle Edward Eubank besucht europäische Soziologen im Sommer 1934* (Opladen, 1985), *passim*.

11 Melchior Palyi (ed.), *Hauptprobleme der Soziologie: Erinnerungsgabe für Max Weber*, 2 vols (Munich and Leipzig, 1923). In a review of vol. 2, 'Der Max-Weber-Kreis in Heidelberg', in *Kölner vierteljahrshefte für Soziologie*, 5 (1926), pp. 270-1, Paul Honigsheim argued that there was a 'Max Weber circle', not a 'school', and explained the absence of the latter in terms of Weber's radical individualism, or rather 'the metaphysics of human heroism': 'Max Weber hat einer jeden Institution, Staat, Kirche, Partei, Trust, Schulzusammenhang, d.h. jedem überindividuellen Gebilde, den Kampf bis aufs Messer angesagt.' ('Max Weber declared he would resist to the last every institution whatsoever - state, church, party, concern and academic "school" - in other words, every suprapersonal formation.')

12 Bernhard Pfister, *Die Entwicklung zum Idealtypus. Eine methodologische Untersuchung über das Verhältnis von Theorie und Geschichte bei Menger, Schmoller und Max Weber* (Tübingen, 1928).

13 Alexander von Schelting, *Max Webers Wissenschaftslehre* (Tübingen, 1934).

14 Joachim Wach, *Das Verstehen*, 2 vols (Tübingen, 1926-29).

15 Karl Löwith, 'Max Weber und Karl Marx', *AfSSP*, 67 (1932), pp. 175-214; reprinted in Karl Löwith, *Gesammelte Abhandlungen: Zur Kritik der geschichtlichen Existenz*, 2nd edn (Stuttgart, 1960).

16 Siegfried Landshut, 'Max Webers geistesgeschichtliche Bedeutung', in *Neue Jahr-*

bücher für Wissenschaft und Jugendbildung, 7 (1931), pp. 507–16.

17 On Carl Schmitt's relationship to Max Weber, see Mommsen, *Max Weber*, pp. 407–15, 478–81; English edn, pp. 382–9, 448–50.

18 Cf. also M. Rainer Lepsius's observation: 'Das von Weber verfolgte Programm einer Soziologie auf dem Boden eines methodologischen Individualismus und einer vergleichenden Analyse von Sozialstruktur und Kultursystem hat die Entwicklung in den zwanziger Jahren nicht prägen können'; 'Die Soziologie der Zwischenkriegszeit', p. 10. ('The plan Weber pursued for sociology based on methodological individualism and a comparative analysis of social structure and cultural systems had no significant impact on developments in the twenties.')

19 Eduard Baumgarten, *Max Weber: Werk und Person* (Tübingen, 1964), p. 554.

20 It is significant that Nietzsche's influence on Weber had been a neglected theme for a long time. However, Wilhelm Hennis in his recently published book *Max Webers Fragestellung* (Tübingen, 1987) considerably overstates Nietzsche's influence on Weber.

21 Cf. Roland Eckert, 'Die Kulturtheorie Alfred Webers – Überlegungen zur Wissenssoziologie des Bildungsbürgertums', in Eberhard Demm (ed.), *Alfred Weber als Politiker und Gelehrter* (Wiesbaden, 1986), pp. 69ff.

22 Cf. the informative treatment by Beate Riesterer, 'Alfred Weber's position in German intellectual history', in Demm (ed.), *Alfred Weber als Politiker und Gelehrter*, pp. 82ff.

23 Hans Freyer, *Soziologie als Wirklichkeitswissenschaft: Logische Grundlegung des Systems der Soziologie* (Leipzig, 1930), p. 158.

24 Ibid., p. 258.

25 Cf. Iring Fetcher, 'Von der Soziologie als Kulturwissenschaft zum Angebot an den Faschismus', in Karl Corino (ed.), *Intellektuelle im Bann des Nationalsozialismus* (Hamburg, 1980), pp. 185ff.

26 See note 3.

27 Christoph Steding, *Politik und Wissenschaft bei Max Weber* (Breslau, 1932).

28 C. Hans Linde, 'Soziologie in Leipzig 1925–1945', in Lepsius (ed.), *Soziologie in Deutschland und Österreich*.

29 Cf. Jerry Z. Muller, 'Enttäuschung und Zweideutigkeit: Zur Geschichte rechter Sozialwissenschaftler im "Dritten Reich"', *Geschichte und Gesellschaft*, 12 (1986), pp. 292ff.; see also Carsten Klingemann, 'Heimatsoziologie oder Ordnungsinstrument? Fachgeschichtliche Aspekte der Soziologie in Deutschland zwischen 1933 und 1945', in Lepsius (ed.), *Soziologie in Deutschland und Österreich*, pp. 274ff.

30 This is the basic conclusion of the recent study by Otthein Rammstaedt, *Deutsche Soziologie 1933–1945* (see note 5).

31 Ibid., p. 297.

32 See Alfred Müller-Armack, *Genealogie der Wirtschaftsstile: Die geistesgeschichtlichen Ursprünge der Staats- und Wirtschaftsformen bis zum Ausgang des 18. Jahrhunderts* (Stuttgart, 1941), pp. 64, 80–1. Cf. also p. 67: 'However astonishing this may appear at first

sight, it was not the material and technical requirements of economic activity which resulted in the emergence of the new system of an entrepreneurial economy. Rather its development was determined by changes in the dominant system of world-views.' It goes without saying that this is a massive distortion of Weber's own views, which considered the new economic ethic to be just one among several others, including material factors.

33 Hans Freyer, 'Gegenwartsaufgaben der deutschen Soziologie', *Zeitschrift für die gesamte Staatswissenschaft*, 95 (1935), p. 138.

34 Cf. Hans Freyer, 'Ferdinand Tönnies und seine Stellung in der deutschen Soziologie', *Weltwirtschaftliches Archiv*, 44, II (1936), pp. 347–67.

35 Cf. the interesting account of Weber's influence on French thought by Michael Pollak, 'Max Weber en France: l'itinéraire d'une œuvre', *Cahiers de l'Institut du Temps Présent* (manuscript July 1986). See also his essay 'Max Weber in Frankreich', *KZSS*, 38 (1986), pp. 670–84.

36 R. H. Tawney, *Religion and the Rise of Protestantism* (London, 1926).

37 Maurice Halbwachs, 'Les Origines puritaines du capitalisme moderne', *Revue d'histoire et de philosophie religieuses*, 5 (1925), pp. 132–54.

38 Henri Sée, *Les Origines du capitalisme moderne* (Paris, 1926). Cf. Pollak, 'Max Weber en France', p. 683.

39 Cf. David Kettler, Volker Meja and Nico Stehr, introduction to *Karl Mannheim, Konservativismus: Ein Beitrag zur Soziologie des Wissens* (Frankfurt, 1984), p. 39, n. 16.

40 See Eva Karadi, 'Der Sonntagskreis und die Weimarer Kultur', in H. Gassner (ed.), *Wechselwirkungen: Ungarische Avantgarde in der Weimarer Republik* (Marburg, 1986), pp. 526–34.

41 Cf. the rather hostile but substantially correct analysis by Georg Lukács in his *Zerstörung der Vernunft*, pp. 553ff.

42 Letter to Oskar Jászi, 25 April 1933. Cf. Kettler et al., *Karl Mannheim, Konservativismus*, p. 37.

43 Here reference is made to the second edition (London, 1948).

44 Ibid., pp. 58ff.

45 Cf. also Martin Albrow, 'Die Rezeption Max Webers in der britischen Soziologie', to be published in the *Proceedings of a Conference of the Deutsche Soziologische Gesellschaft at Kassel in 1985*, ed. Johannes Weiss (forthcoming). Quoted here from the manuscript with the kind permission of the author.

46 Cf. Günther Roth und Reinhard Bendix, 'Max Webers Einfluss auf die amerikanische Soziologie', *KZSS*, 11 (1959), p. 41.

47 Max Weber, *The Methodology of the Social Sciences*, trans. and ed. Edward A. Shils and Henry A. Finch (New York, 1949), p. viii.

48 For an assessment of the misunderstandings of Weber's ideal type of bureaucracy, see Wolfgang J. Mommsen, '"Toward the iron cage of future serfdom"? On the methodological status of Max Weber's ideal-typical concept of bureaucratization', *Transactions of the Royal Historical Society*, 5th series (London, 1980), pp. 176ff.

49 For an impressive account of the shortcomings of the English translations of Weber's *Sociology of Religion*, see Detlef Kantowsky, 'Die Fehlrezeption von Max Webers Studie über "Hinduismus und Buddhismus" in Indien: Ursachen und Folgen', in *Max Weber e India, Atti del Convegno Internazionale su la tesi Weberiana della razionalizzazione in rapporto all'induismo e al buddhismo* (Turin, 1986), pp. 125ff.

50 The continuing strong interest of Japanese scholarship in Max Weber has so far received no adequate attention in the West, despite considerable research achievements by Japanese scholarship. For a survey, see Uchida Yoshiaki, 'Max Weber in den Japanischen Sozialwissenschaften 1905–1978', *Bochumer Jahrbuch für Ostasienforschung*, 4 (1981), pp. 71–109.

51 For instance, Reinhard Bendix, 'Max Weber's interpretation of conduct and history', *American Journal of Sociology*, 51 (1945/46), pp. 518–26.

52 Benjamin Nelson, *The Idea of Usury: From Tribal Brotherhood to Universal Otherhood* (Princeton, 1949).

53 *From Max Weber: Essays in Sociology*, ed. H. H. Gerth and C. Wright Mills (London, 1948).

54 H. Stuart Hughes, *Consciousness and Society: The Reorientation of European Social Thought 1890–1930* (London, 1959). See also Wolfgang J. Mommsen, *Introduction to Max Weber and his Contemporaries*, ed. Wolfgang J. Mommsen and Jürgen Osterhammel (London, 1987), p. 3.

55 Reinhard Bendix, *Max Weber: An Intellectual Portrait* (London, 1960); German edn, *Max Weber – Das Werk: Darstellung, Analyse, Ergebnisse* (Munich, 1964).

56 Admittedly Bendix himself emphasized that he wanted to present 'das empirisch-soziologische Werk Max Webers' while neglecting the methodological and theoretical aspects; German edn, p. 14.

57 Eduard Baumgarten, *Die Sammlung*, 5 (1950), p. 398.

58 Dieter Henrich, *Die Einheit der Wissenschaftslehre Max Webers* (Tübingen, 1952), p. 68.

59 See in particular Theodor Schieder, 'Der Typus in der Geschichtswissenschaft', in Theodore Schieder, *Staat und Gesellschaft im Wandel unserer Zeit* (Munich, 1958), pp. 172–87; Schieder, *Geschichte als Wissenschaft: Eine Einführung* (Munich, 1965), pp. 167, 201–7.

60 *KZSS*, 11 (1959), pp. 625ff.

61 See C. von Ferber, 'Der Werturteilsstreit 1909–1956: Versuch einer wissenschaftsgeschichtlichen Interpretation', *KZSS*, 11 (1959), pp. 21–37.

62 Ibid., p. 78.

63 For an assessment of the tendencies and results of this dispute, see the Postscript to Mommsen, *Max Weber*, pp. 442–77; English edn, pp. 415–47.

64 Arnold Bergstraesser, 'Max Webers Antrittsvorlesung in zeitgeschichtlicher Perspektive', *Vierteljahrsheft für Zeitgeschichte*, 5 (1957), p. 217.

65 *Vierteljahrshefte für Zeitgeschichte*, 7 (1959), p. 21ff.

66 Tübingen, 1952.

67 On this subject see Mommsen, *Max Weber*, pp. 478–83; English edn, pp. 448–54.

68 *GPS*, p. xii.

69 Mommsen, *Max Weber*, 1st edn (Tübingen, 1959), 2nd edn (Tübingen, 1974); English edition *Max Weber and German Politics, 1890–1920* (Chicago, 1985).

70 Jacob Peter Mayer, *Max Weber in German Politics*, 2nd edn (London, 1956).

71 Raymond Aron, 'Max Weber und die Machtpolitik', in Otto Stammer (ed.), *Max Weber und die Soziologie heute: Verhandlungen des 15. Deutschen Soziologentages* (Tübingen, 1965), pp. 103–20; English edn, *Max Weber and Sociology Today* (Oxford, 1971), pp. 83–100.

72 Ibid., p. 66.

73 Ibid., pp. 133–51.

74 Ibid., p. 25.

75 Wolfgang Schluchter, *Aspekte bürokratischer Herrschaft: Studien zur Interpretation der fortschreitenden Industriegesellschaft* (Munich, 1972), 2nd edn (Munich, 1985).

76 See in particular S. N. Eisenstadt, *Tradition, Change and Modernity* (New York, 1973).

77 Cf. Wolfgang J. Mommsen and Jürgen Osterhammel (eds), *Max Weber and his Contemporaries* (London, 1987), pp. 574–80.

78 In this connection particular mention should be made of Wolfgang Schluchter's studies *Die Entwicklung des okzidentalen Rationalismus: Eine Analyse von Max Webers Gesellschaftsgeschichte* (Tübingen, 1979) and *Rationalismus der Weltbeherrschung: Studien zu Max Weber* (Frankfurt, 1980).

79 Cf. Wolfgang J. Mommsen, 'Personal conduct and societal change', in Sam Whimster and Scott Lash (eds), *Max Weber: Rationality and Modernity* (London, 1987), pp. 35–51.

80 For a good survey of the new developments in this field, see Jürgen Kocka (ed.), *Max Weber, der Historiker* (Göttingen, 1986), being the papers on Max Weber presented on the occasion of the 14th International Congress of Historians at Stuttgart (1985).

81 Wilhelm Hennis, *Max Webers Fragestellung* (Tübingen, 1987). However, this study, though thoughtful, decisive and full of insight, stops short of a substantive analysis of Weber's historical sociology proper which alone could prove his argument, namely, that Weber wanted to pave the way for a new understanding of man in the post-modern age.

Index